the FLYING McCOYS

DON'T WORRY, DOROTHY. I'M SURE THEY'LL OUTGROW THIS.
HAPPY MOTHER'S DAY MOM!
GLENN
GARY

the FLYING McCOYS

COMICS FOR A BOLD NEW WORLD

Glenn and Gary McCoy

Andrews McMeel
Publishing, LLC

Kansas City

The Flying McCoys is syndicated internationally by Universal Press Syndicate.

The Flying McCoys copyright © 2006 by Glenn and Gary McCoy. All rights reserved. Printed in the United States of America. No part of this book may be used or reproduced in any manner whatsoever without written permission except in the case of reprints in the context of reviews. For information, write Andrews McMeel Publishing, LLC, an Andrews McMeel Universal company, 4520 Main Street, Kansas City, Missouri 64111.

07 08 09 10 BBG 10 9 8 7 6 5 4 3 2

ISBN-13: 978-0-7407-6044-0
ISBN-10: 0-7407-6044-0

Library of Congress Catalog Control Number: 2006926008

www.andrewsmcmeel.com

The Flying McCoy Brothers would like to thank: God, Mom and Dad, Mark McCoy, Kent McCoy, Laura, Michael Eisner, Whoopi Goldberg, Judge Judith Sheindlin, Charles Addams, Woody Allen, Tex Avery, Carl Barks, Frank Baum, The Beatles, Jim Borgman, Ray Bradbury, Edgar Rice Burroughs, Johnny Carson, Oliver Christianson, Todd Clark, Samuel Coldridge, Bill Cosby, Robert Crumb, Steve Dickenson, Walt Disney, Dogs, Bob Duffy, Doug Eskra, Frank Frazetta, Fritz Freeling, Erin Friedrich, John Glynn, Sam Gross, Ray Harryhausen, Johnny Hart, Paul Henning, George Herriman, Bahaar Husain, Thomas Jefferson, Chuck Jones, Ron Kanfi, Boris Karloff, Andy Kaufman, Bill Keane, Hank Ketcham, Michael Kilfoy, B. Kliban, Don Knotts, Jeff Koterba, Gary Larson, Led Zeppelin, David Letterman, The Little Rascals, Jeff MacNelly, *Mad* Magazine, Steve Martin, Glenn Myers, Moebius, Earl Musick, National Lampoon, Bob Newhardt, Pat Oliphant, P. J. O'Rourke, Brant Parker, Sean Parkes, Mike Peters, Elvis Presley, Richard Pryor, Albert Pujols, Monty Python, Brian Regan, Norman Rockwell, Charles Rodrigues, Arnold Roth, Early *SNL*, Steve Sack, Lee Salem, Charles Schulz, Ronald Searle, R. J. Shay, Bob Staake, Wayne Stayskal, The Three Stooges, Dale Threlkeld, Hunter Thompson, Mark Twain, Jim Unger, Tomi Ungerer, Michelle Urry, Jerry Van Amerongen, Sister Veronica, Leonardo da Vinci, Mort Walker, Bob Weber, Hank Williams, Gahan Wilson, Jonathan Winters . . . and special thanks to the late Rowley Stout McCoy.

For Mom and Dad,
who despite our successes, always kept us grounded.
Often for weeks at a time.

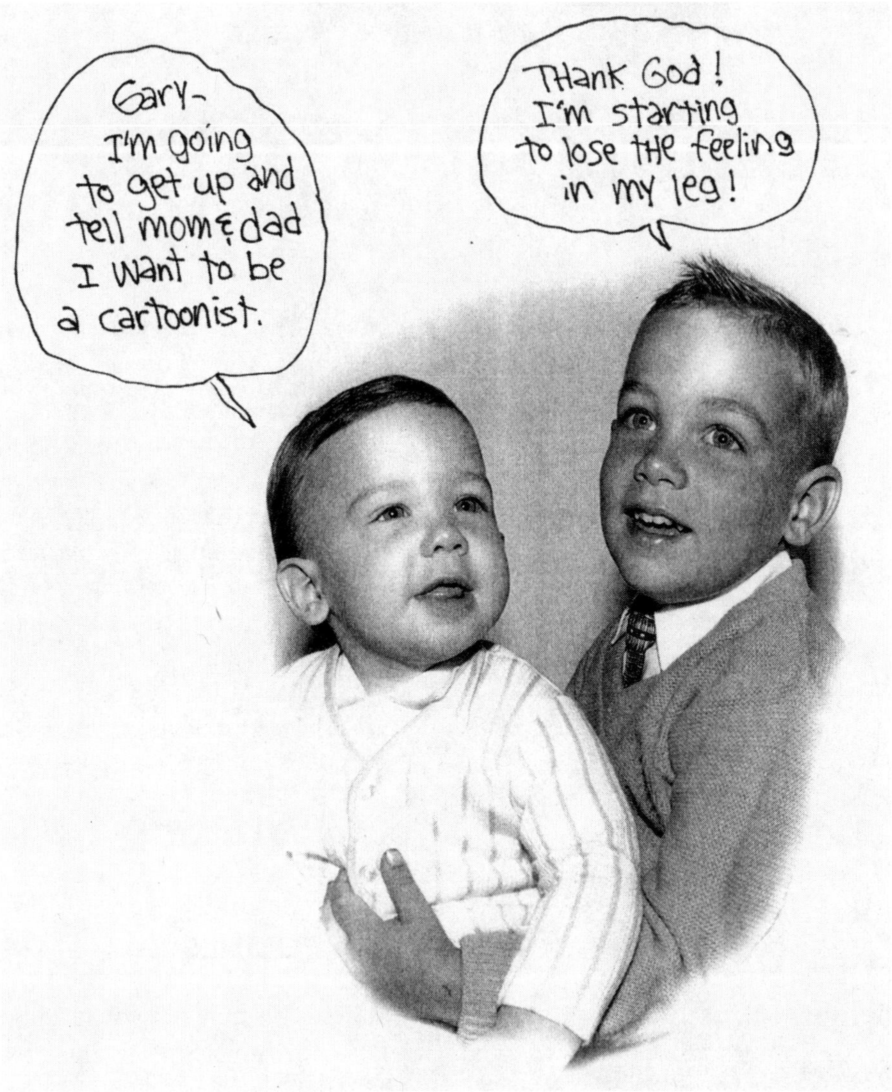
Gary- I'm going to get up and tell mom & dad I want to be a cartoonist.
Thank God! I'm starting to lose the feeling in my leg!

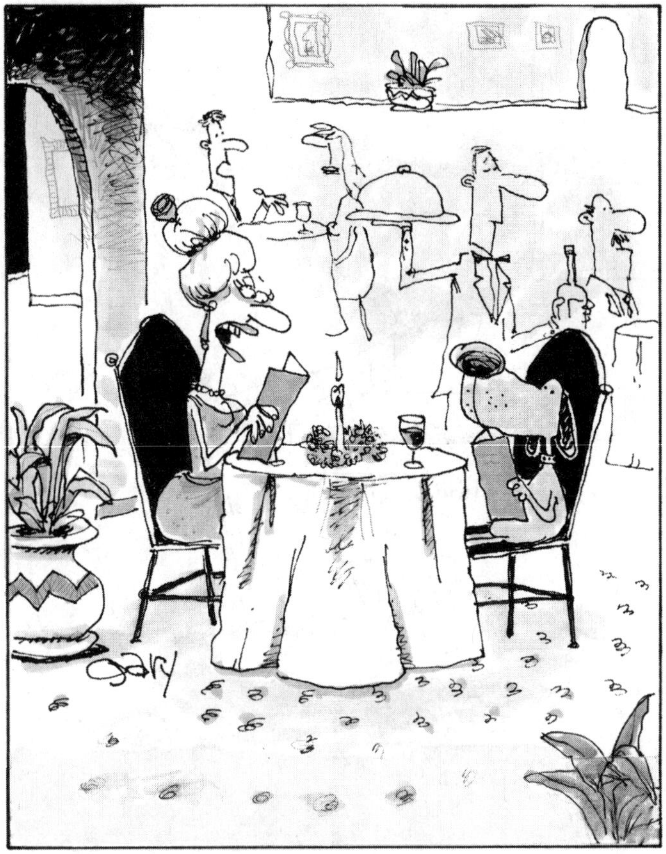

“Well yes, I admit your ad clearly stated that you like to go on long walks in the park.”

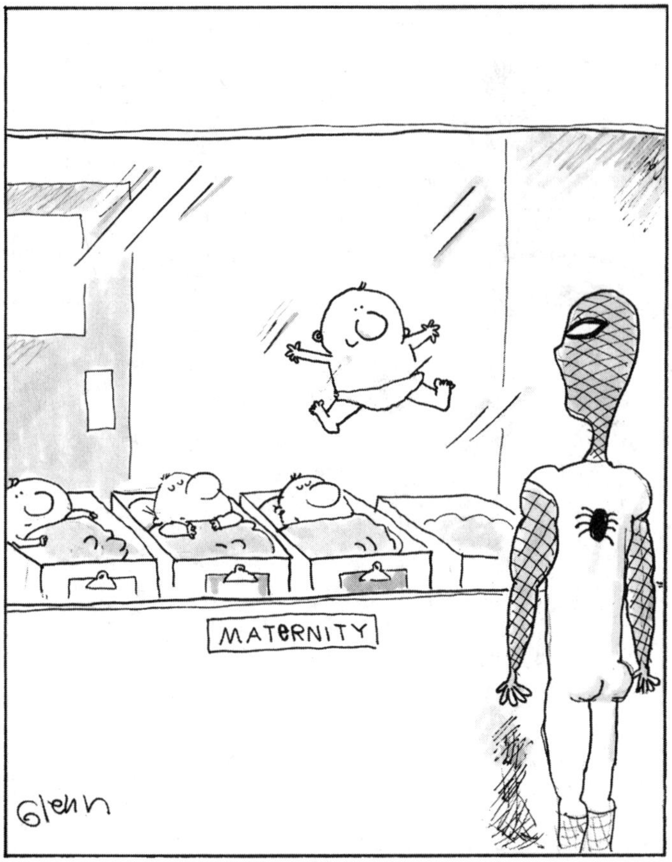
MATERNITY

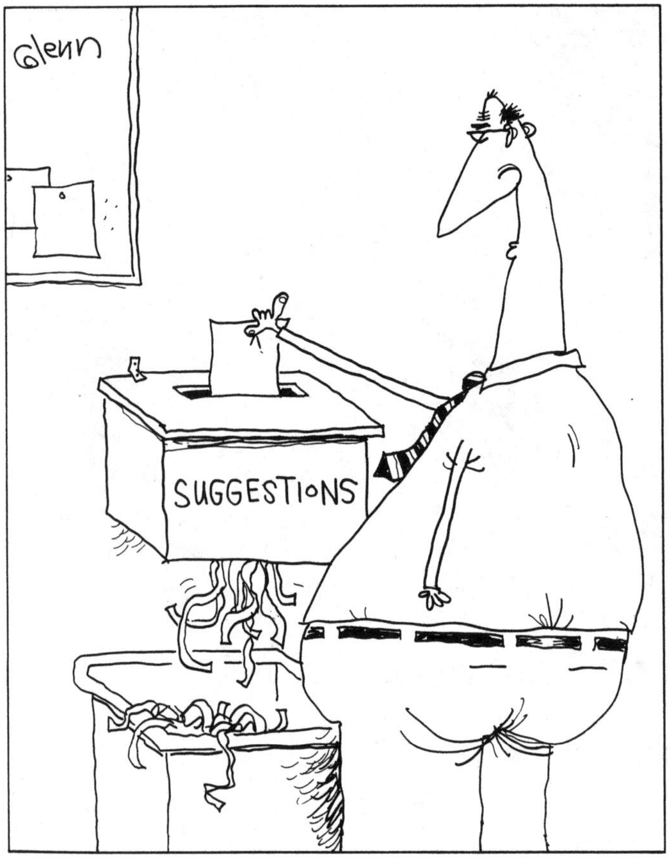
Glenn
SUGGESTIONS

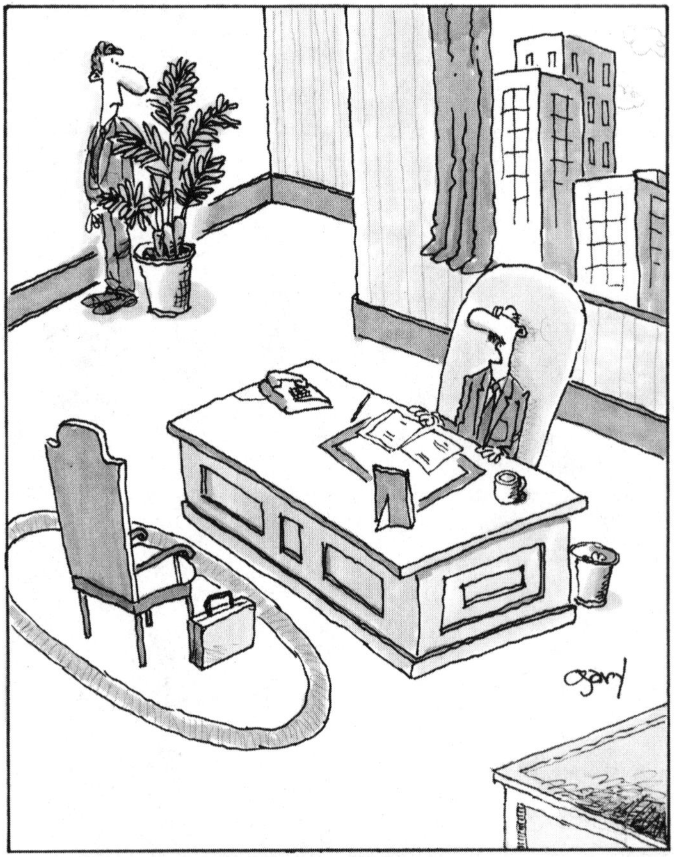
Gary

"That is not what I meant when I asked if you'd be willing to relocate."

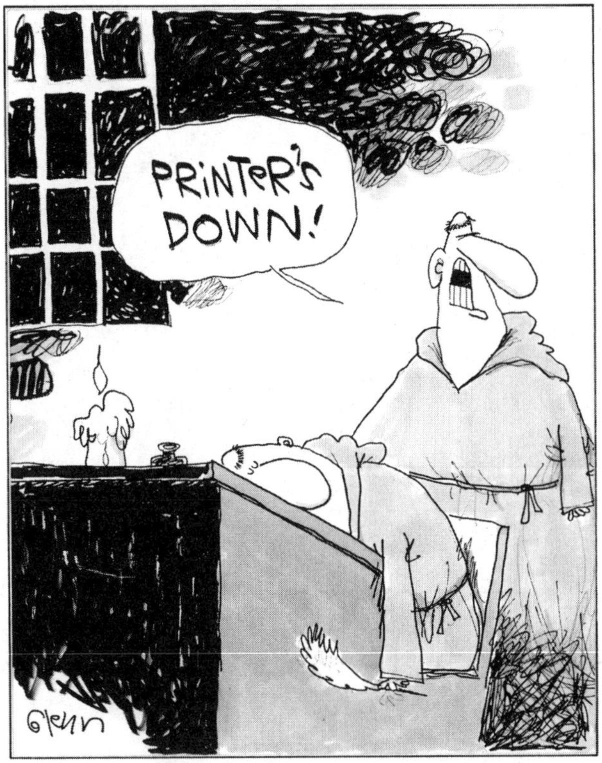
PRINTER'S DOWN!
Glenn

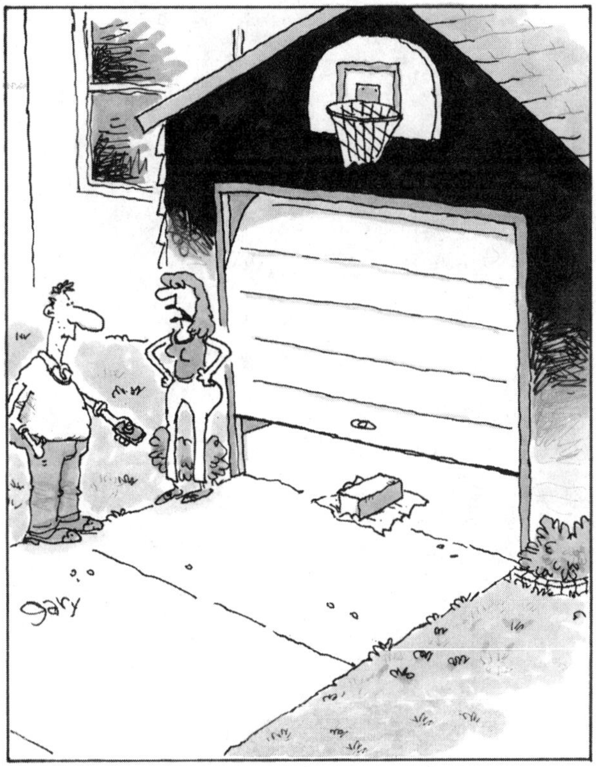
Gary

"Why don't you just buy a new cheese slicer?"

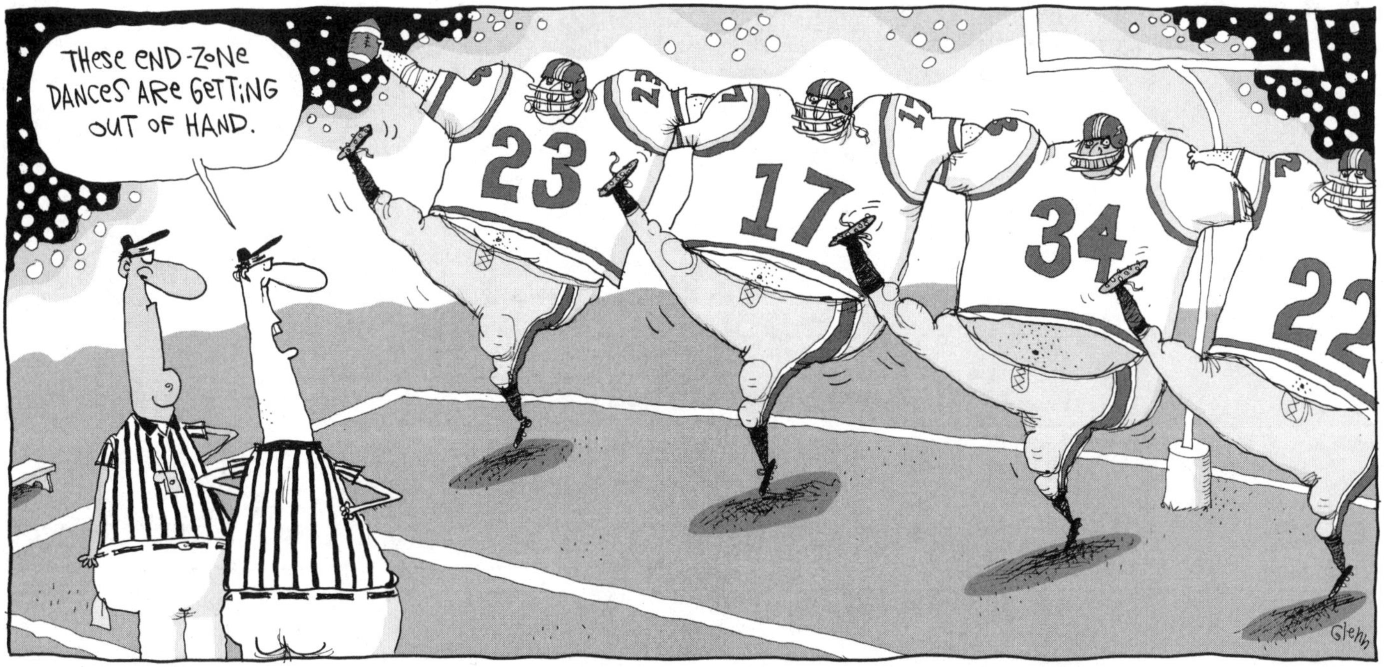
THESE END-ZONE DANCES ARE GETTING OUT OF HAND.
23
17
34
22
Glenn

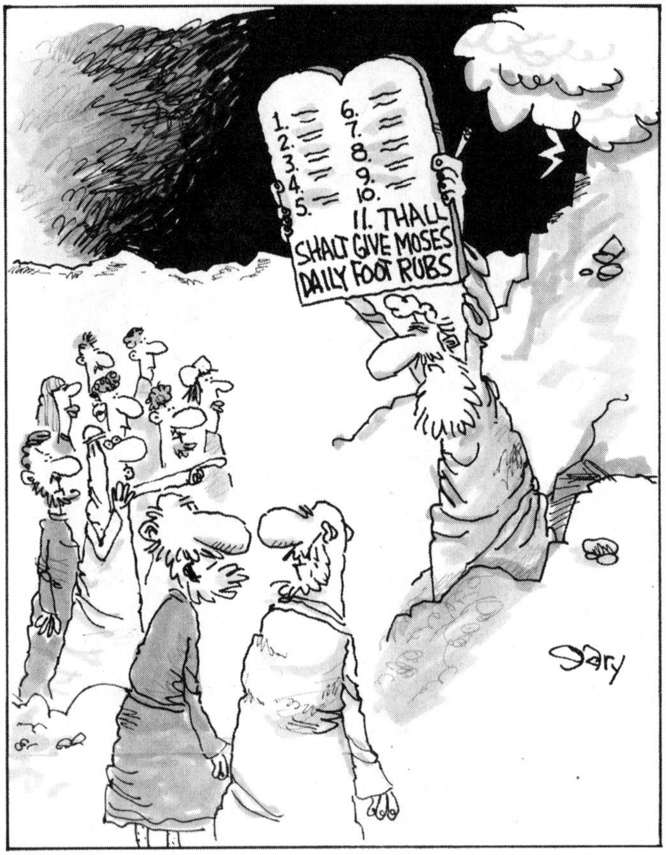
1.
2.
3.
4.
5.
6.
7.
8.
9.
10.
11. THALL SHALT GIVE MOSES DAILY FOOT RUBS
Gary

"I've gotta question the handwriting on that 11th Commandment."

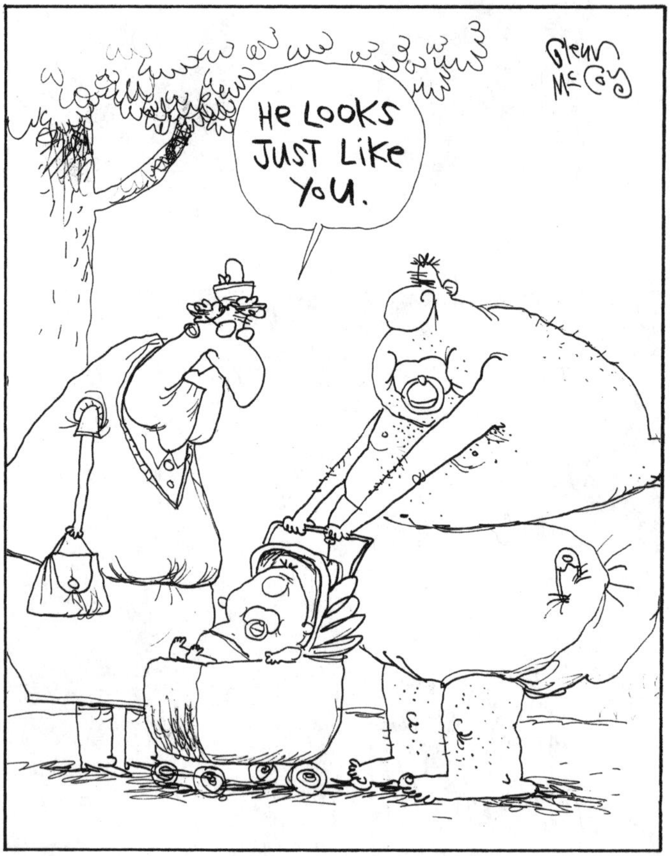
Glenn McCoy
HE LOOKS JUST LIKE YOU.

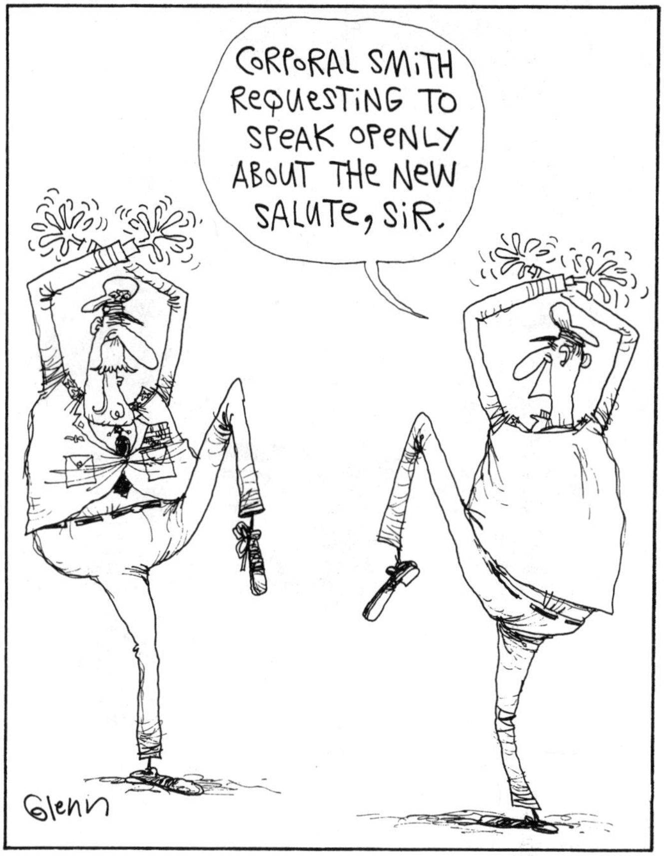
CORPORAL SMITH REQUESTING TO SPEAK OPENLY ABOUT THE NEW SALUTE, SIR.

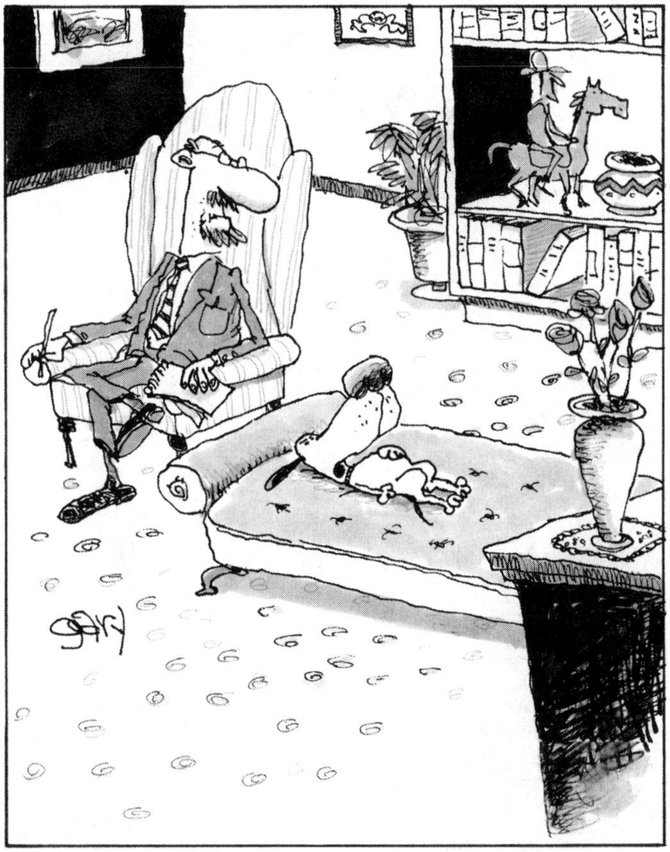

"One hundred and forty bucks an hour, and all you can tell me is to get down off the couch?"

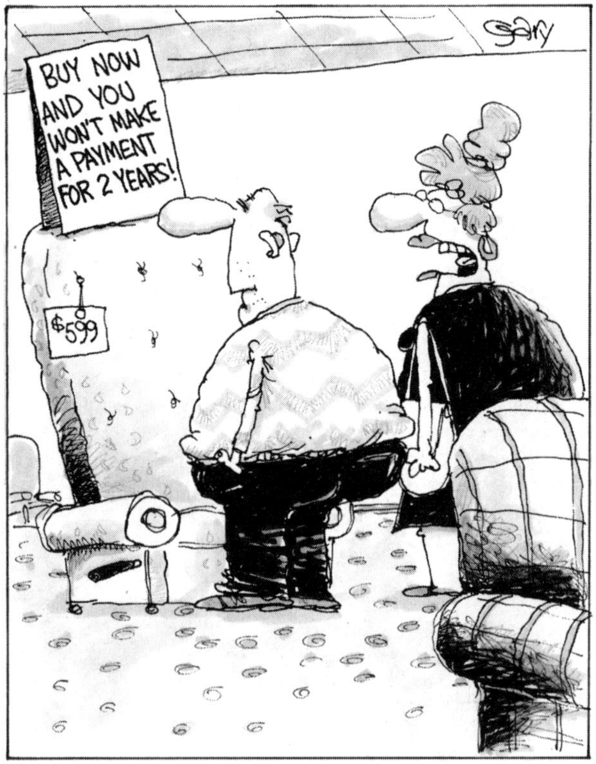
BUY NOW AND YOU WON'T MAKE A PAYMENT FOR 2 YEARS!
$599

"They know you."

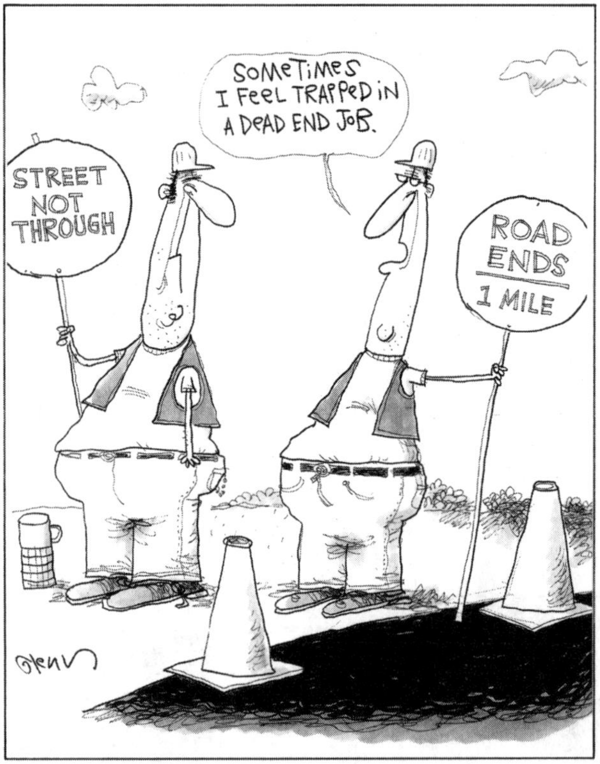
SOMETIMES I FEEL TRAPPED IN A DEAD END JOB.
STREET NOT THROUGH
ROAD ENDS 1 MILE

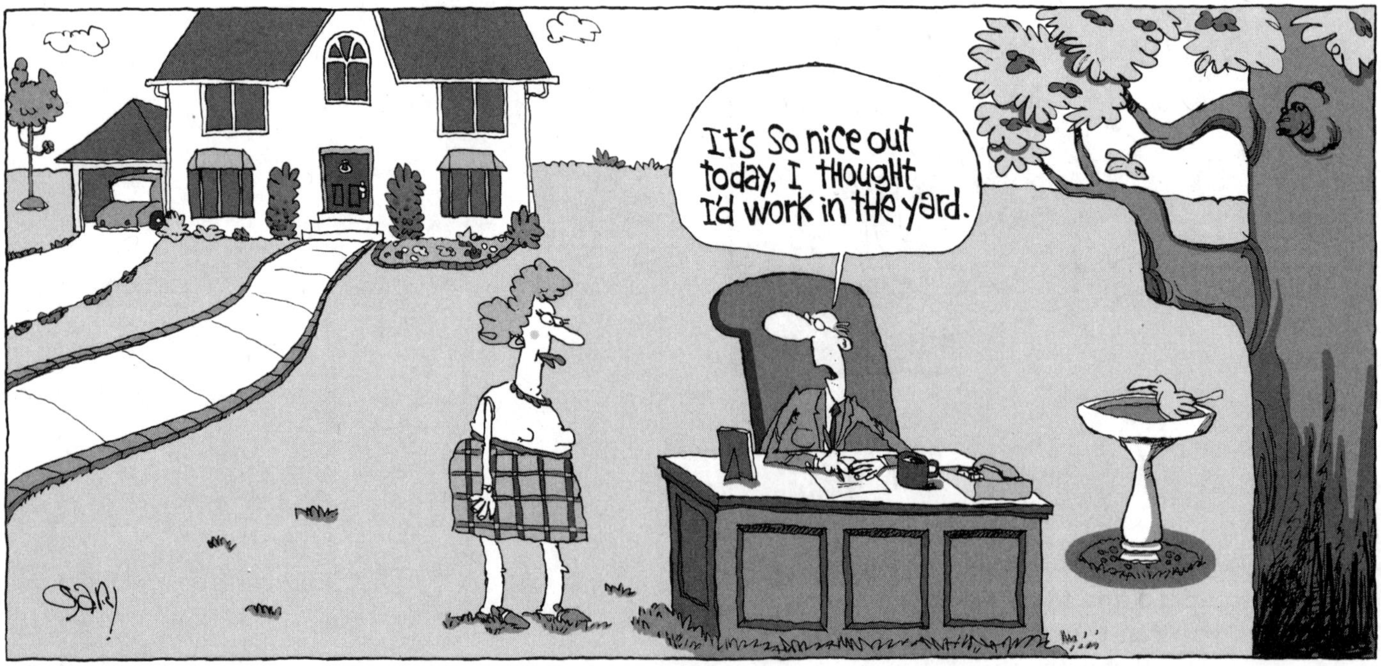
It's So nice out today, I THOUGHT I'd work in THE yard.

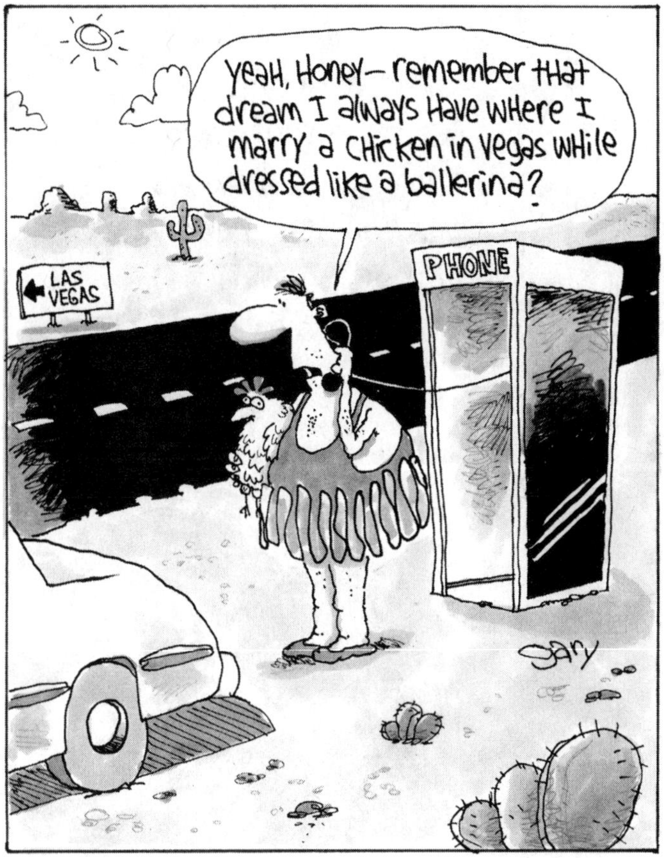
YEAH, HONEY— REMEMBER THAT DREAM I ALWAYS HAVE WHERE I MARRY A CHICKEN IN VEGAS WHILE DRESSED LIKE A BALLERINA?
LAS VEGAS
PHONE
Gary

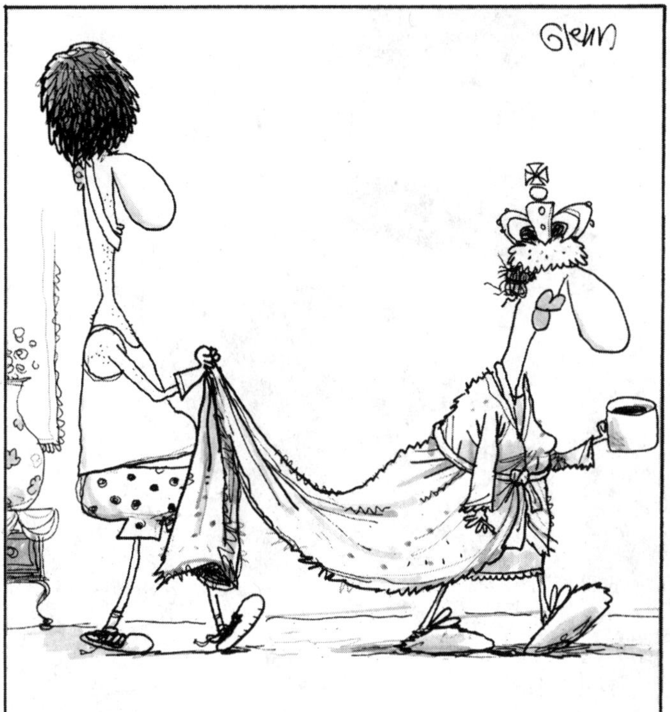
Glenn

CASUAL FRIDAY AT BUCKINGHAM PALACE

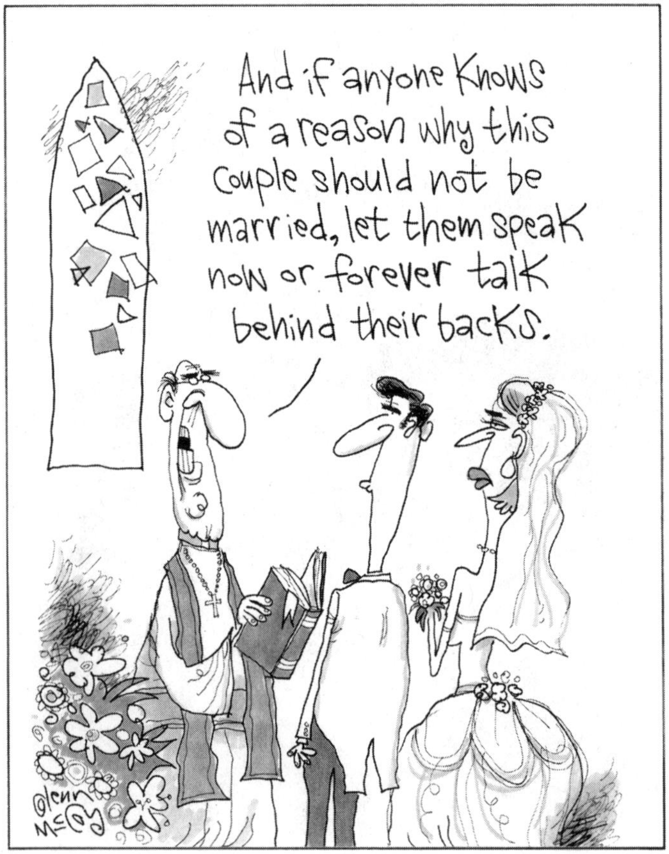
And if anyone Knows of a reason why this couple should not be married, let them speak now or forever talk behind their backs.

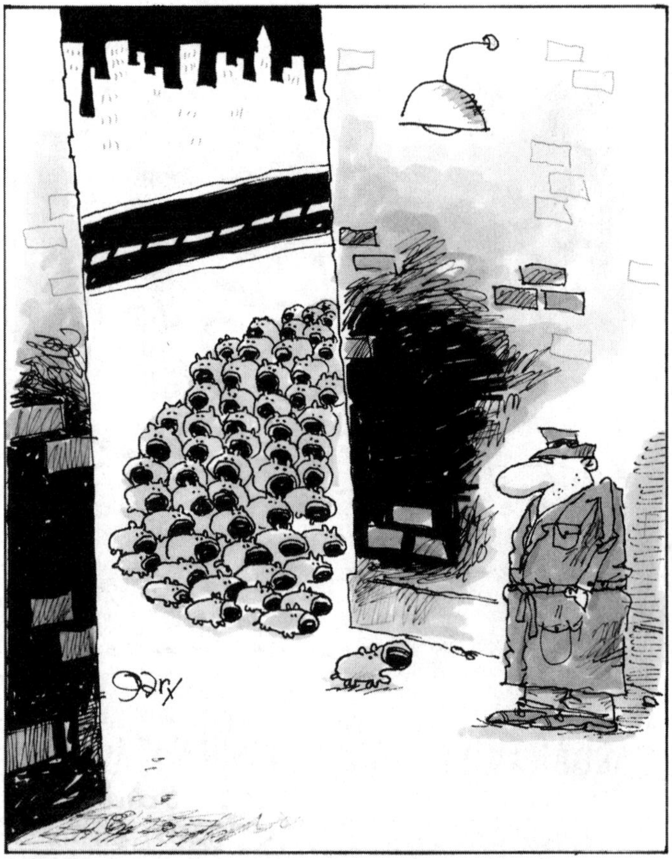

"What kind of a stupid question is that?
I'm a lemming, remember?
Of course I was followed."

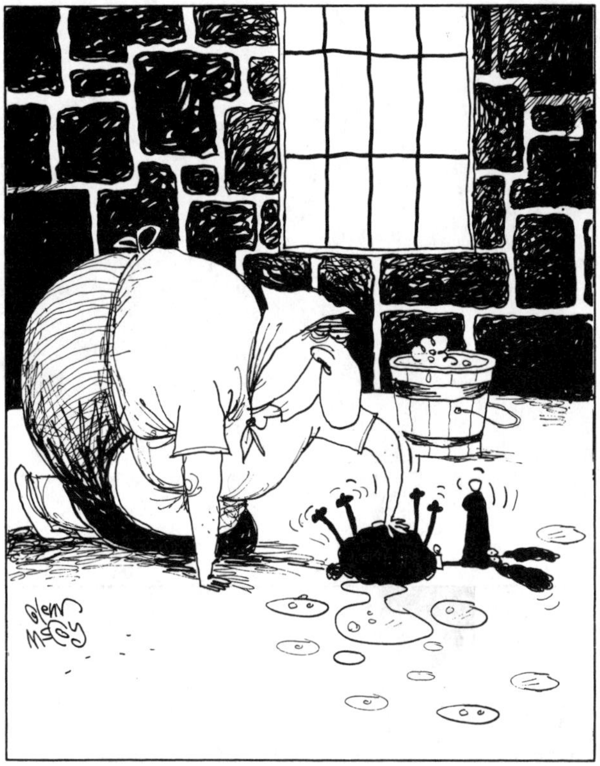
Glenn McCoy

Poodles once served a purpose.

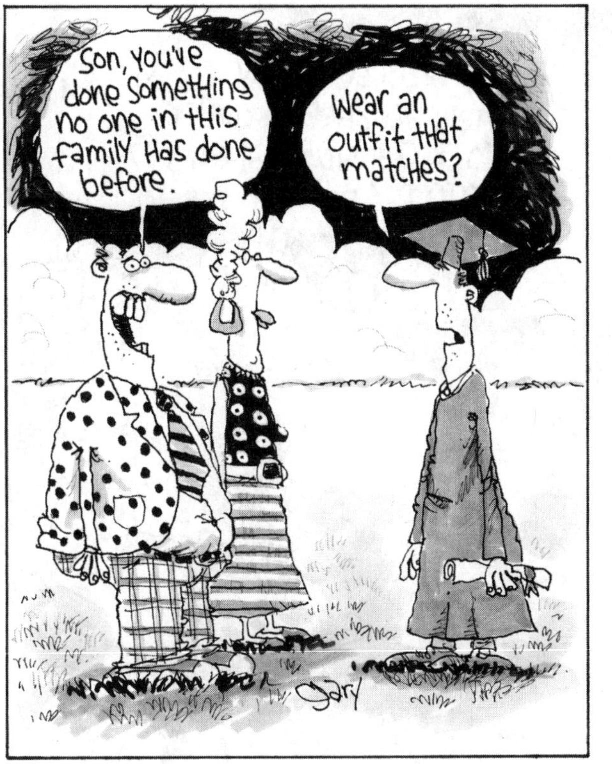
Son, you've done something no one in this family has done before.
Wear an outfit that matches?
Gary

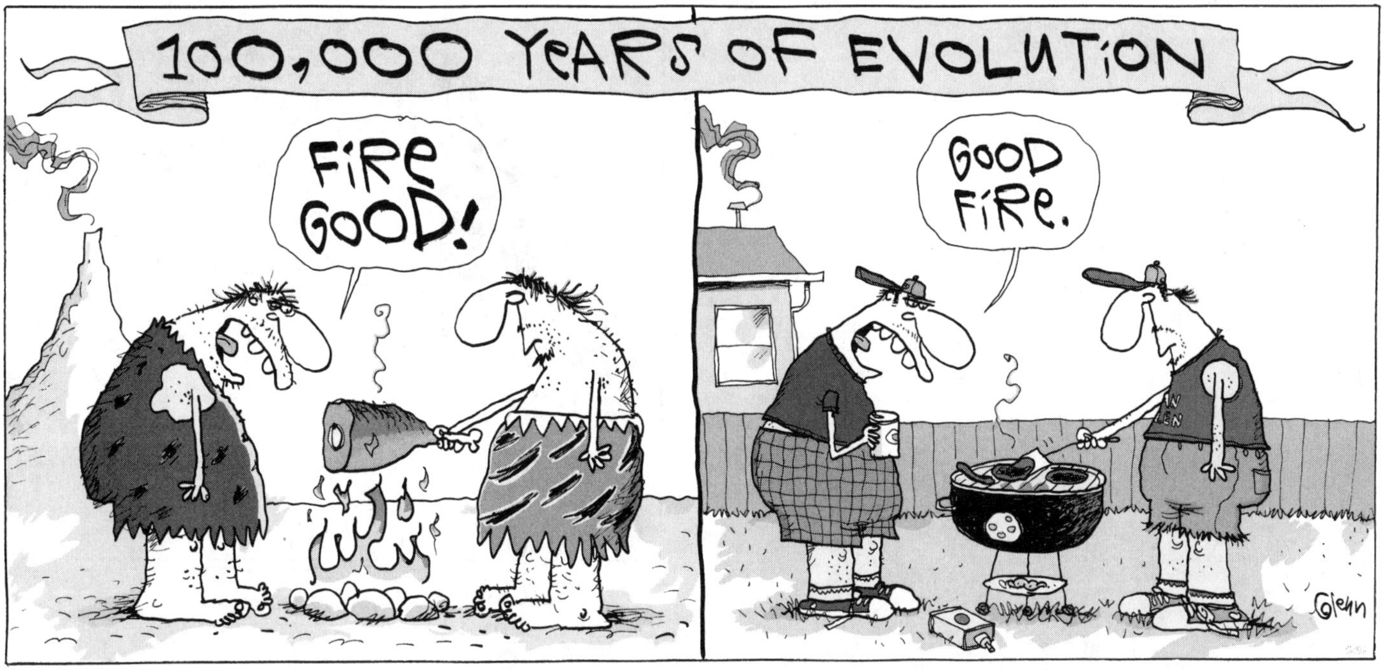
100,000 YEARS OF EVOLUTION
FIRE GOOD!
GOOD FIRE.
Glenn

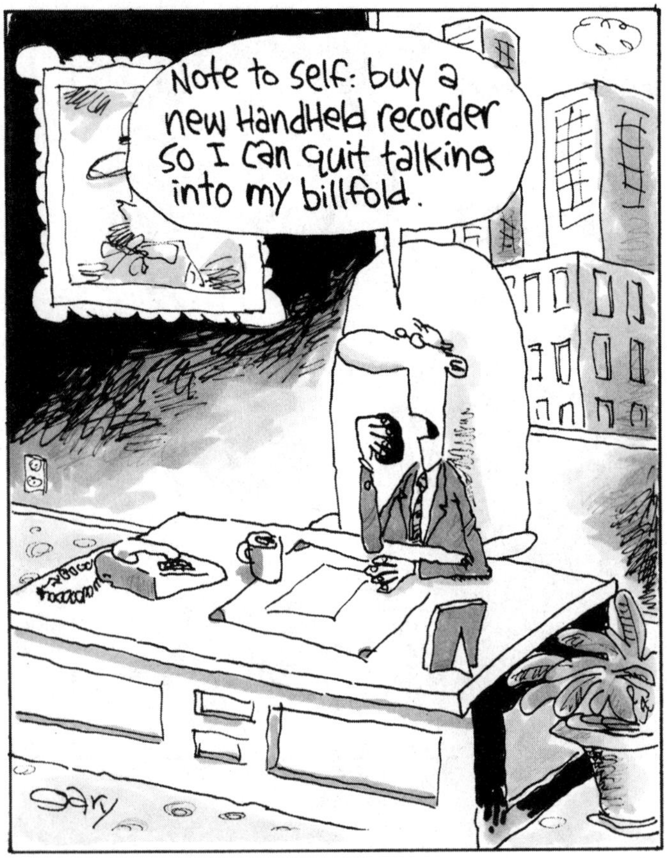
Note to self: buy a new HandHeld recorder so I can quit talking into my billfold.
Gary

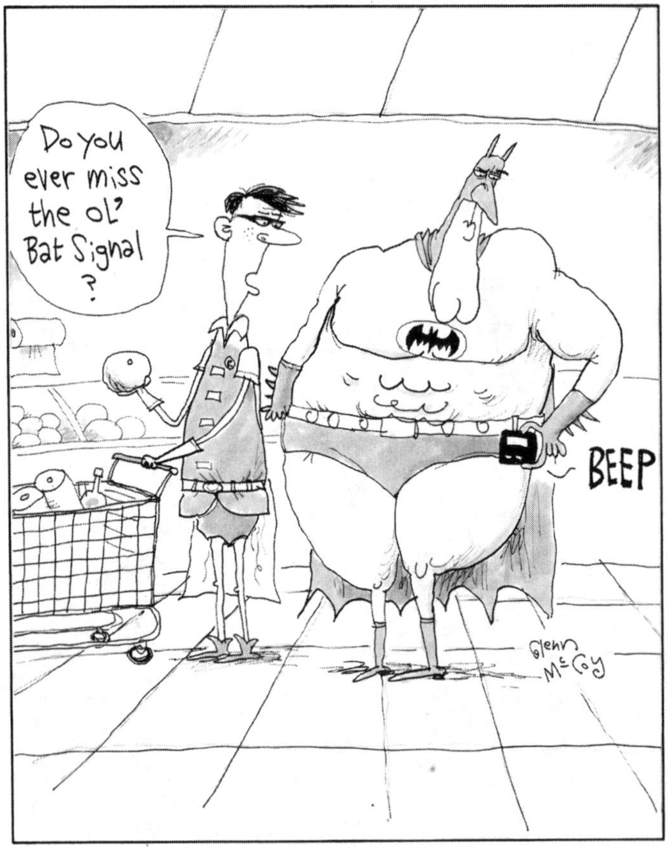
Do you ever miss the ol' Bat Signal ?
BEEP
Glenn McCoy

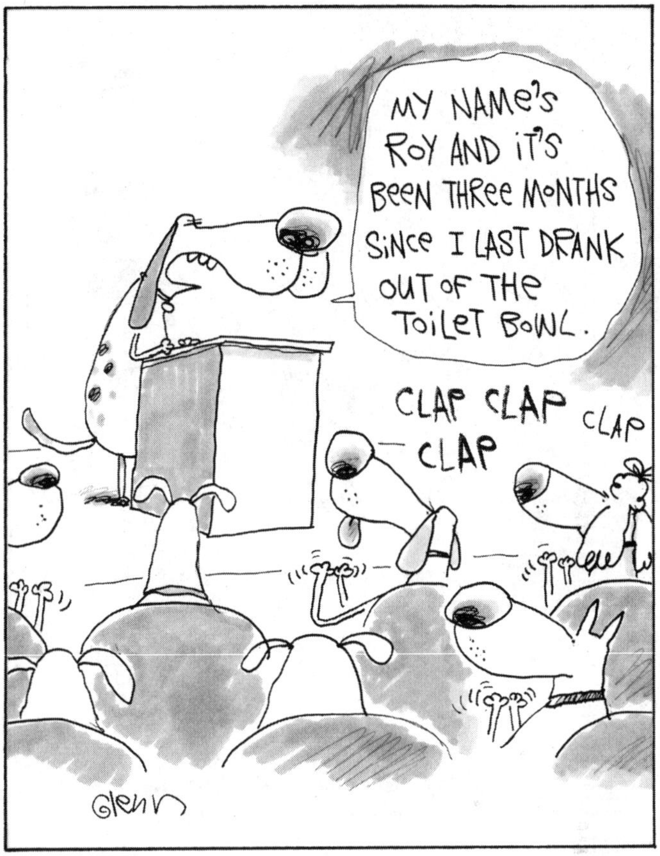
MY NAME'S ROY AND IT'S BEEN THREE MONTHS SINCE I LAST DRANK OUT OF THE TOILET BOWL.
CLAP CLAP CLAP
CLAP
Glenn

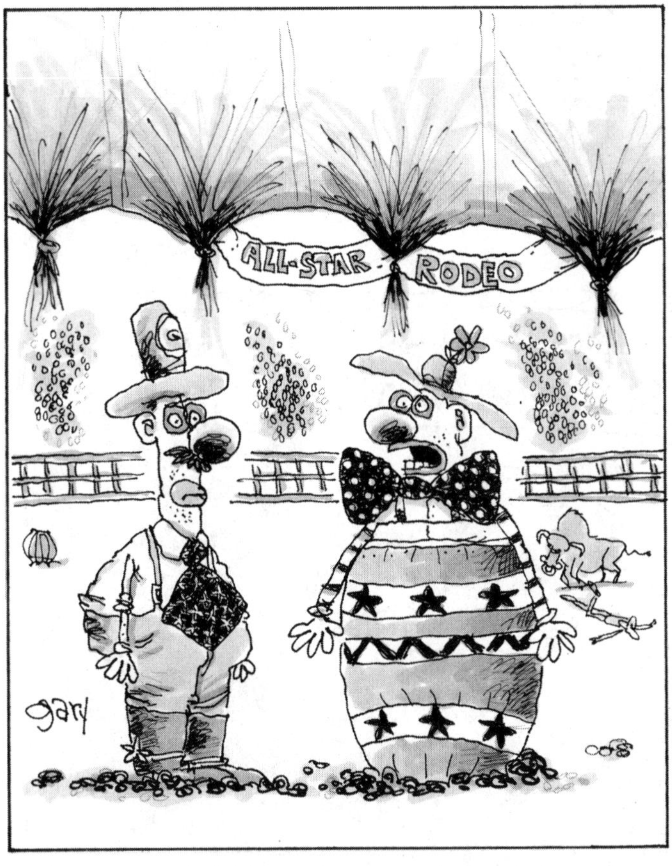
ALL-STAR RODEO
gary

"Someday I'd like to have a job that doesn't require me to wear a tie to work."

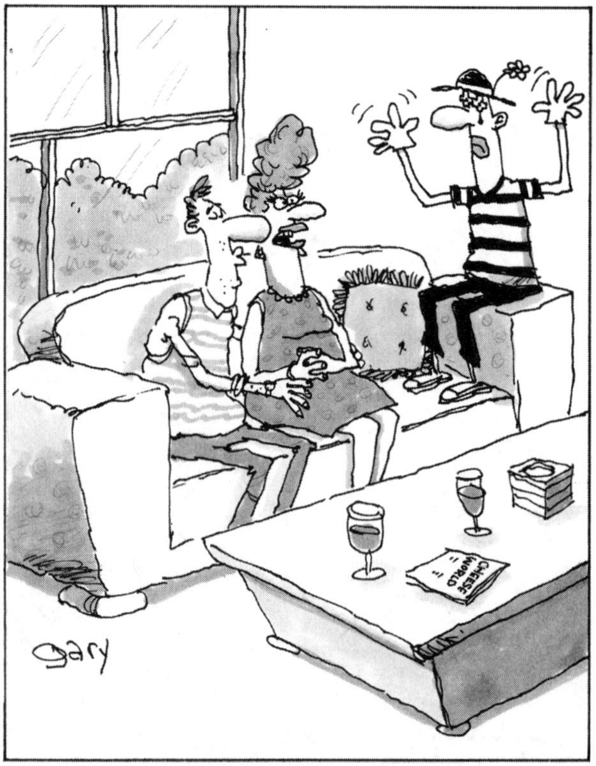

"My heart says 'yes,' but my mime says 'no.'"

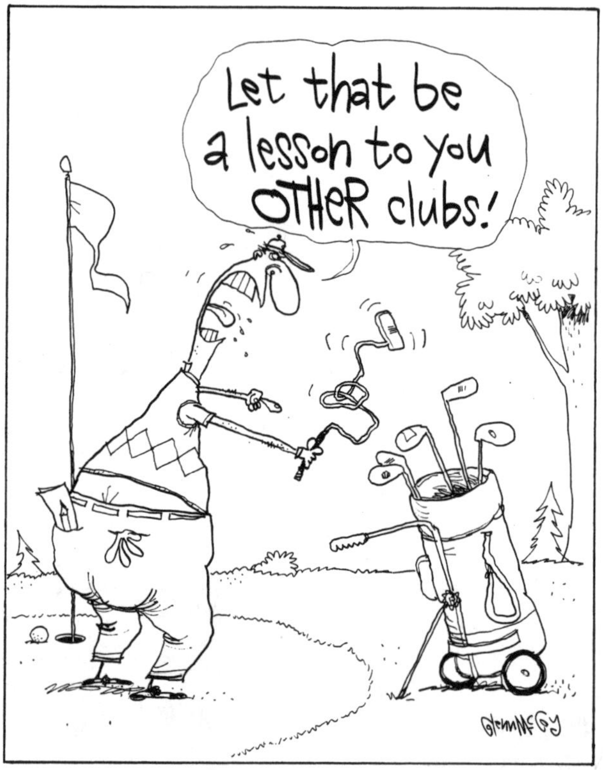
Let that be a lesson to you OTHER clubs!

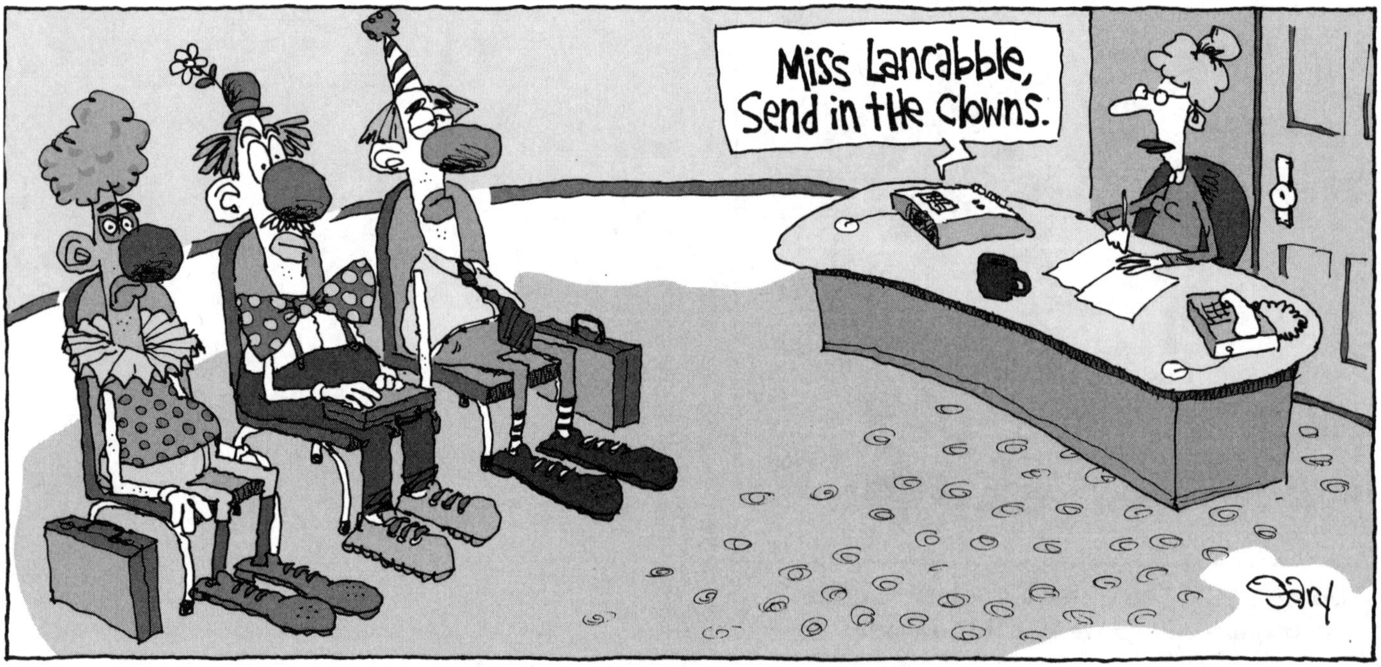
Miss Lancabble, Send in the Clowns.

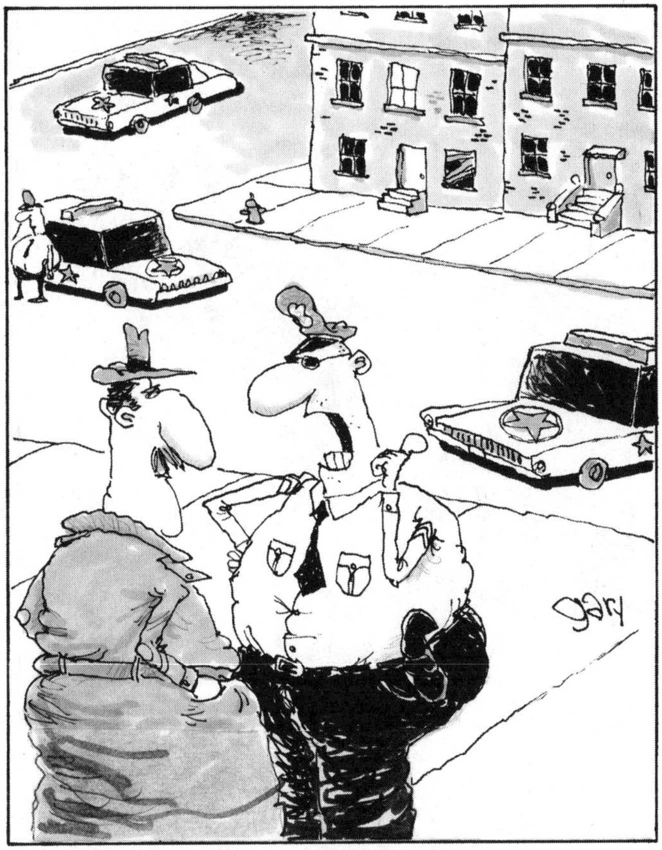
Gary

"We've got a real crisis on our hands. Some nut's in there holding our top three hostage negotiators."

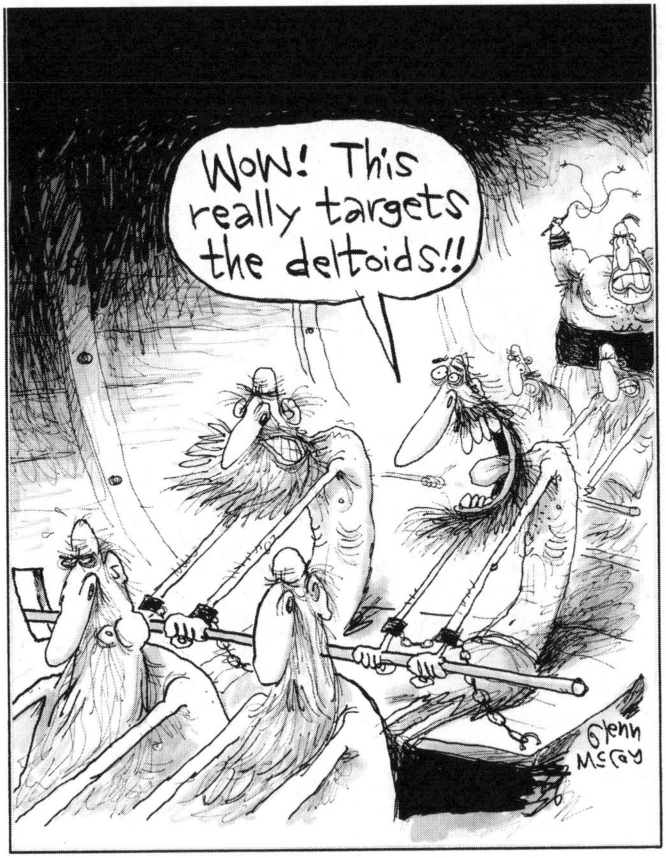
WOW! This really targets the deltoids!!
Glenn McCoy

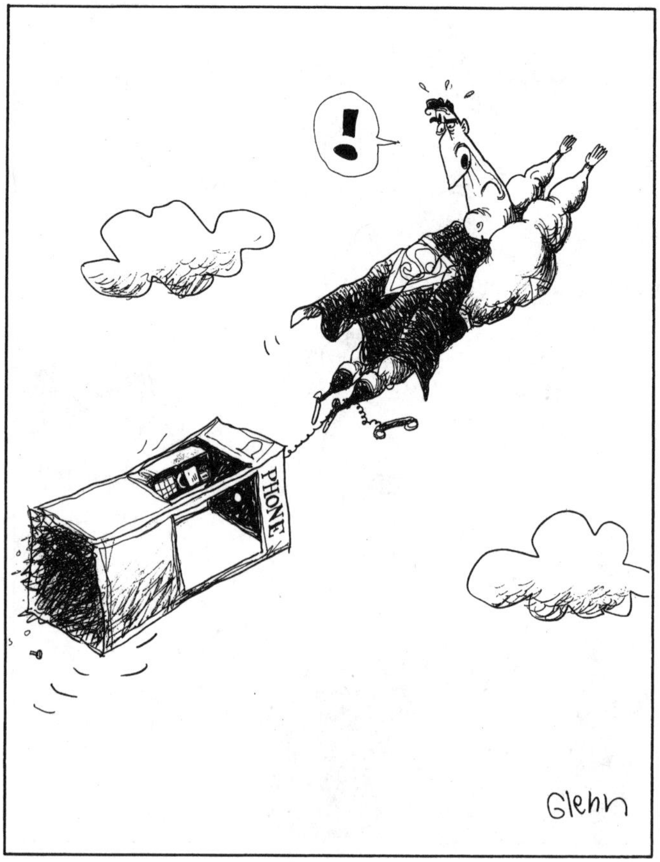
!
PHONE
Glenn

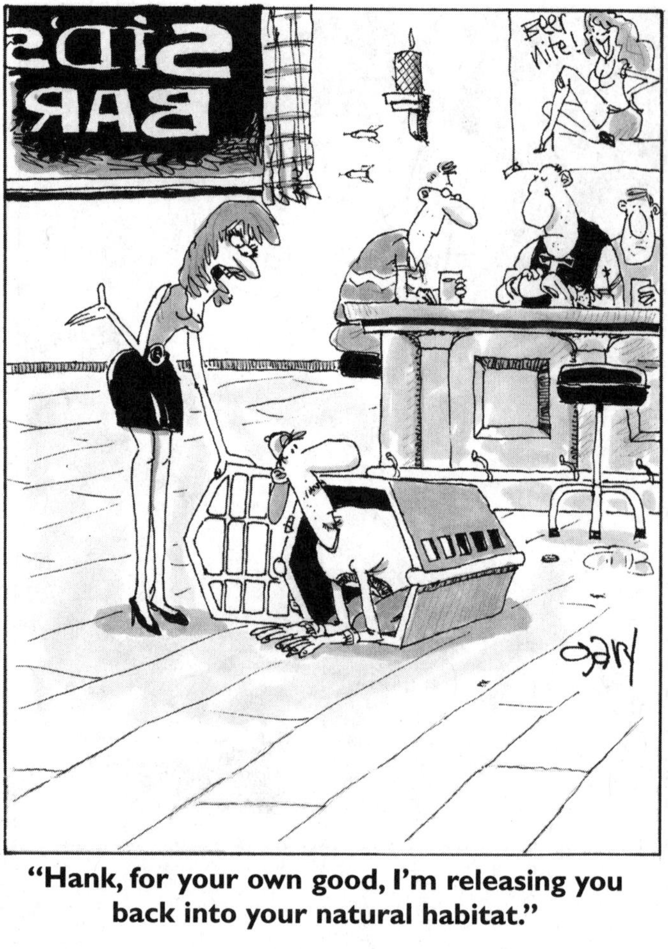
Beer nite!
gary

"Hank, for your own good, I'm releasing you back into your natural habitat."

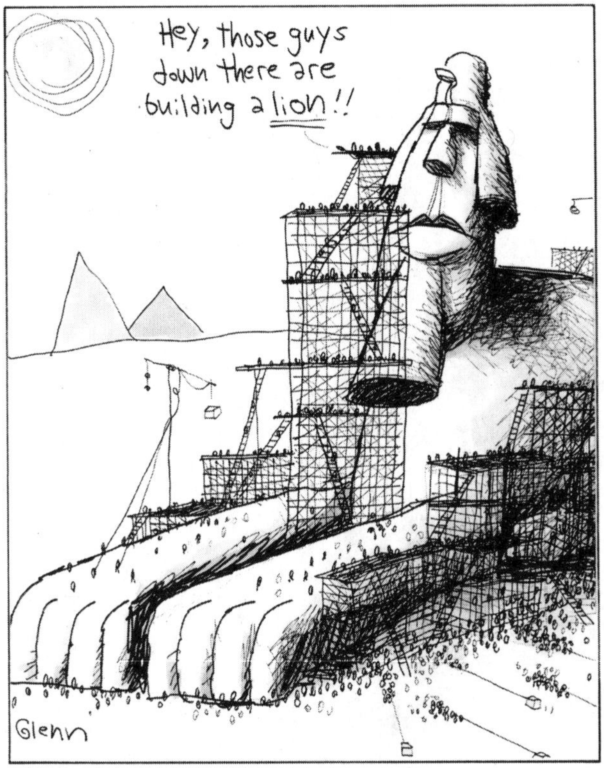
Hey, those guys down there are building a lion!!
Glenn

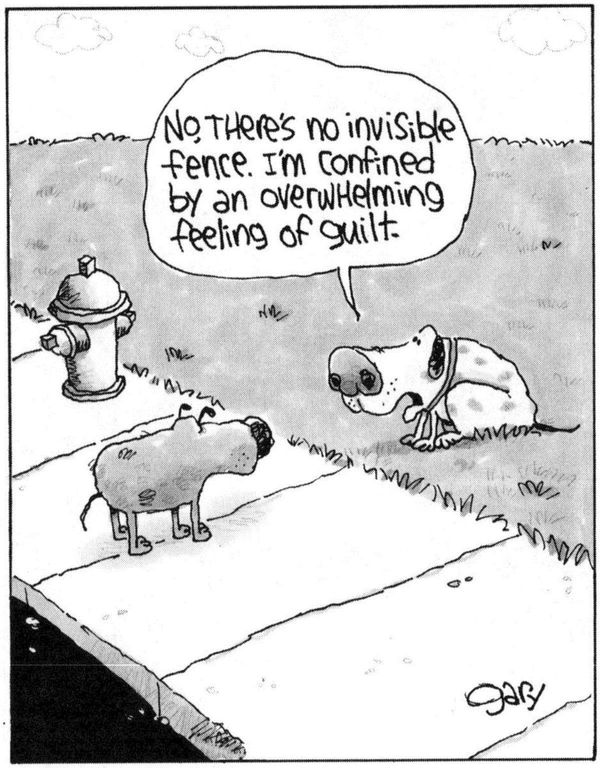
No, There's no invisible fence. I'm confined by an overwhelming feeling of guilt.
Gary

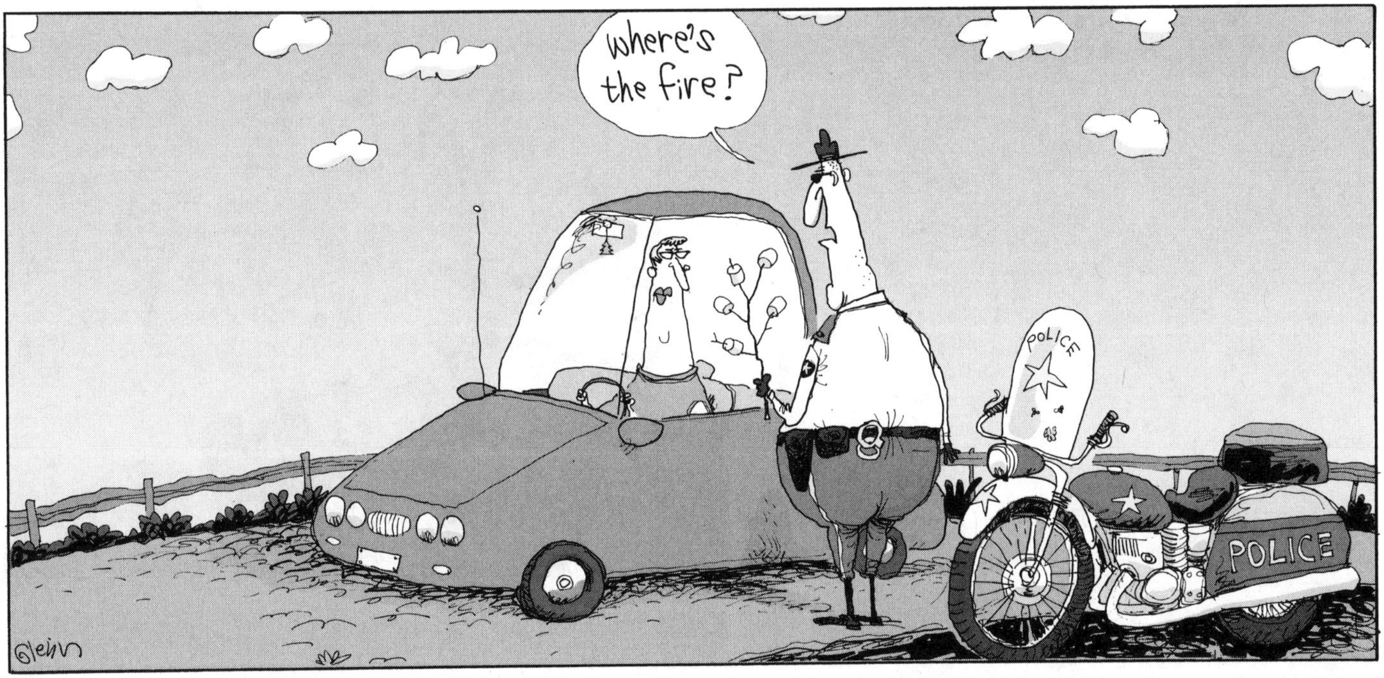
Where's the fire?
POLICE
POLICE
Glenn

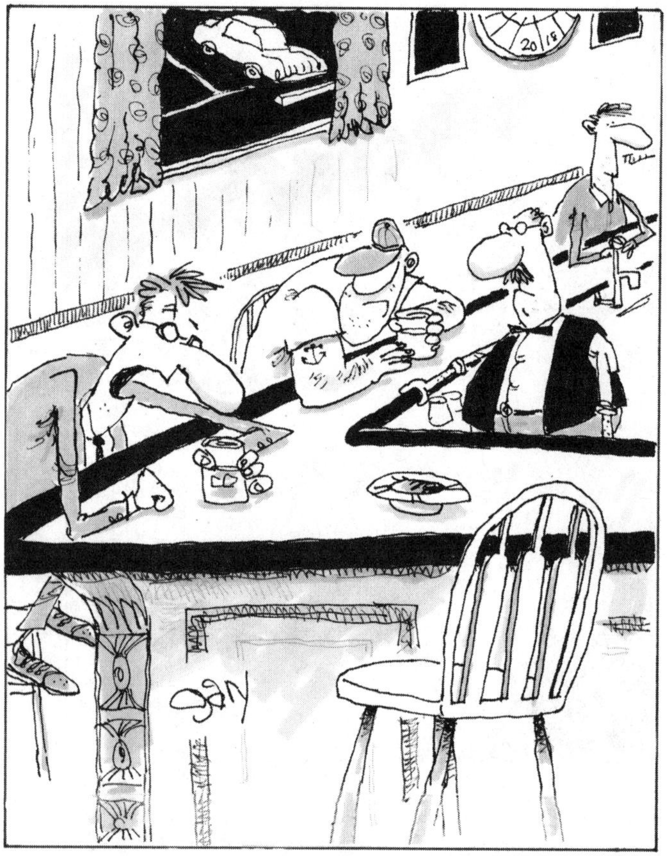

"My ex-wife's lawyer doesn't understand me."

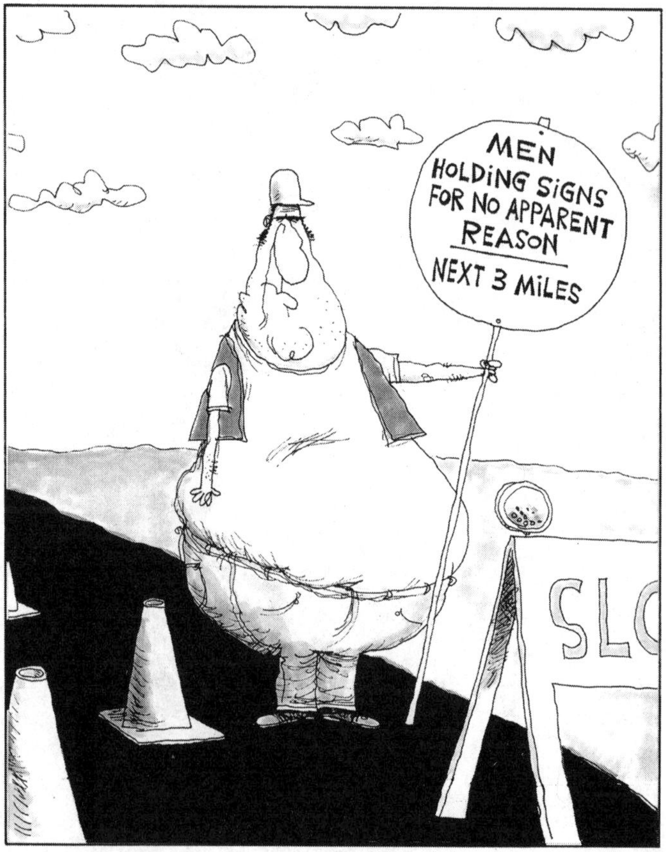
MEN
HOLDING SIGNS
FOR NO APPARENT
REASON
NEXT 3 MILES
SLO

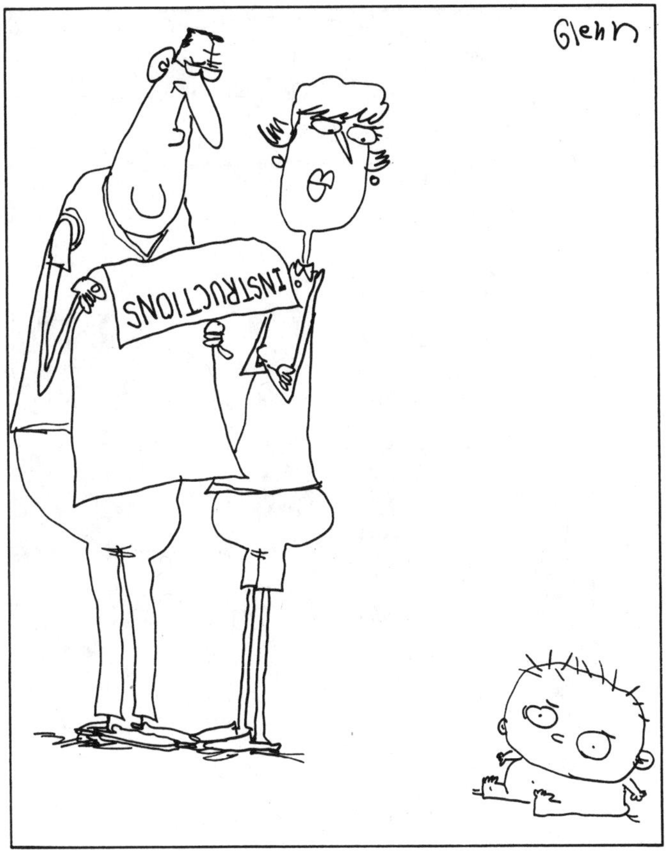
Glenn
INSTRUCTIONS

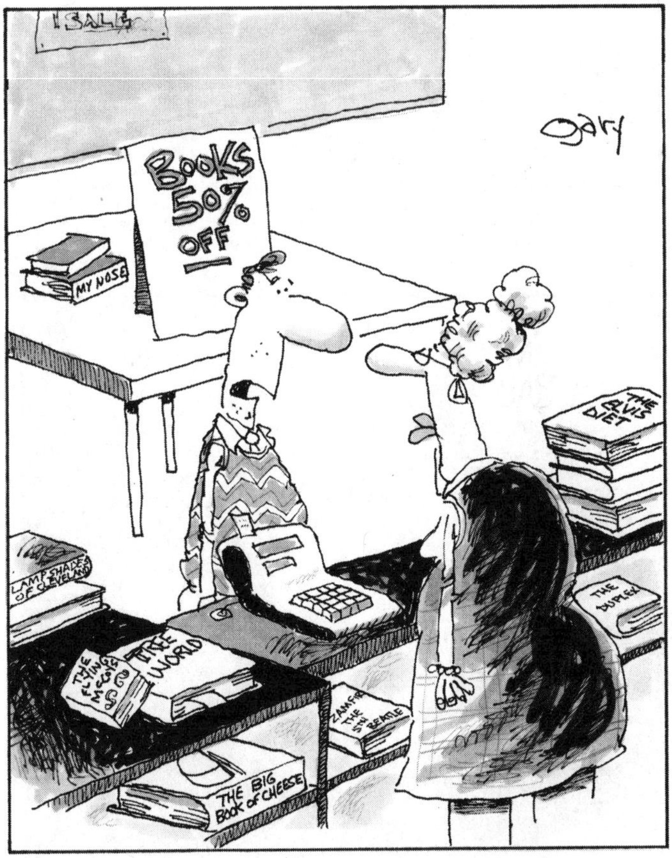
SALE
gary
BOOKS 50% OFF
MY NOSE
LAMP SHADES OF CLEVELAND
THE DUPLEX
THE FLYING McCOYS
WORLD
THE BIG BOOK OF CHEESE

"Do you have *Building Your Self-Esteem for Dummies?*"

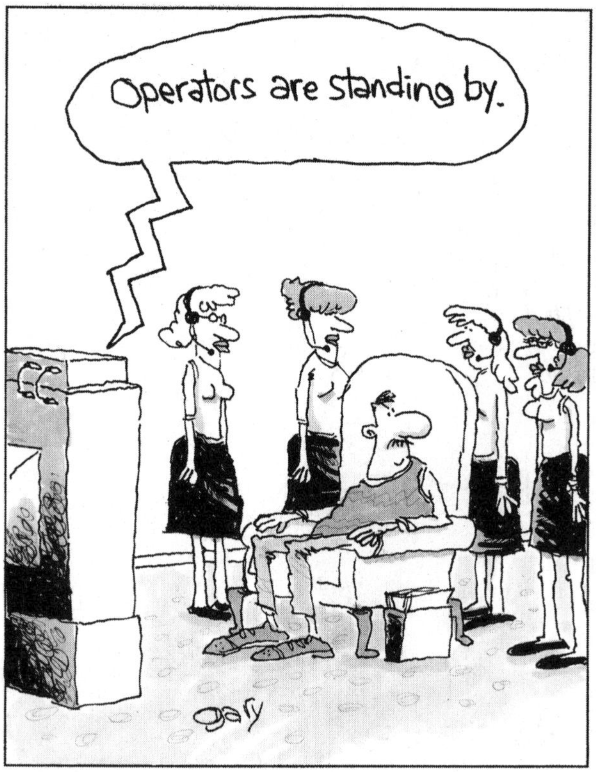
Operators are standing by.
gary

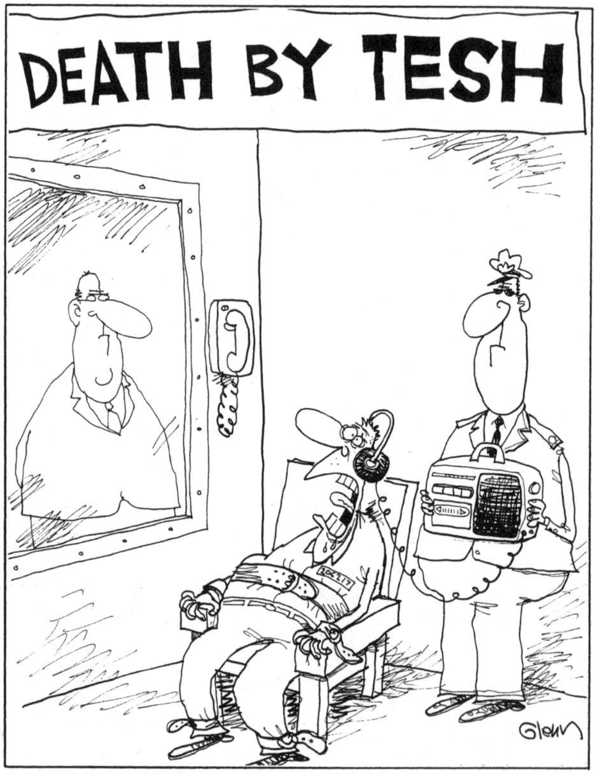
DEATH BY TESH
Glenn

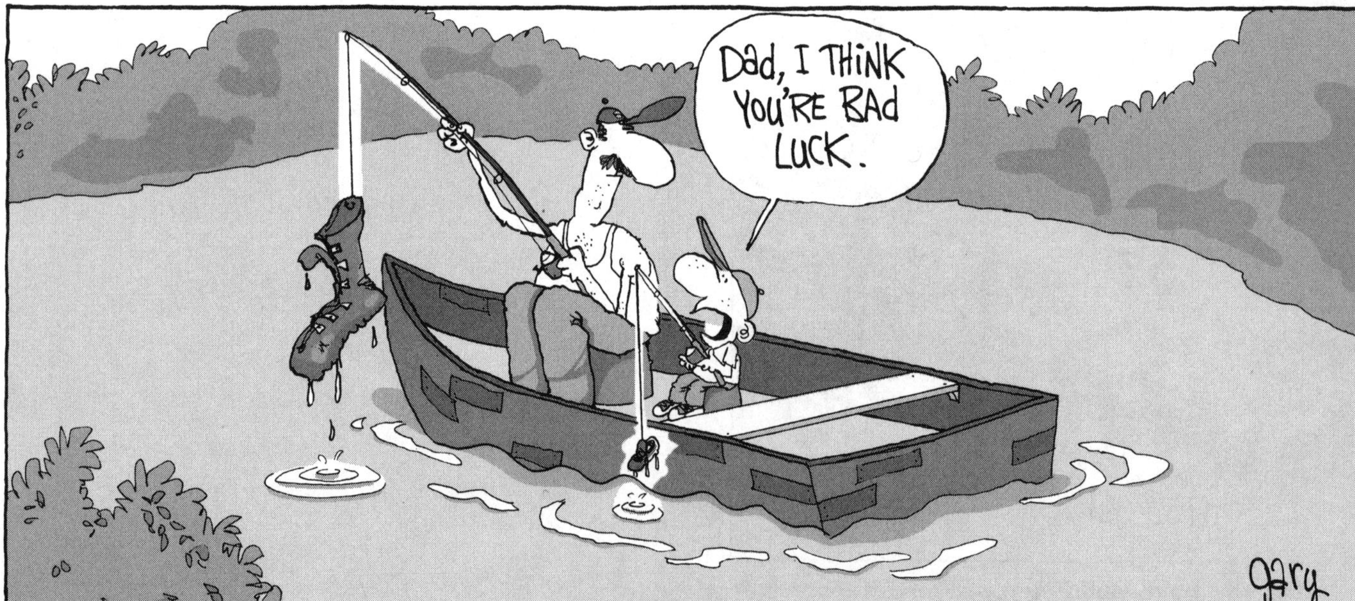
Dad, I THINK YOU'RE BAD LUCK.
gary

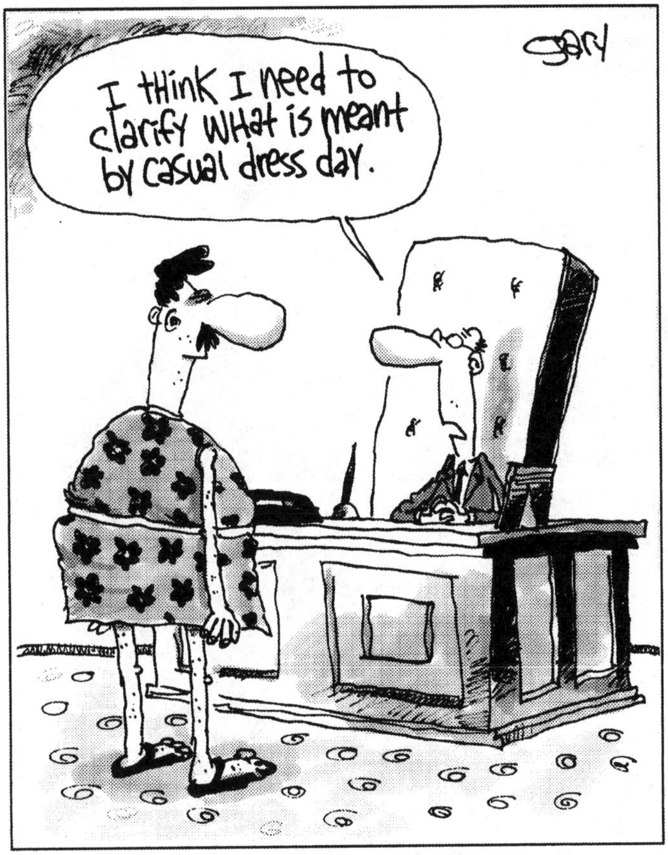

I THINK I NEED TO CLARIFY WHAT IS MEANT BY CASUAL DRESS DAY.

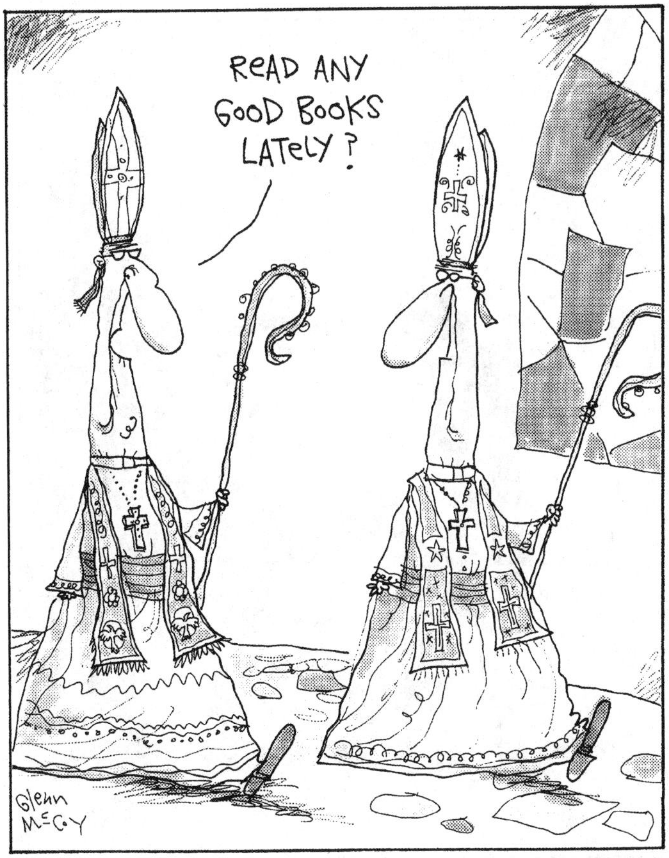

READ ANY GOOD BOOKS LATELY?
Glenn McCoy

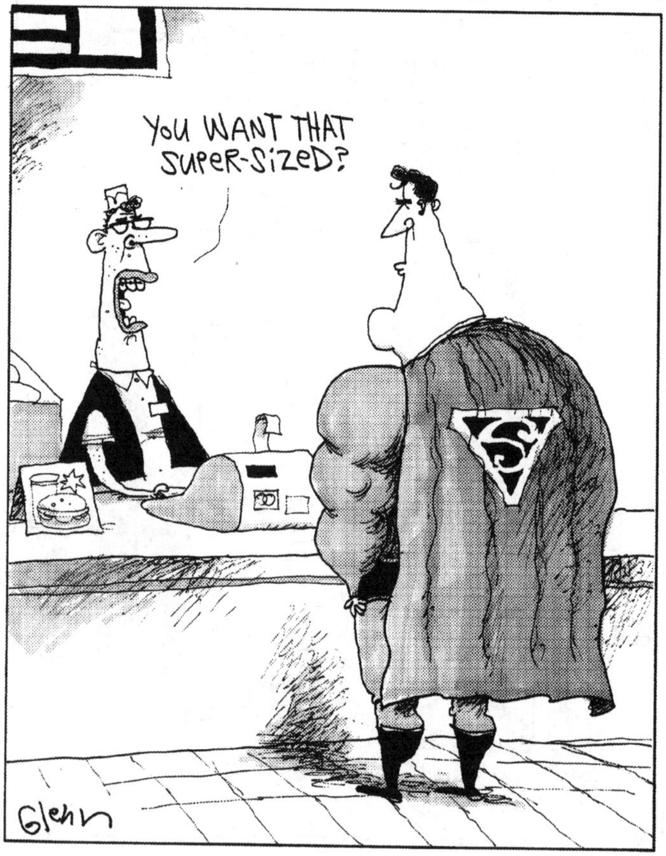
YOU WANT THAT SUPER-SIZED?

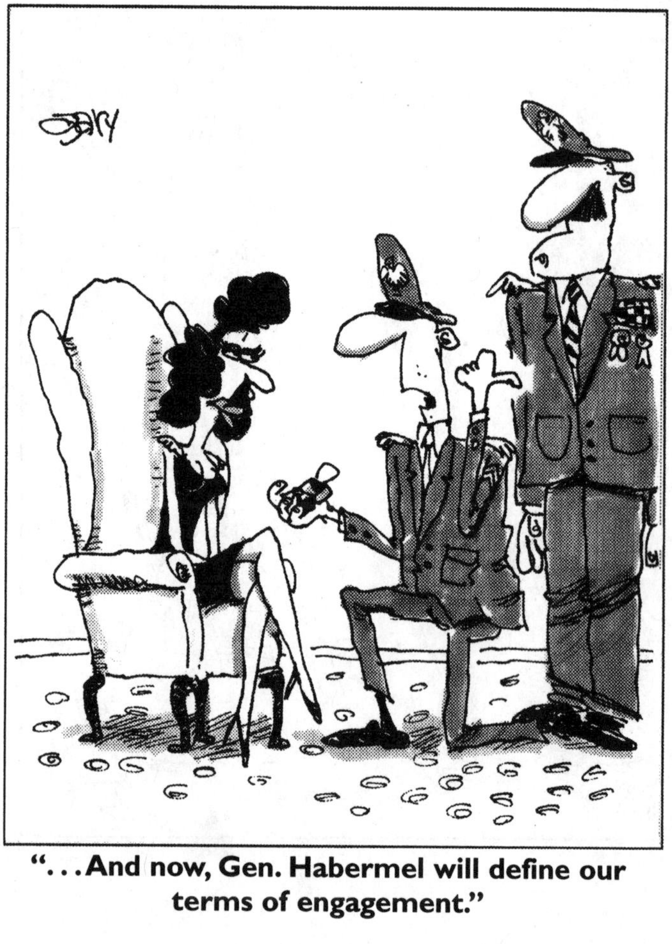

"...And now, Gen. Habermel will define our terms of engagement."

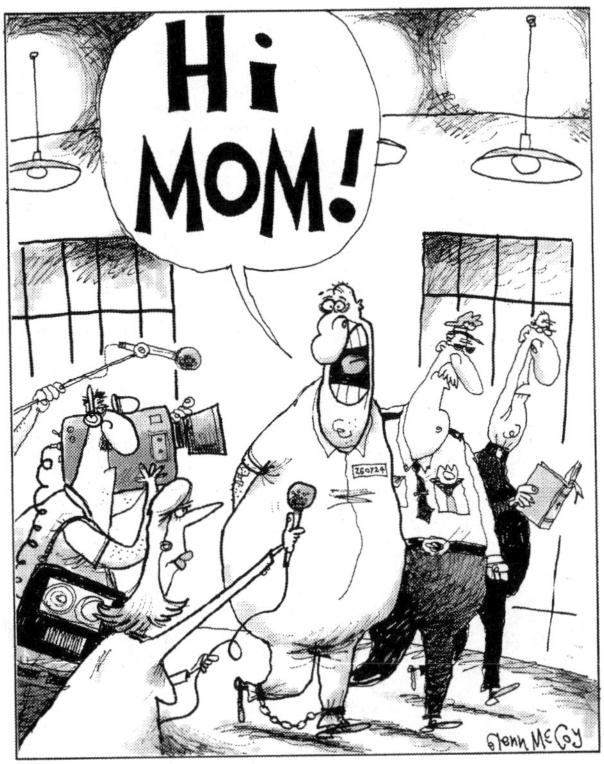
Hi MOM!
Glenn McCoy

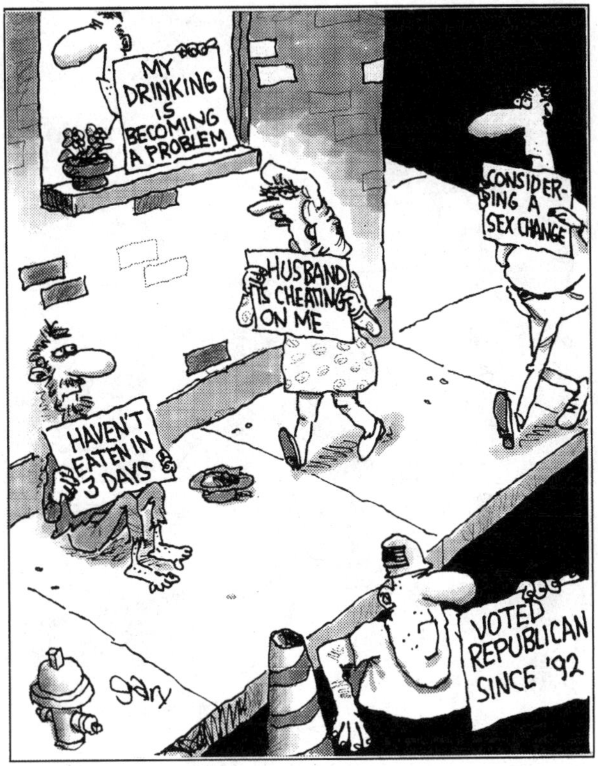
MY DRINKING IS BECOMING A PROBLEM
CONSIDER-ING A SEX CHANGE
HUSBAND IS CHEATING ON ME
HAVEN'T EATEN IN 3 DAYS
VOTED REPUBLICAN SINCE '92
Gary

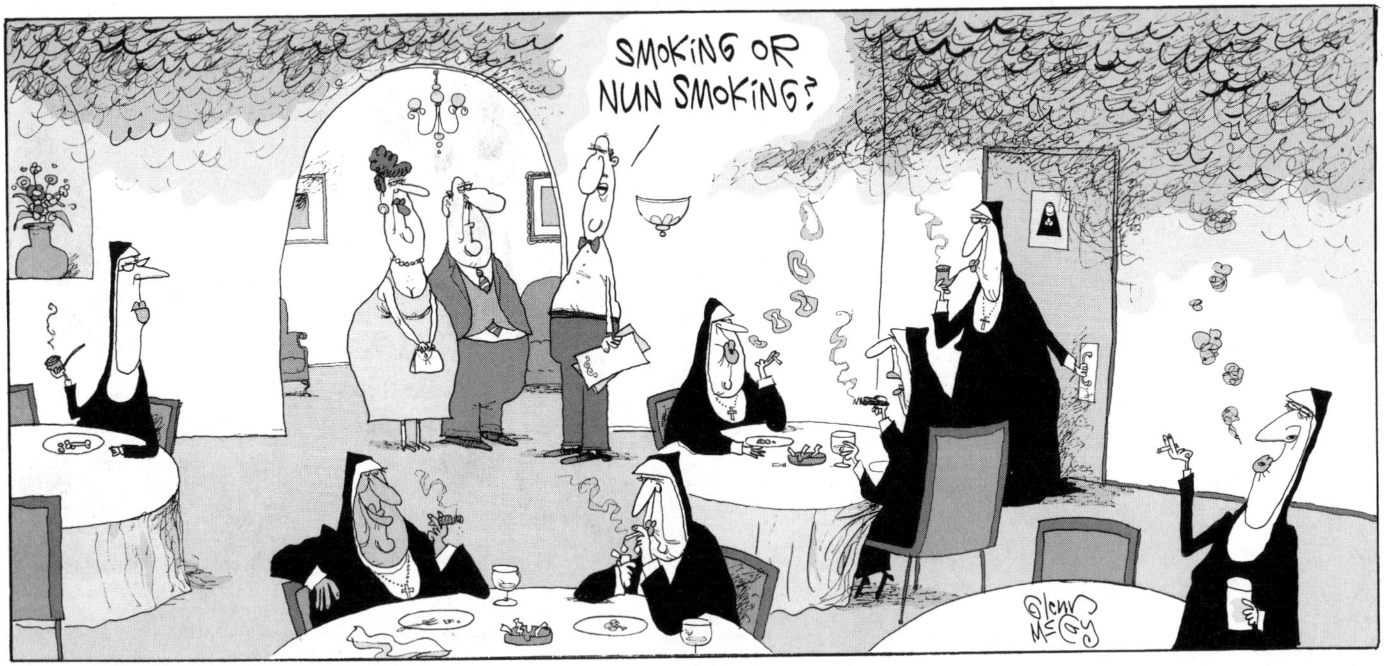
SMOKING OR NUN SMOKING?
Glenn McCoy

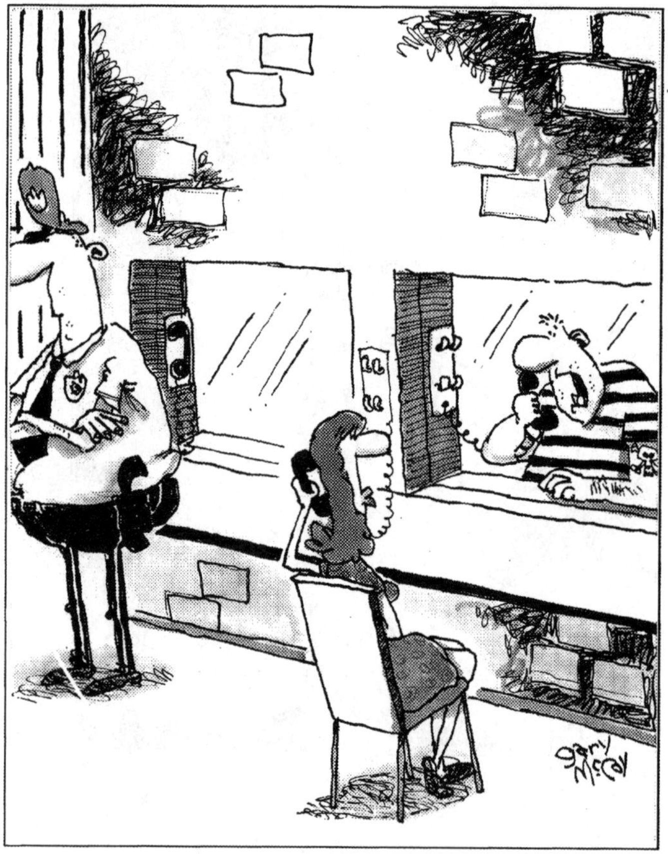
gary McCoy

"Mary Jo, you can't walk out on me now—we've got a good thing going!"

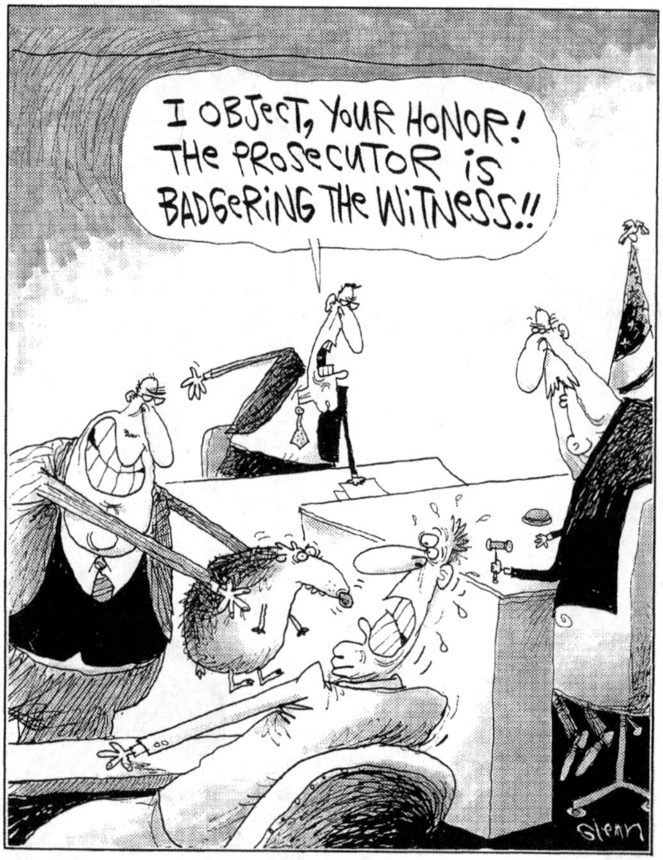
I OBJECT, YOUR HONOR! THE PROSECUTOR IS BADGERING THE WITNESS!!
Glenn

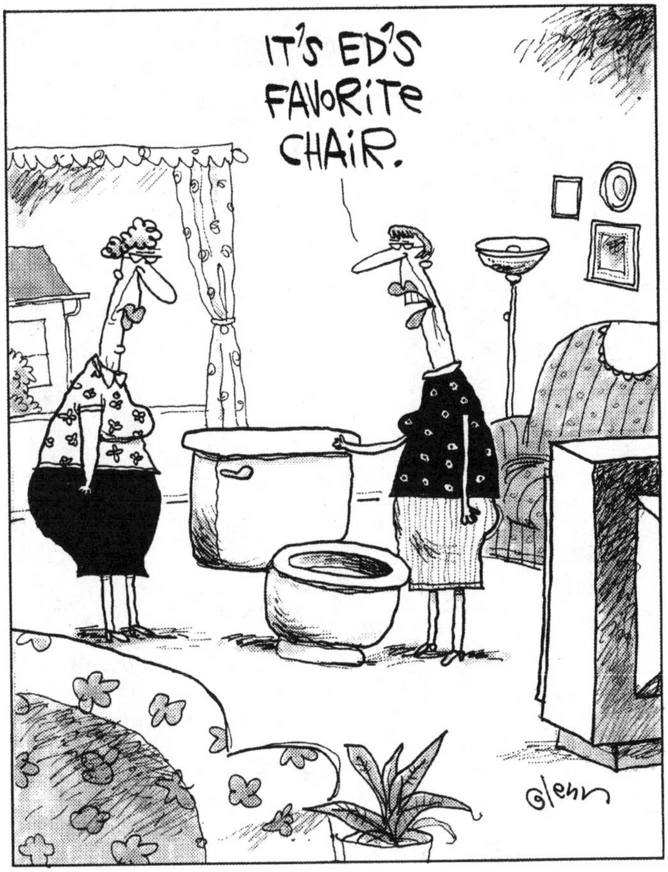
IT'S ED'S FAVORITE CHAIR.
Glenn

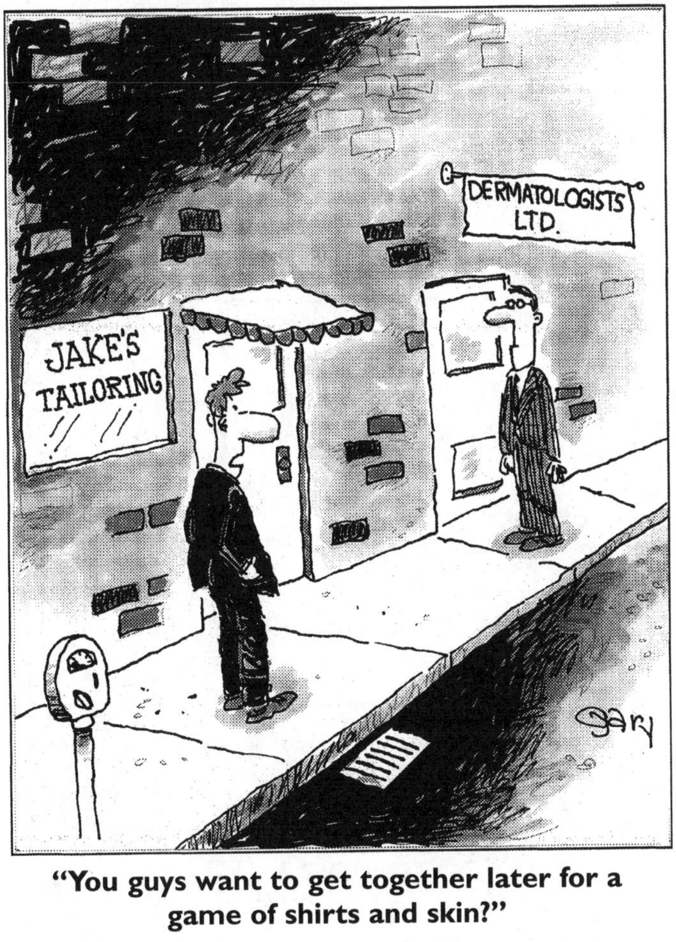
DERMATOLOGISTS LTD.
JAKE'S TAILORING
Gary

"You guys want to get together later for a game of shirts and skin?"

Dropped on my HEAD AS A BABY.
PLEASE HELP

NO. I'M SORRY. I DON'T HAVE MY INSURANCE CARD ON ME.

THIS ONE'S OUR BEST SELLER. IT CREATES A CLOUD OF SMOKE SO THICK THAT YOUR WIFE WILL NEVER BE ABLE TO FIND YOU AND WRING YOUR NECK FOR SPENDING THE GROCERY MONEY ON FIREWORKS.
FIREWORKS

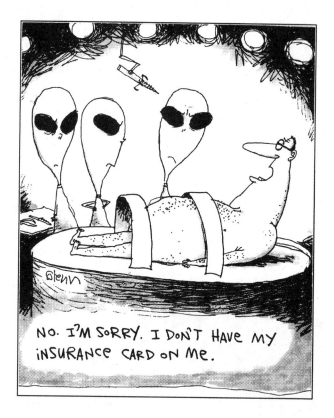

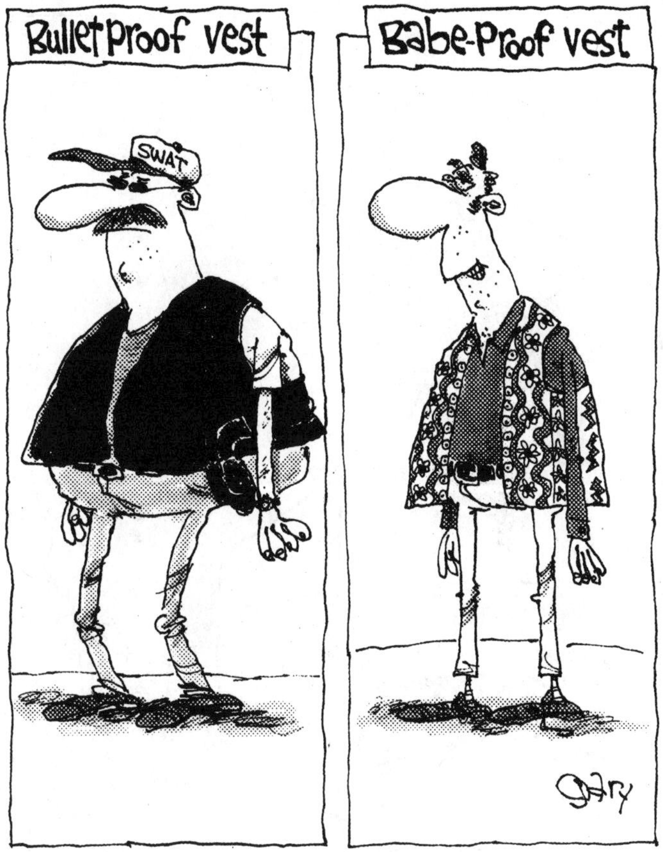
Bulletproof vest
SWAT
Babe-Proof vest
Gary

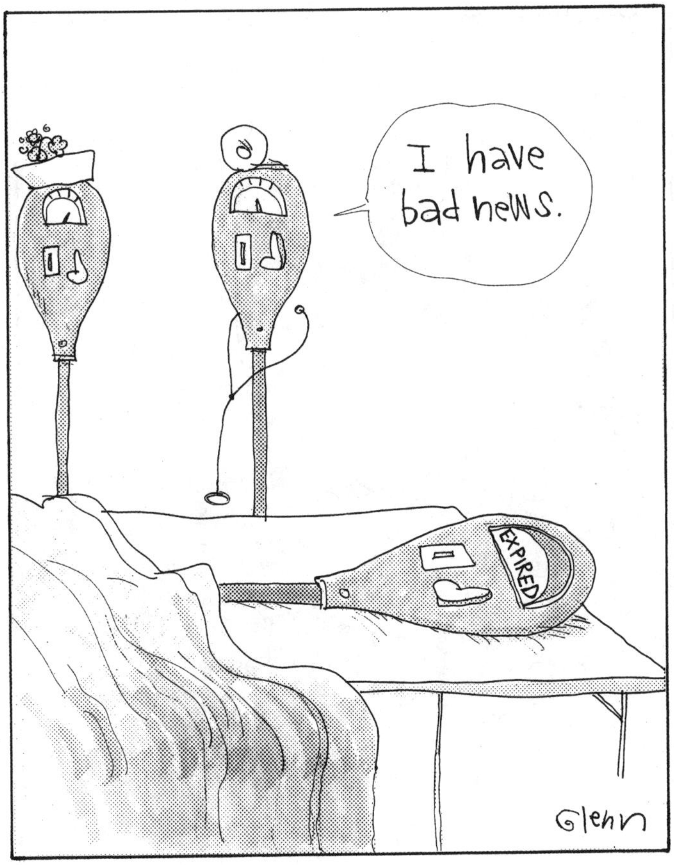
I have bad news.
EXPIRED
Glenn

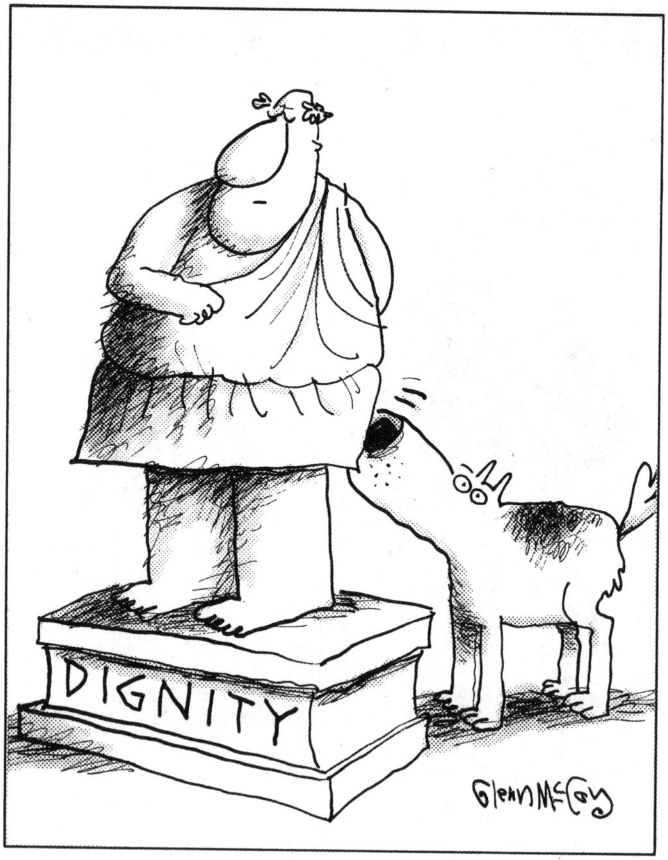
DIGNITY
Glenn McCoy

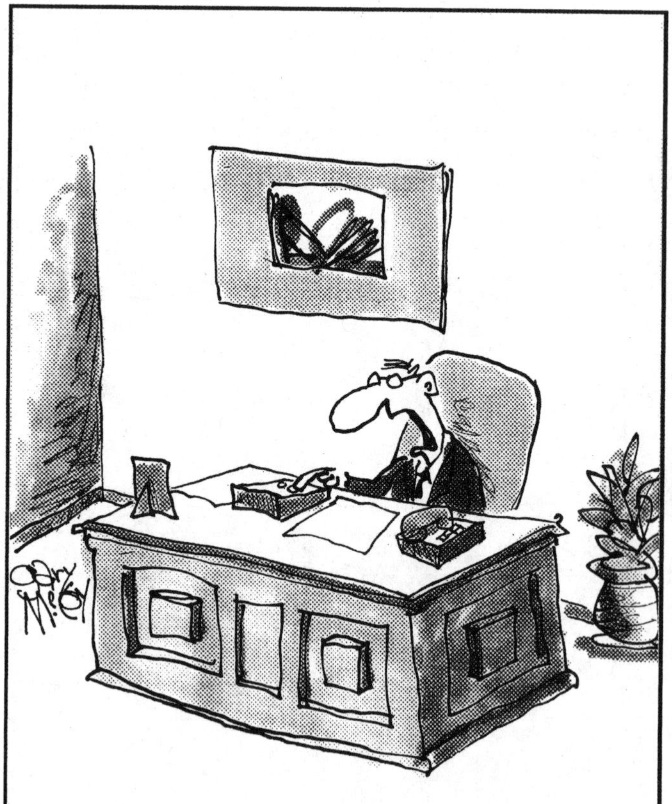
Glenn McCoy

"Miss Fergens, cancel my midlife crisis."

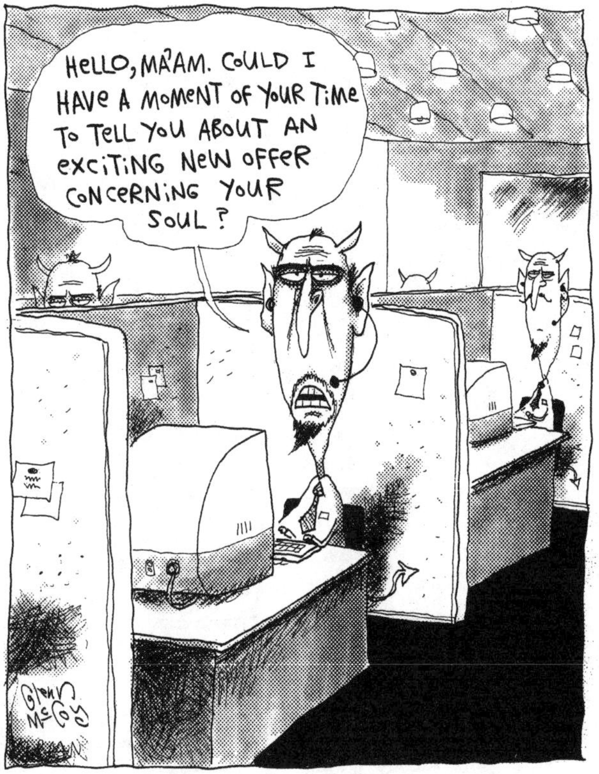
HELLO, MA'AM. COULD I HAVE A MOMENT OF YOUR TIME TO TELL YOU ABOUT AN EXCITING NEW OFFER CONCERNING YOUR SOUL?
Glenn McCoy

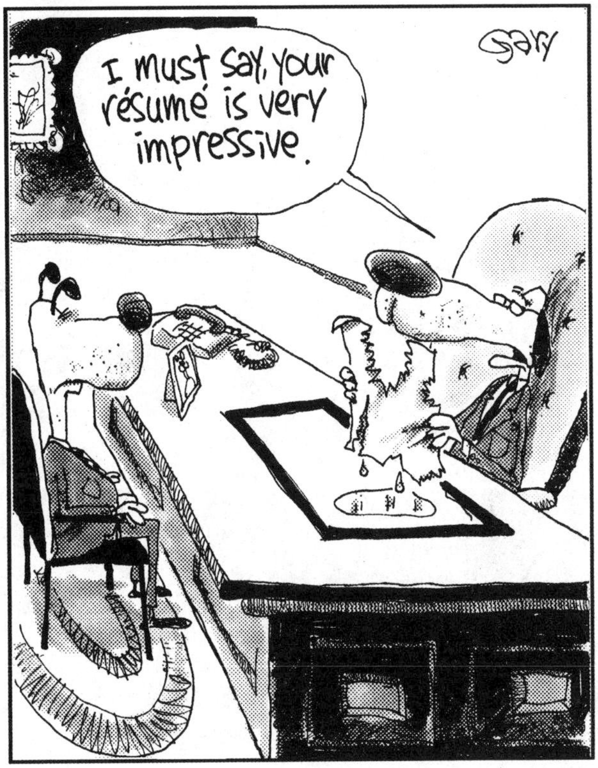
Gary
I must say, your résumé is very impressive.

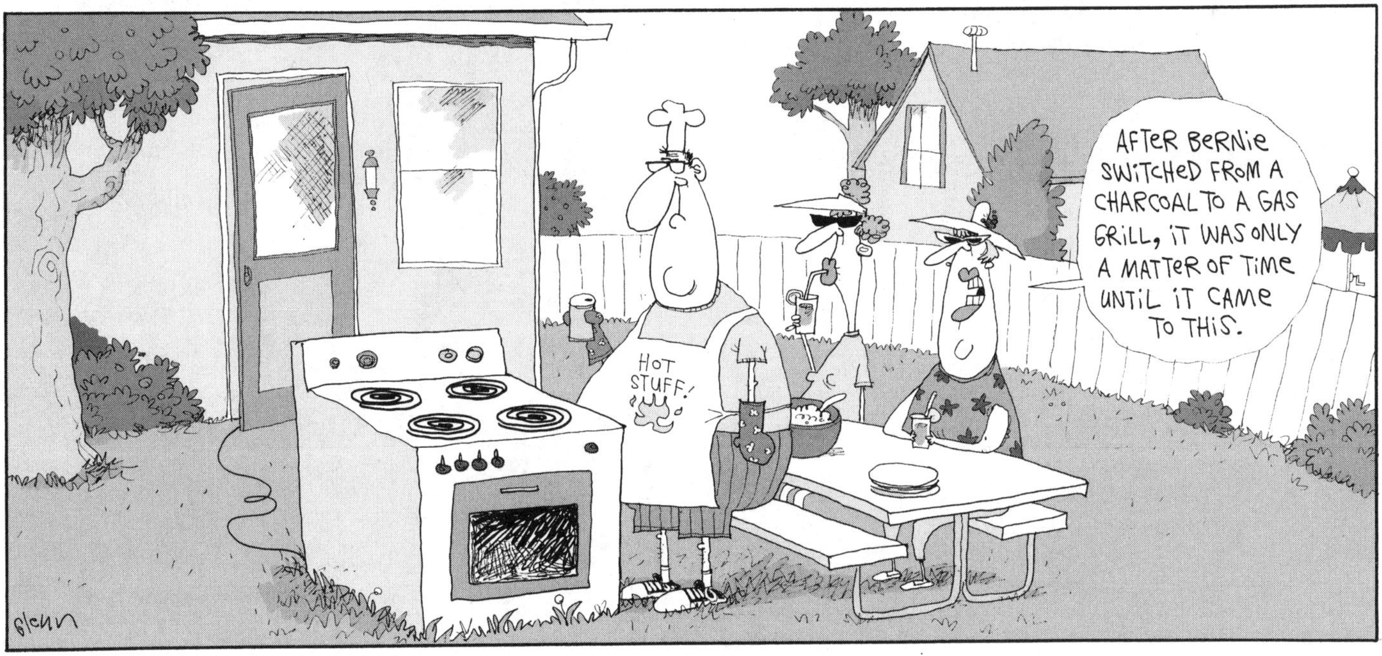
AFTER BERNIE SWITCHED FROM A CHARCOAL TO A GAS GRILL, IT WAS ONLY A MATTER OF TIME UNTIL IT CAME TO THIS.
HOT STUFF!
Glenn

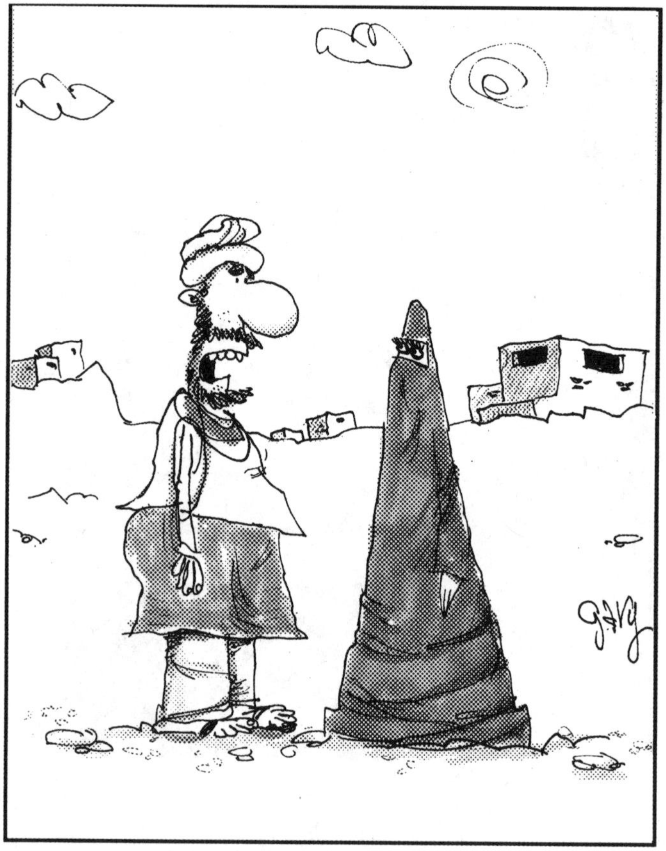
Gary

"Has anyone ever told you that you have beau-
tiful eyes?"

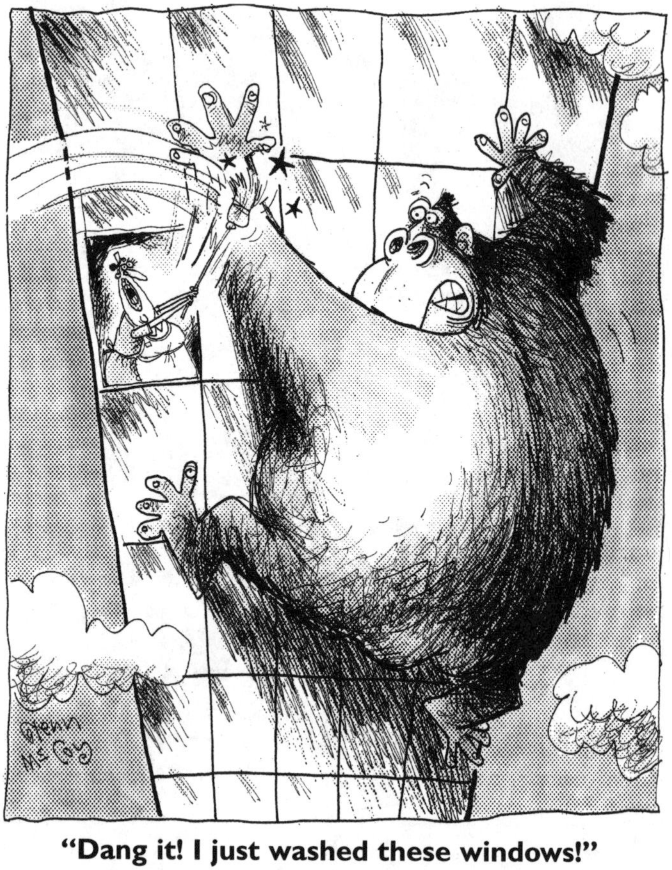
Glenn McCoy

"Dang it! I just washed these windows!"

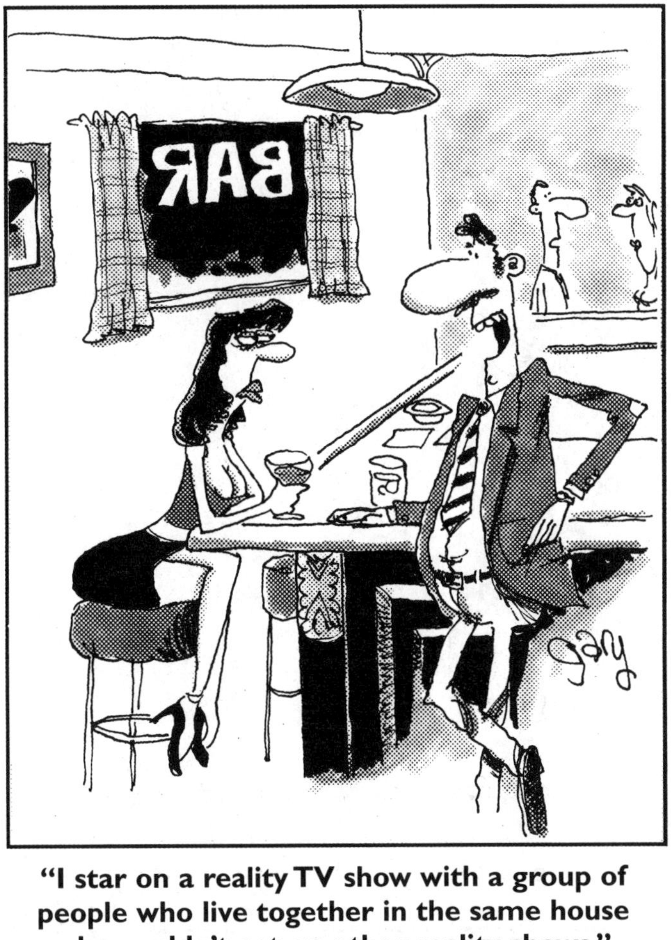
BAR
Gary

"I star on a reality TV show with a group of people who live together in the same house who couldn't get on other reality shows."

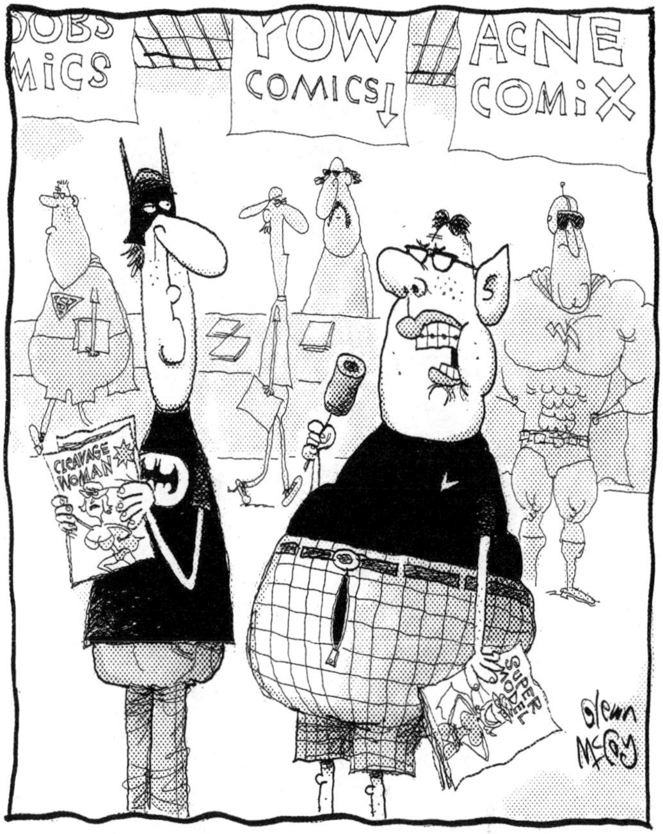
YOW COMICS
ACNE COMIX
CLEAVAGE WOMAN
SUPER MODEL
Glenn McCoy

"The corn dogs at this Comic-Con taste like glok! Pardon my Klingon."

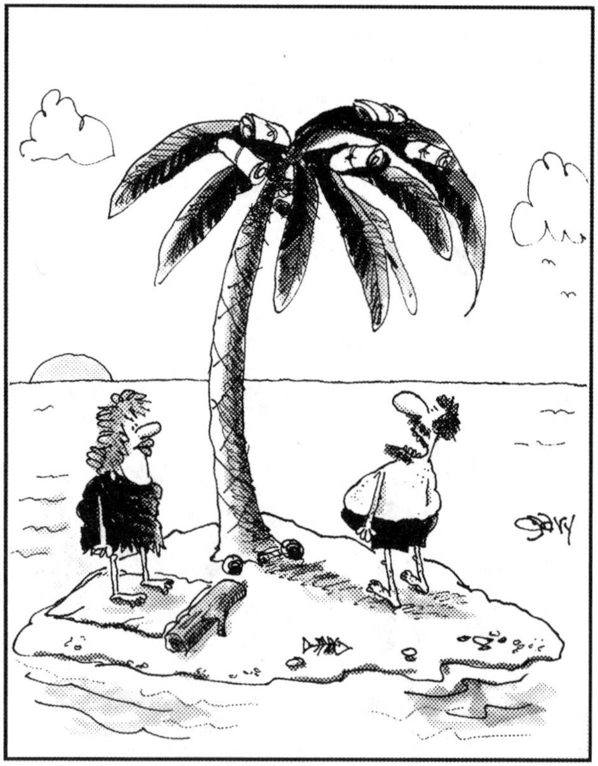

"The darn paper boy threw another one up in the tree!"

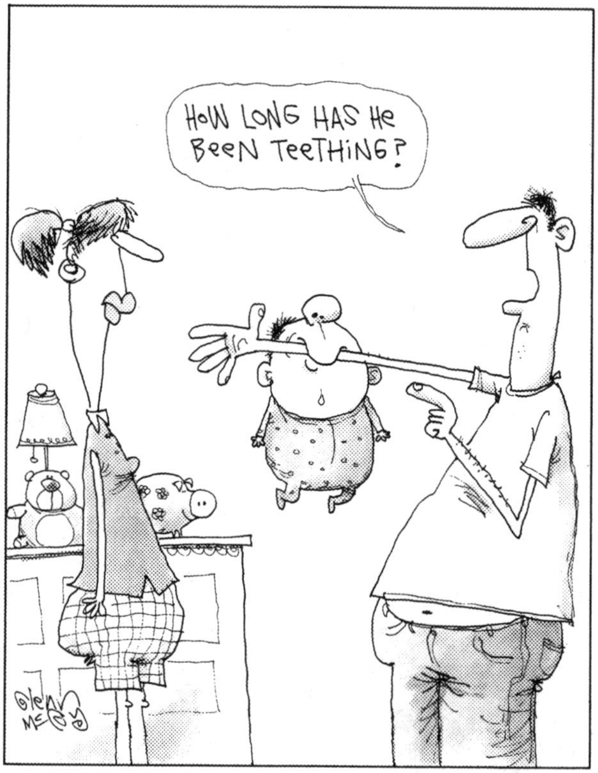
HOW LONG HAS HE BEEN TEETHING?

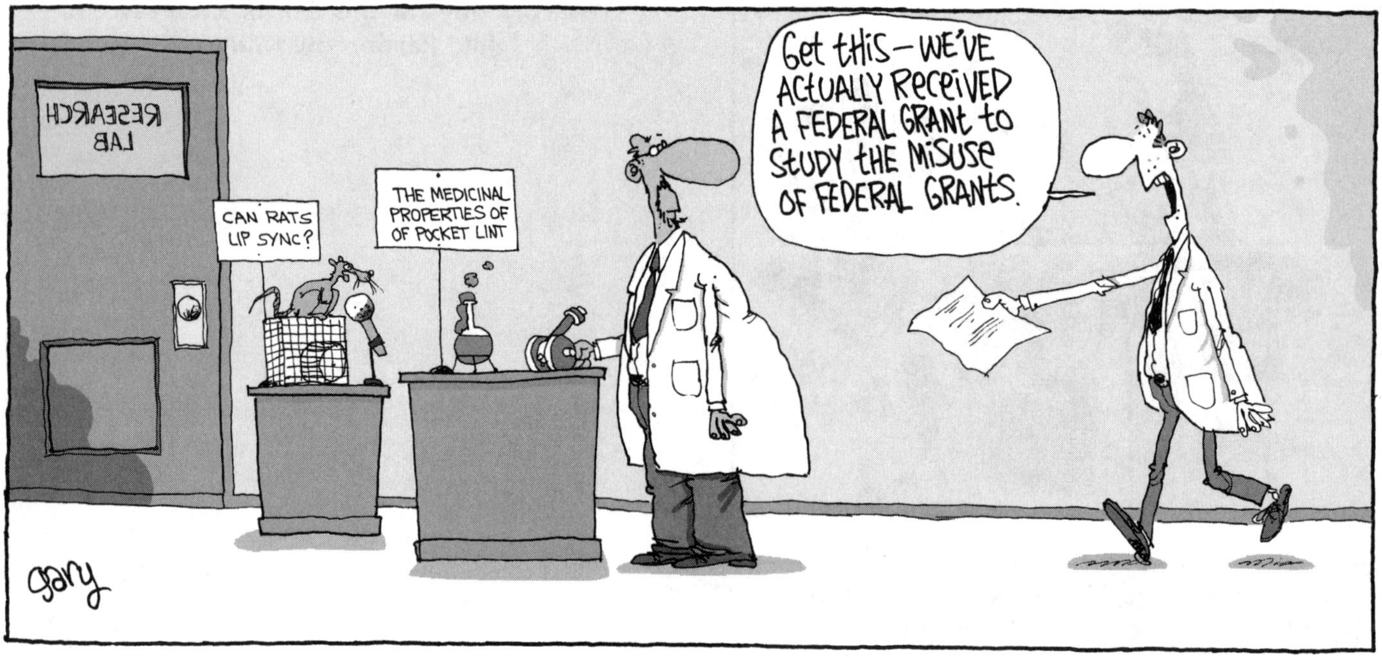
RESEARCH LAB
CAN RATS LIP SYNC?
THE MEDICINAL PROPERTIES OF OF POCKET LINT
Get this—WE'VE ACTUALLY Received A FEDERAL GRANT to Study the MiSUSe OF FEDERAL GRANTS.

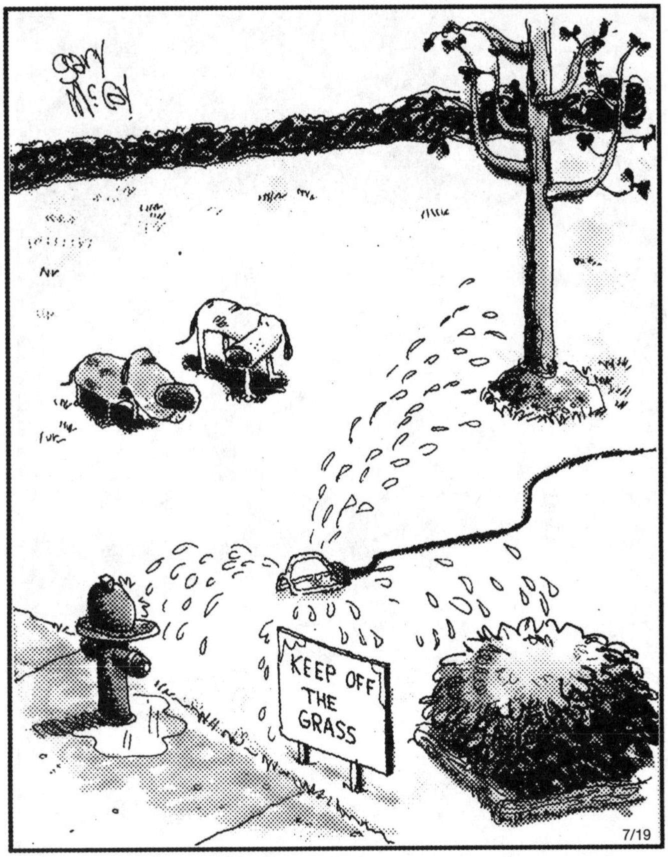
Gary McCoy
KEEP OFF THE GRASS
7/19

"That thing's got me worried. It does the work of four dogs."

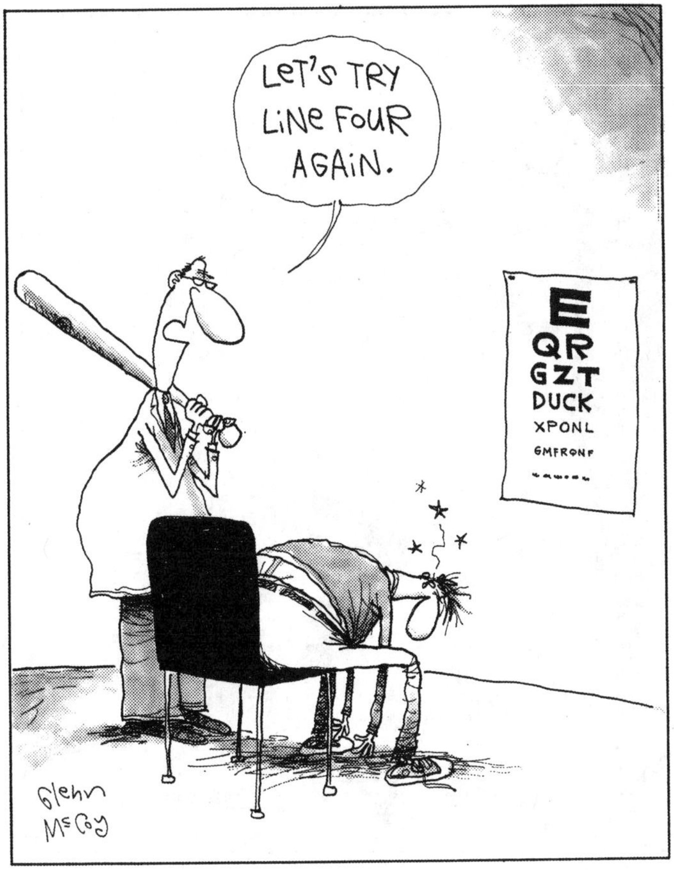
LET'S TRY LINE FOUR AGAIN.
E
QR
GZT
DUCK
XPONL
GMFRONF
Glenn McCoy

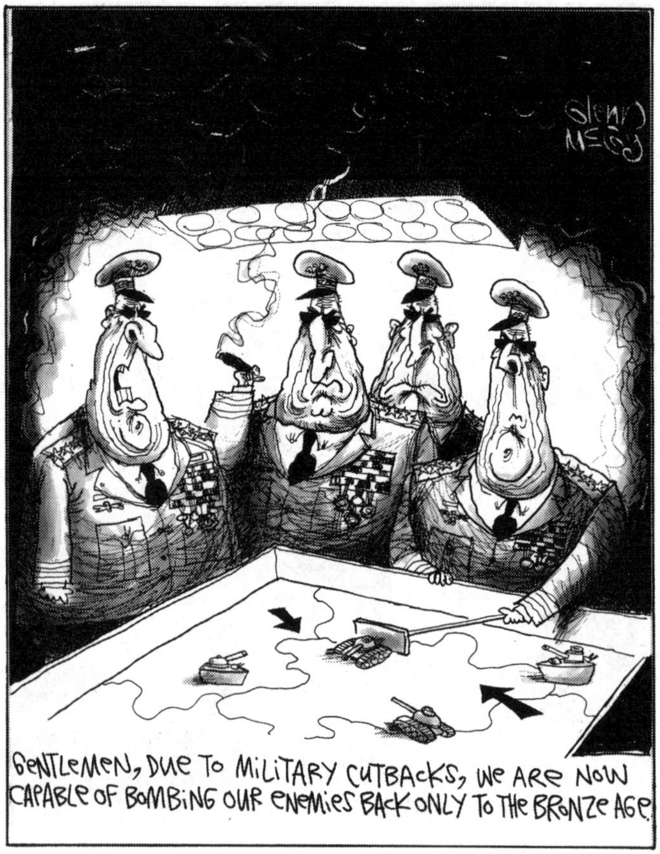
Glenn McCoy
GENTLEMEN, DUE TO MILITARY CUTBACKS, WE ARE NOW CAPABLE OF BOMBING OUR ENEMIES BACK ONLY TO THE BRONZE AGE.

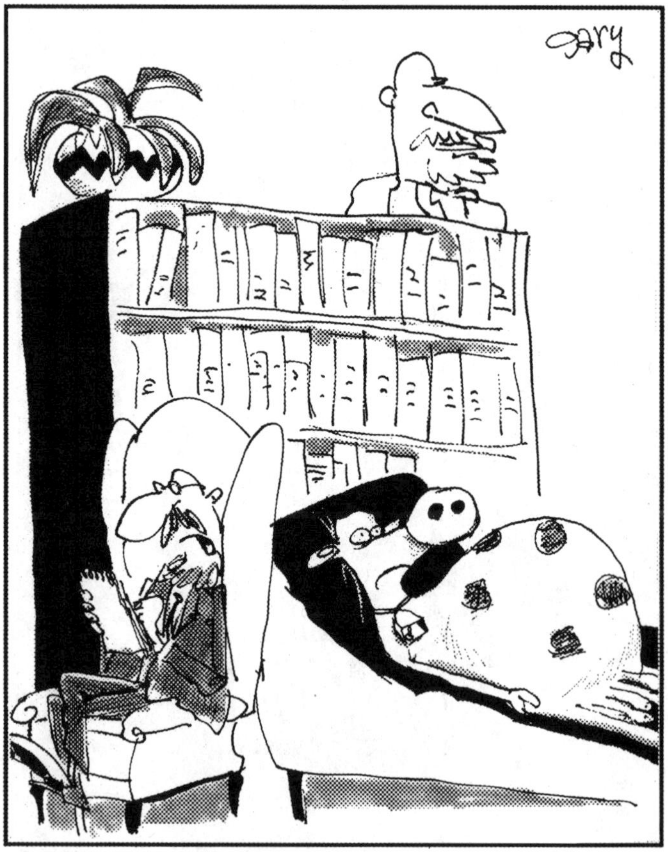
Gary

**"Mad cow? . . . No.
A cow with issues? . . . Yes."**

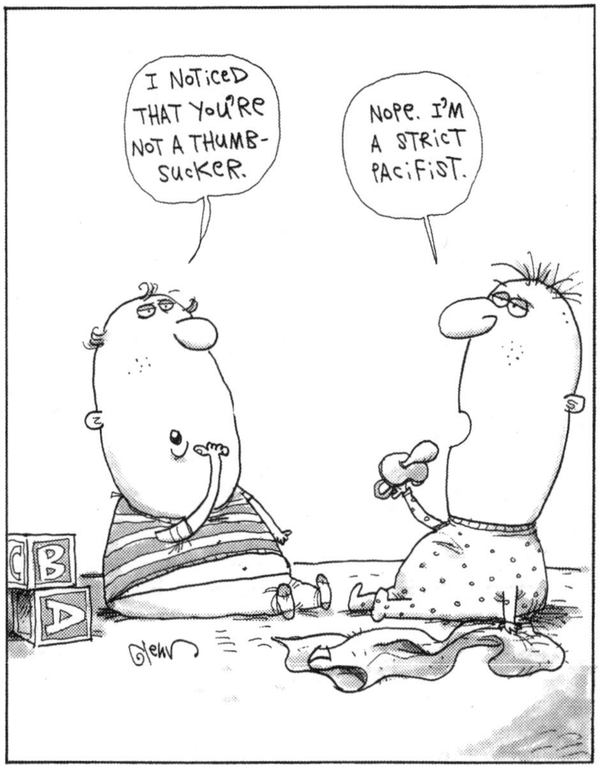
I NOTICED THAT YOU'RE NOT A THUMB-SUCKER.
NOPE. I'M A STRICT PACIFIST.

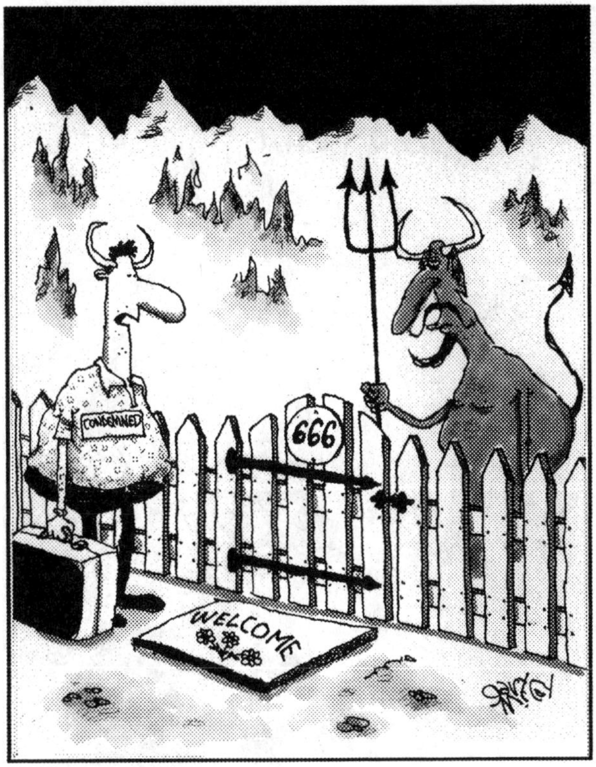
CONDEMNED
666
WELCOME

"It's just that I've always had a different perception of the gates of hell."

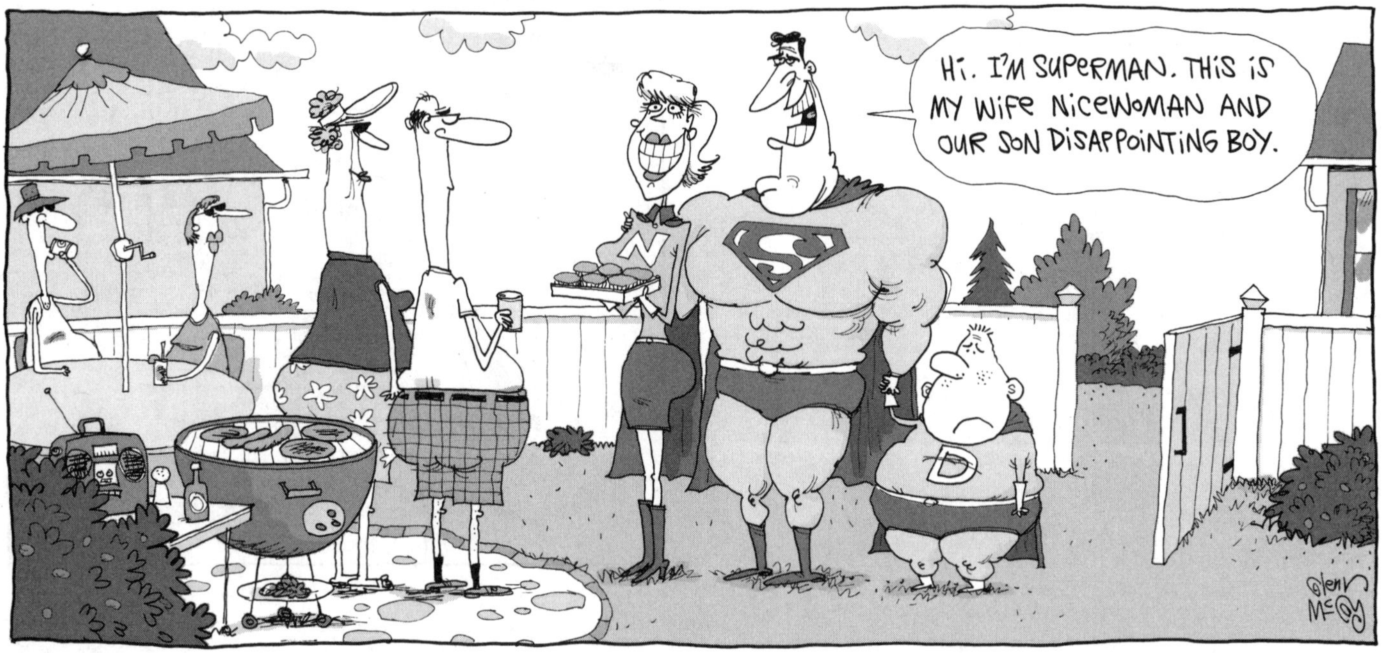
HI. I'M SUPERMAN. THIS IS MY WIFE NICEWOMAN AND OUR SON DISAPPOINTING BOY.
N
S
D

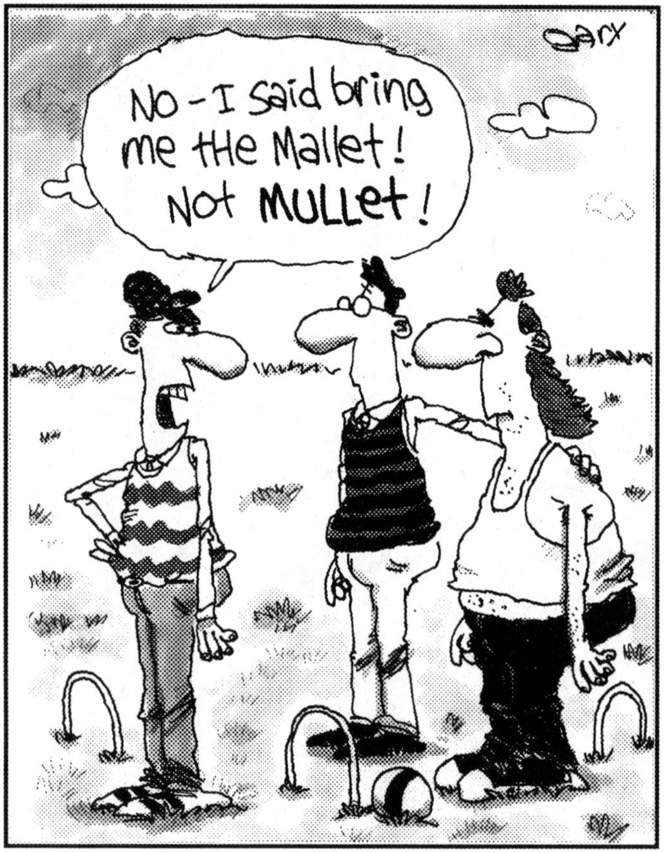
Gary
No - I said bring me the Mallet! Not MULLet!

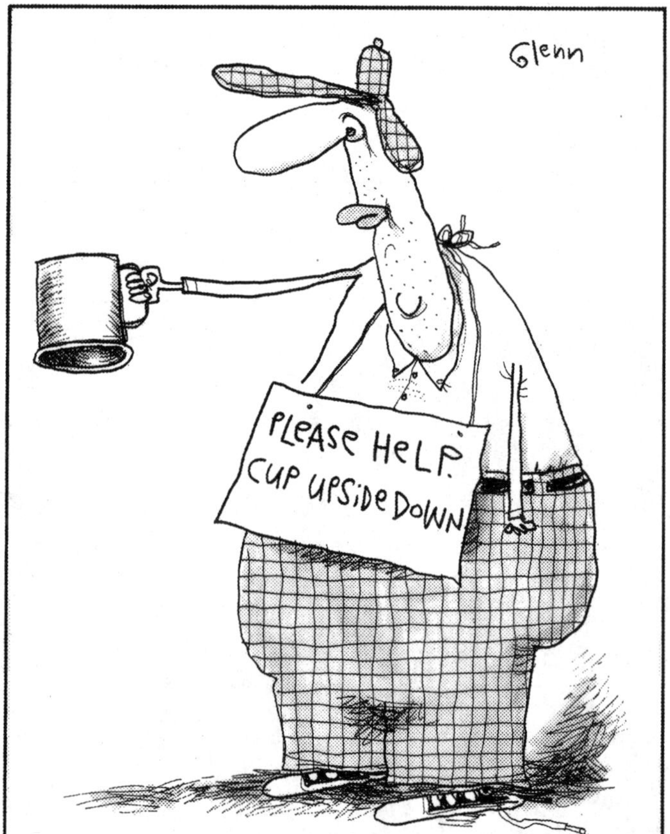
Glenn
PLEASE HELP. CUP UPSIDE DOWN

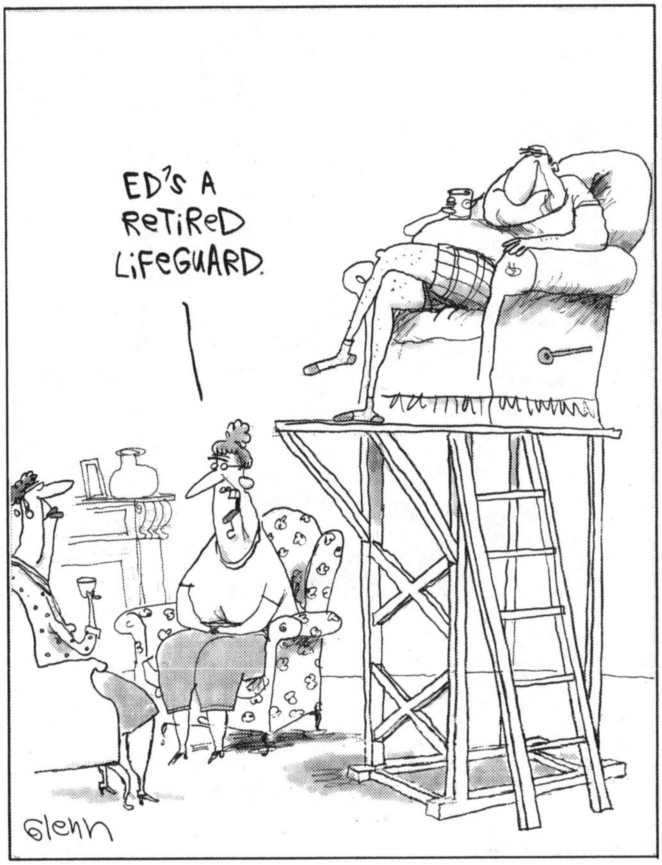
ED'S A
RETIRED
LIFEGUARD.
Glenn

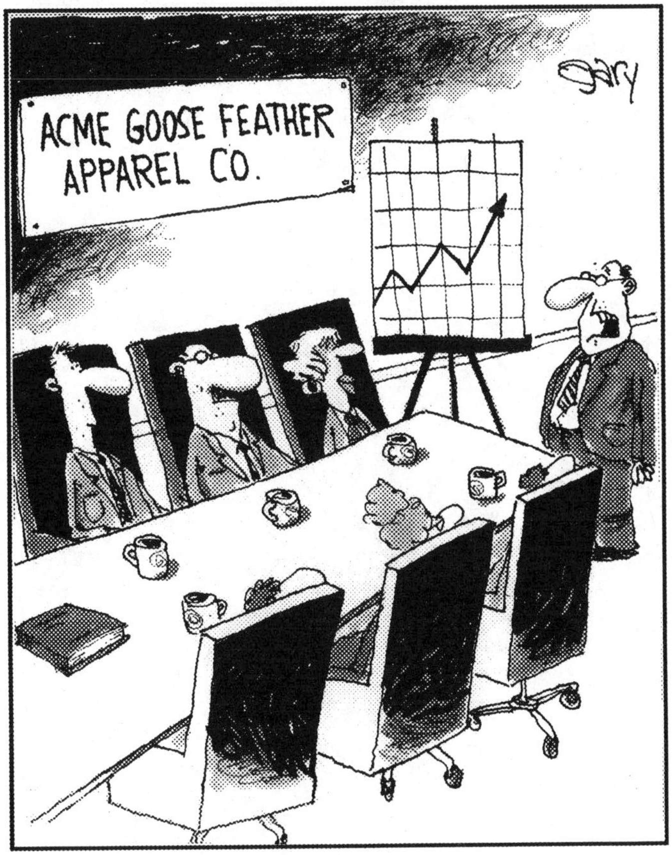
Gary
ACME GOOSE FEATHER
APPAREL CO.

"I'm pleased to announce profits were down last year."

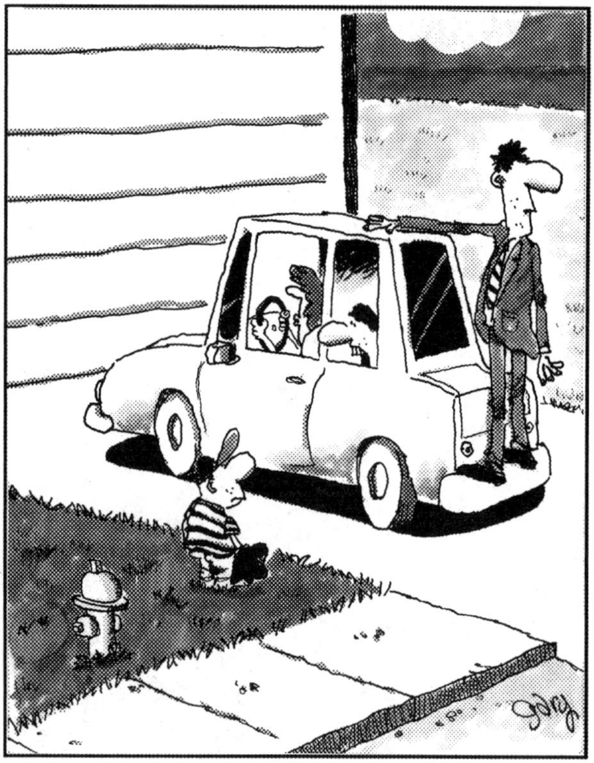

"My dad's a trashman by trade."

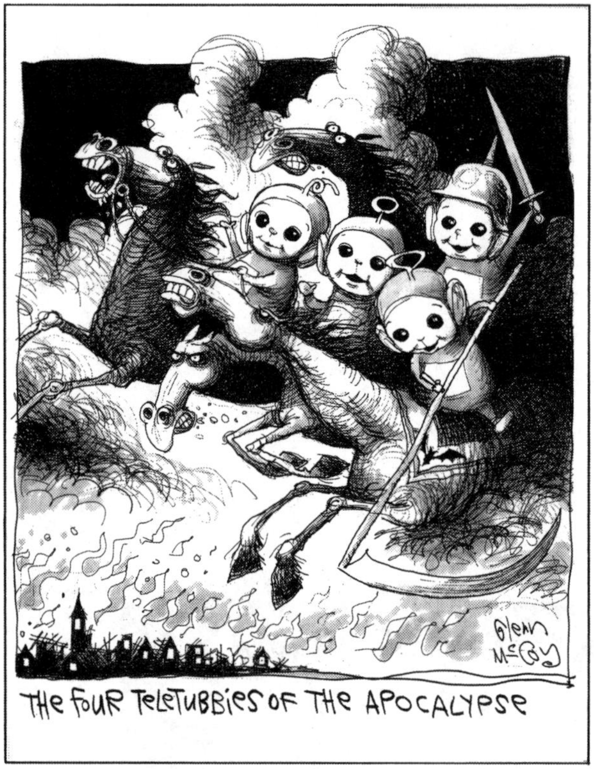
THE FOUR TELETUBBIES OF THE APOCALYPSE

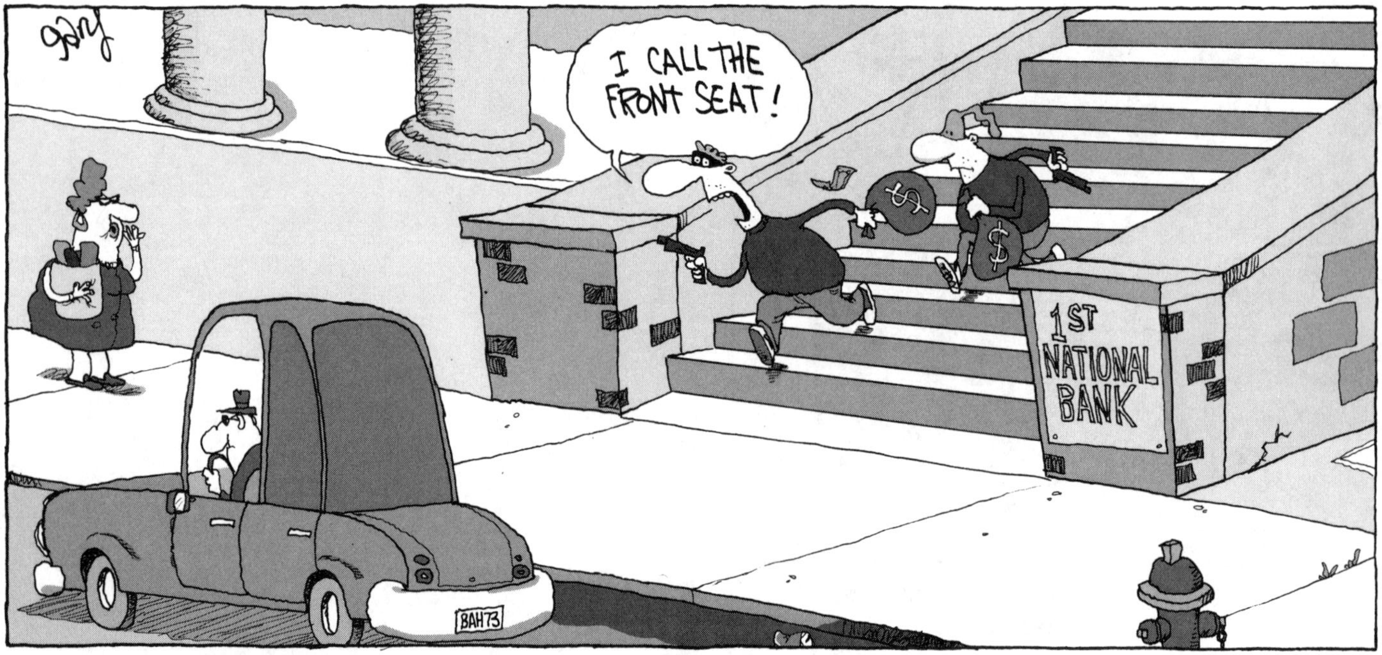
I CALL THE FRONT SEAT!
1ST NATIONAL BANK
BAH73

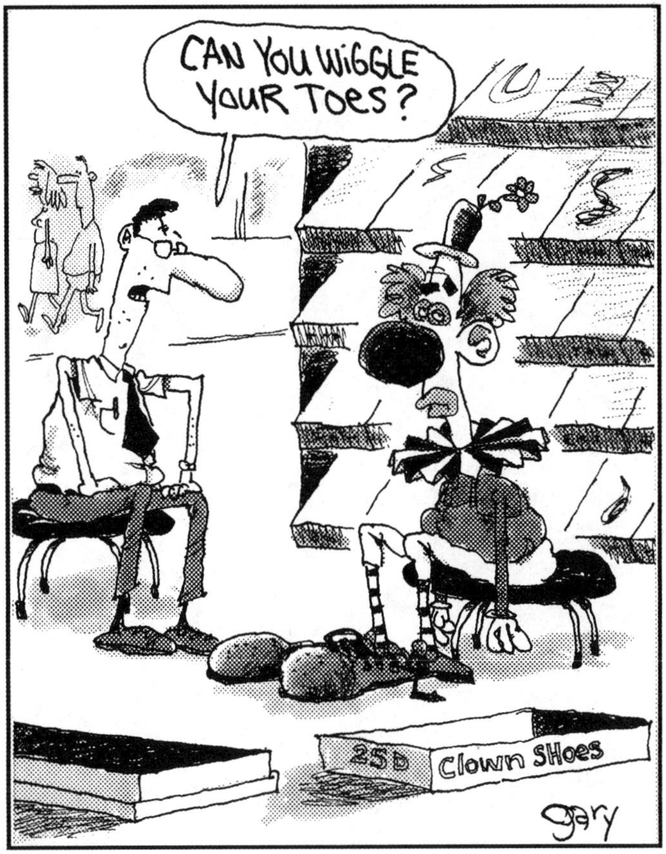
CAN YOU WIGGLE YOUR TOES?
25D
Clown SHoes
Gary

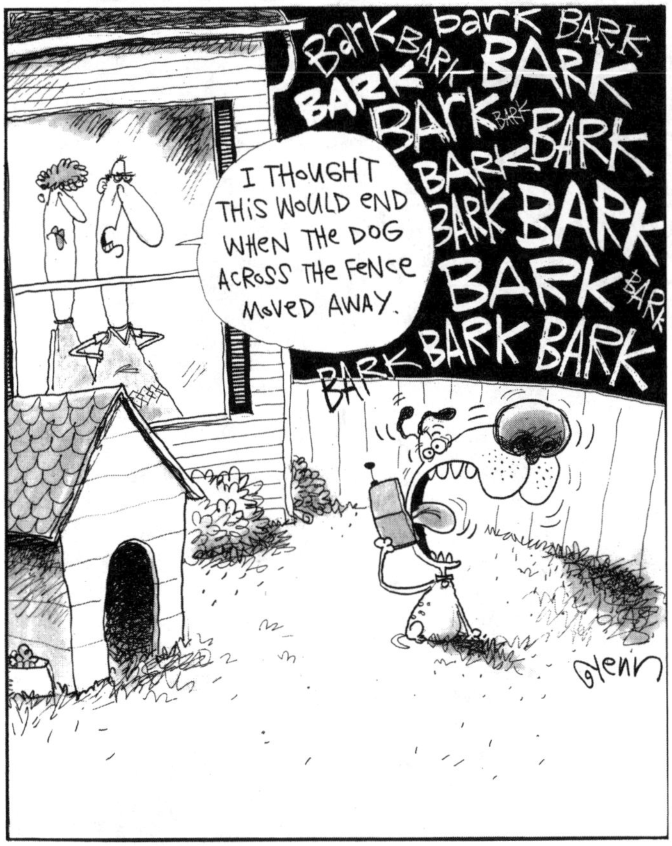
Bark bark BARK BARK BARK BARK BARK BARK BARK BARK BARK BARK BARK BARK BARK BARK BARK BARK
I THOUGHT THIS WOULD END WHEN THE DOG ACROSS THE FENCE MOVED AWAY.
Glenn

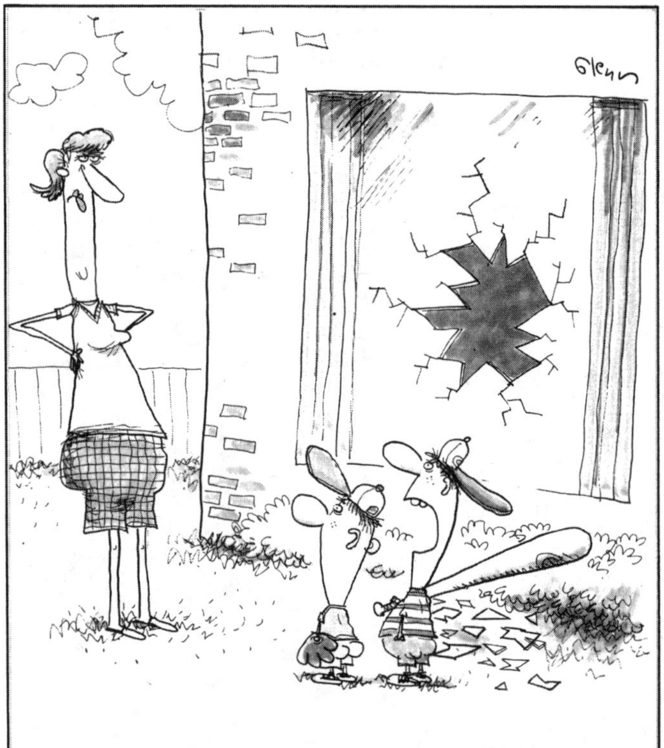
Glenn

YOU'LL BE RELIEVED TO LEARN THAT WE'VE LAUNCHED AN INTERNAL INVESTIGATION.

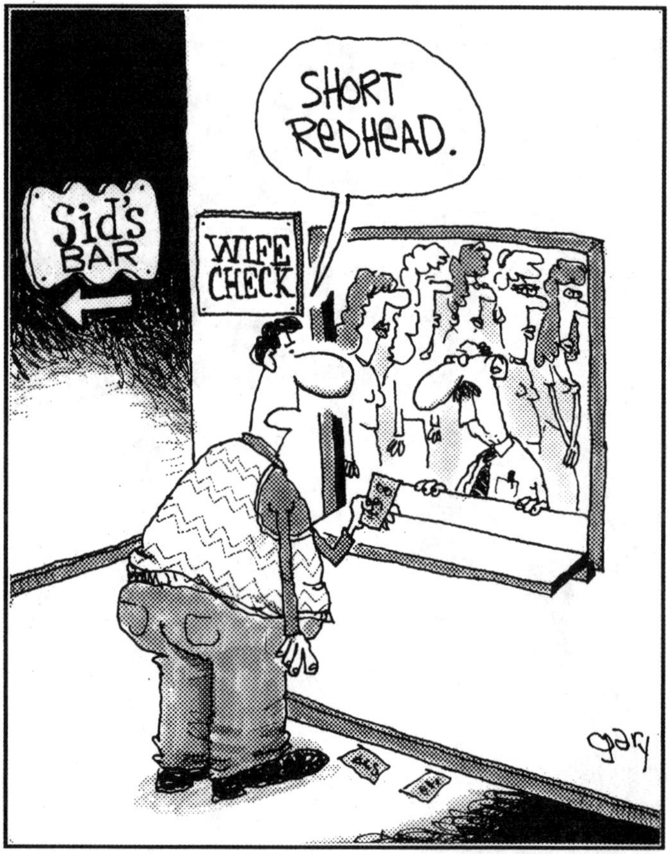
SHORT REDHEAD.
Sid's BAR
WIFE CHECK
gary

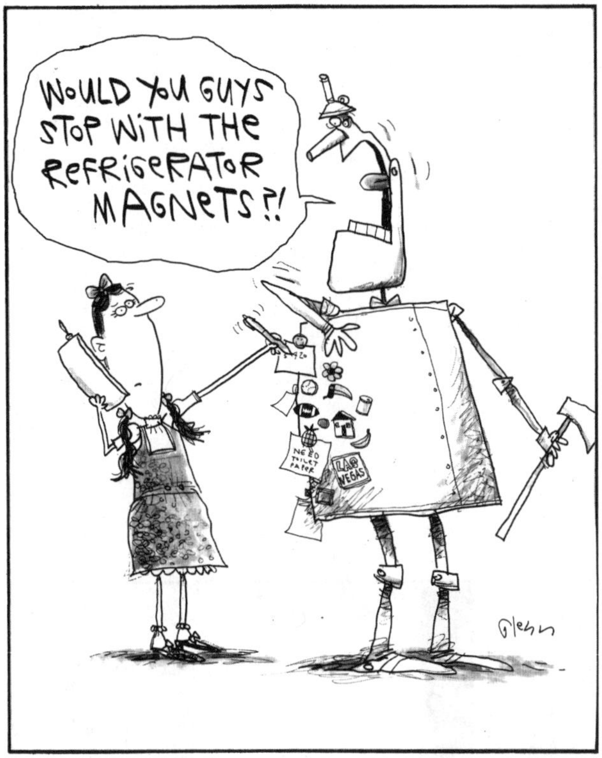
WOULD YOU GUYS STOP WITH THE REFRIGERATOR MAGNETS?!
NEED TOILET PAPER
LAS VEGAS
Glenn

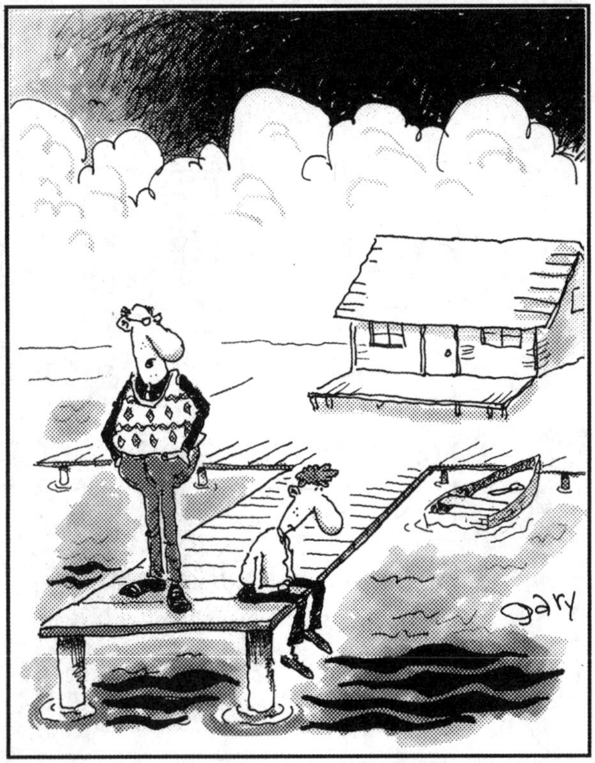
gary

"Son, you'll know when you've found the right woman. Your mother will tell you."

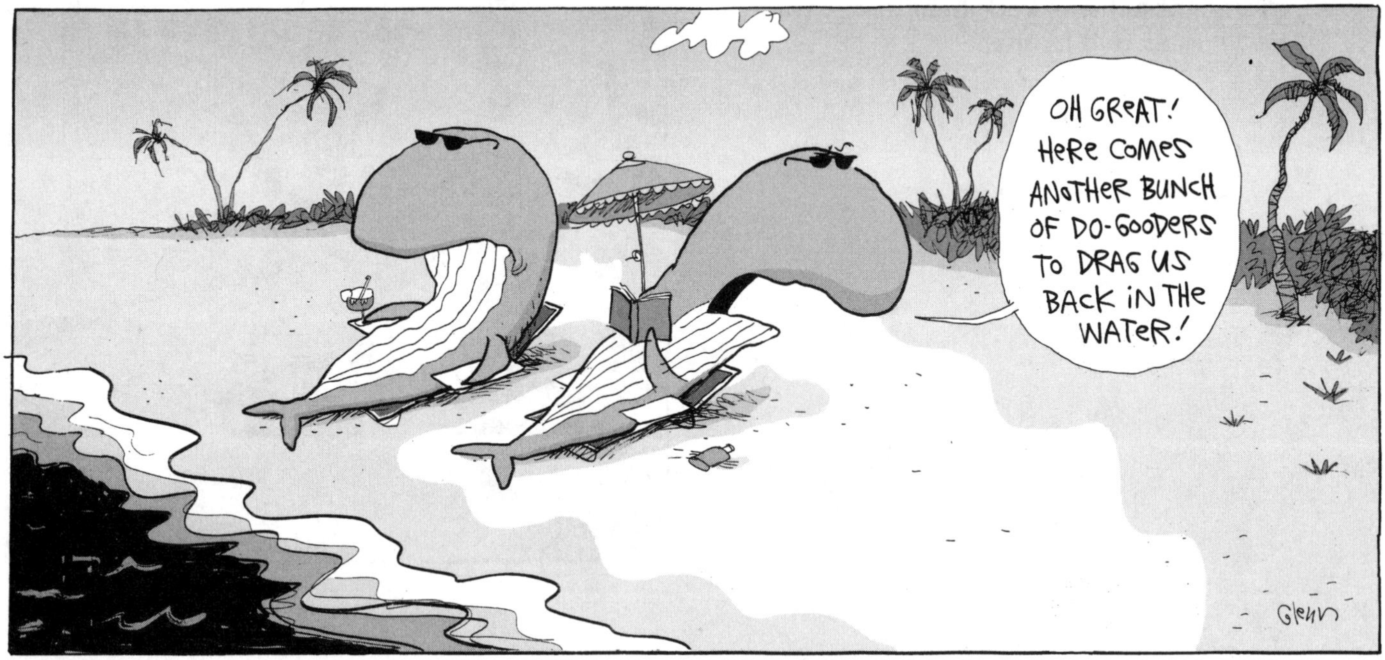
OH GREAT! HERE COMES ANOTHER BUNCH OF DO-GOODERS TO DRAG US BACK IN THE WATER!
Glenn

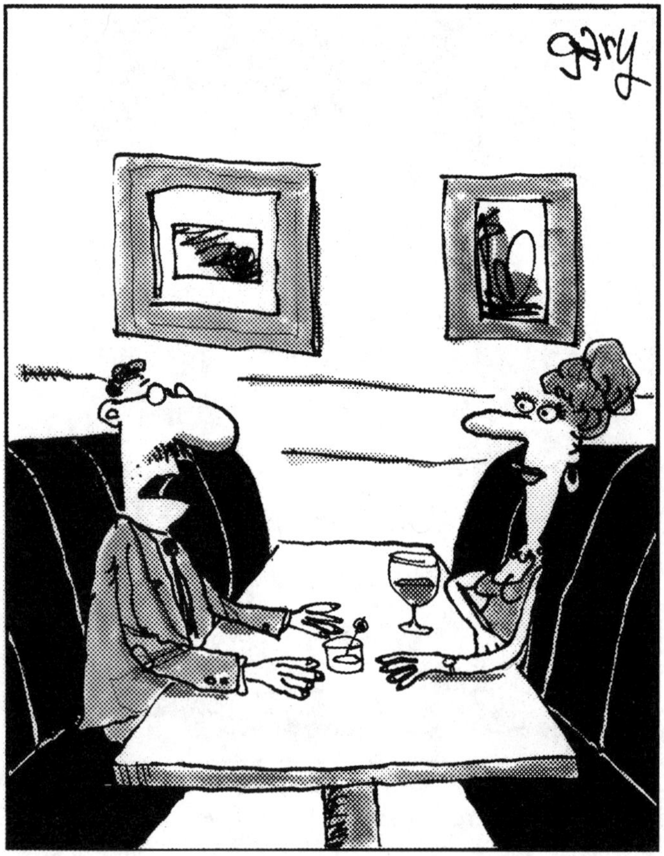
gary

"Well, enough about me. Let's hear about you, as told by me."

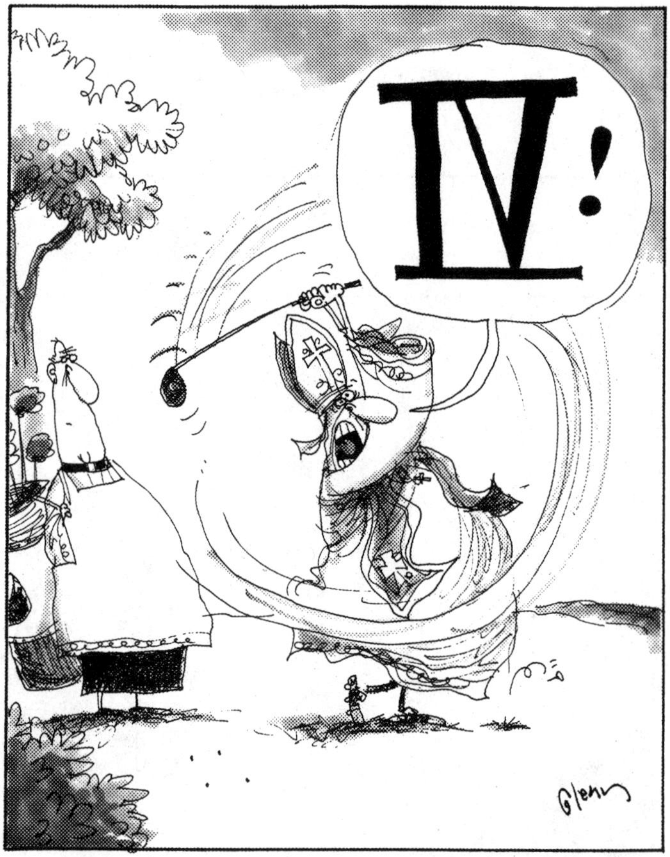
IV!
Glenn

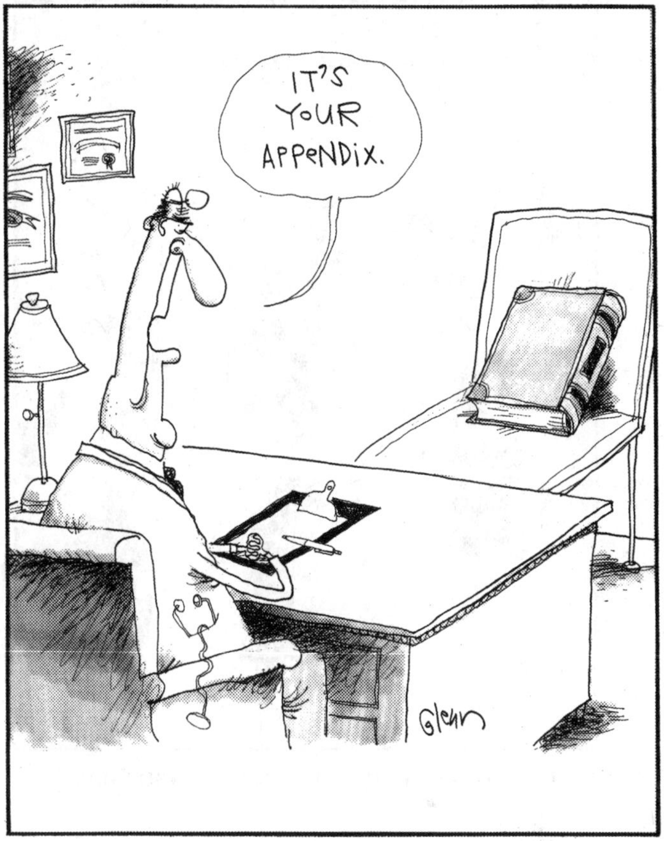
IT'S YOUR APPENDIX.
Glenn

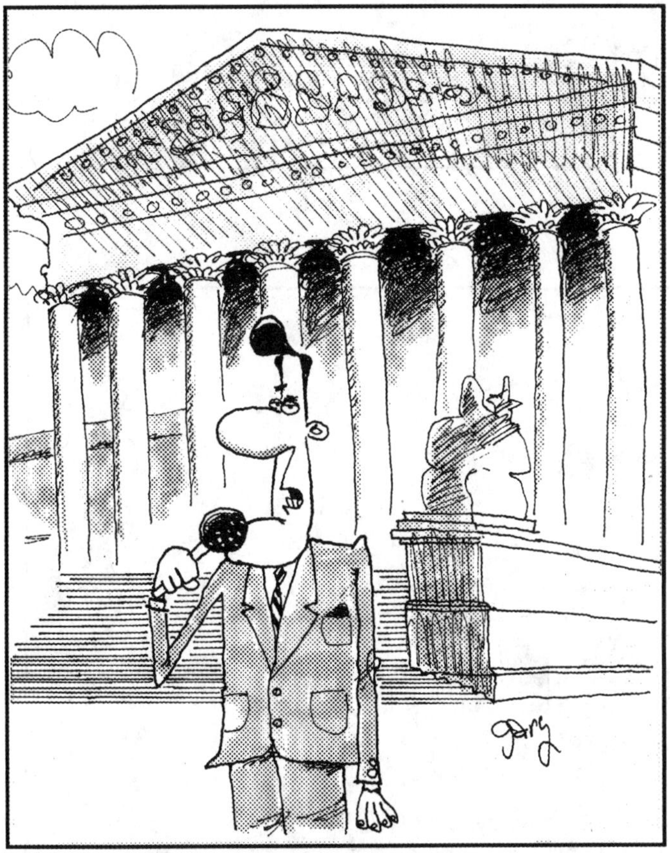
Gary

"As expected today, the Supreme Court, in a 6–3 decision, ruled the lyrics to the 'Hokey Pokey' unconstitutional."

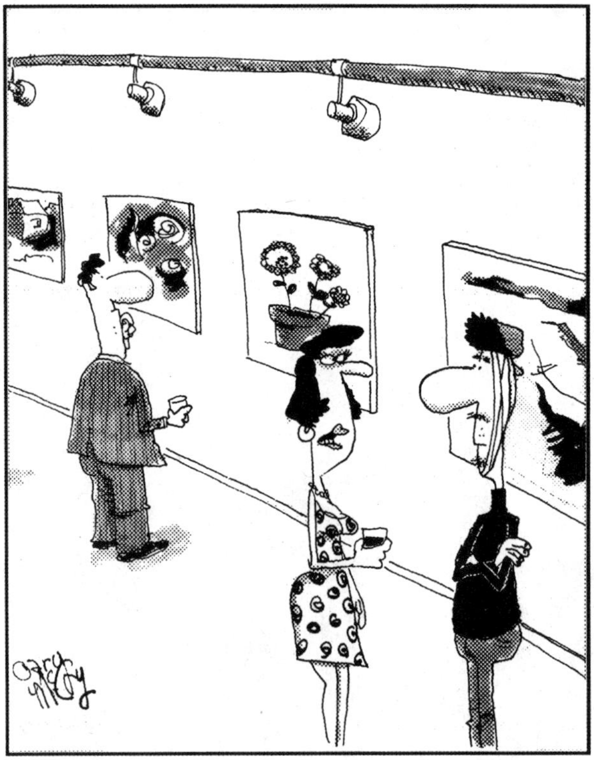
Gary McCoy

"I see you've been influenced by van Gogh."

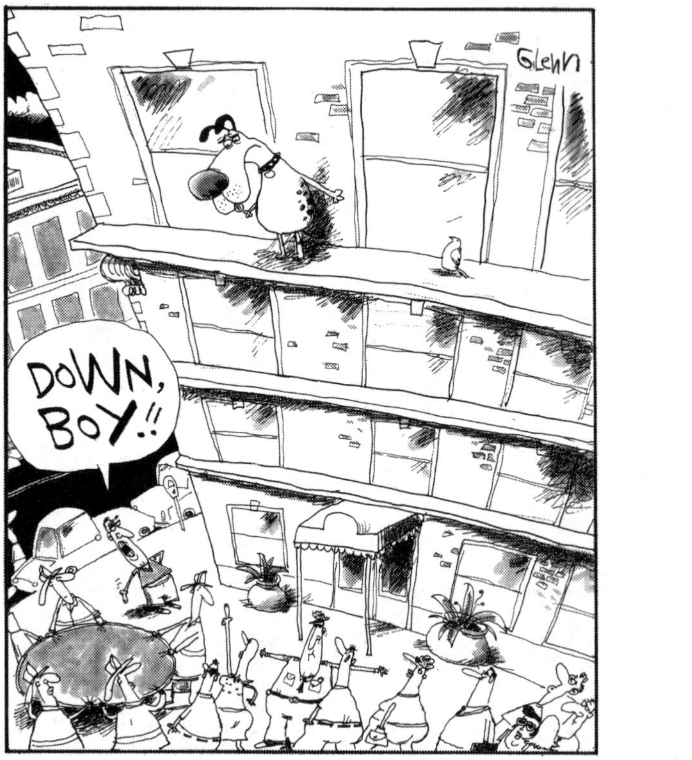
Glenn
DOWN, BOY!!

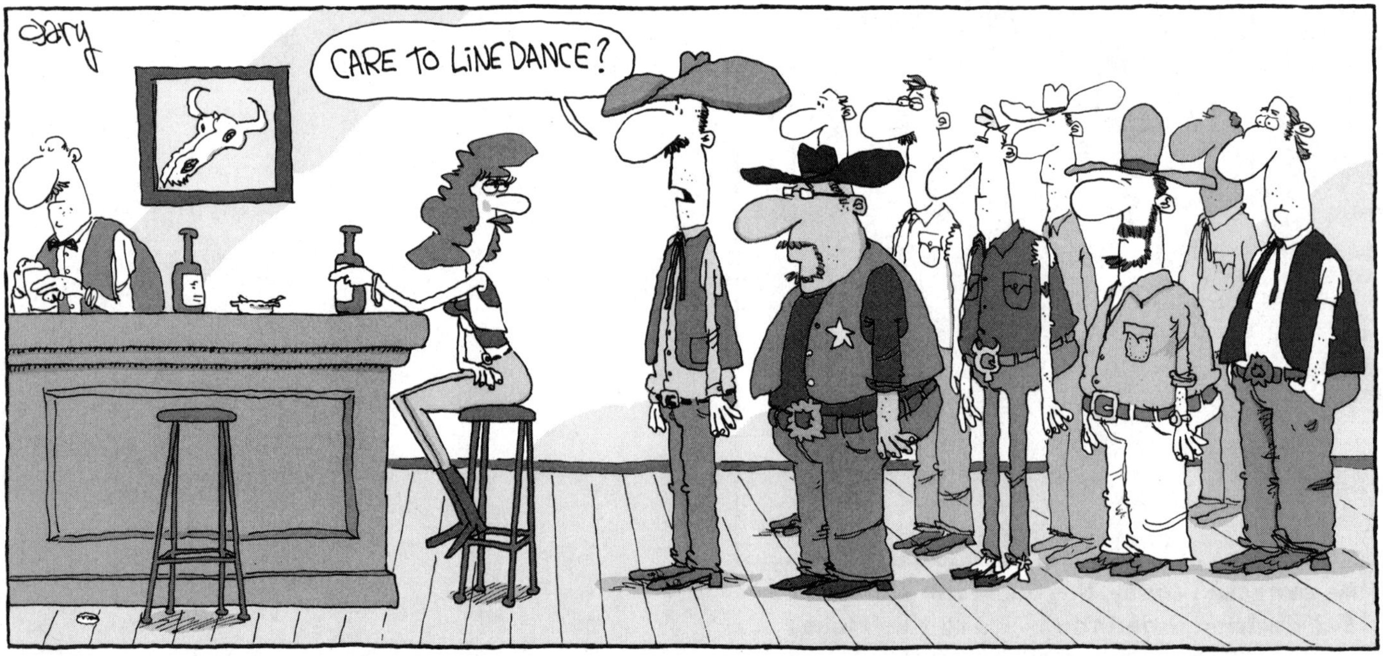
Gary
CARE TO LINE DANCE?

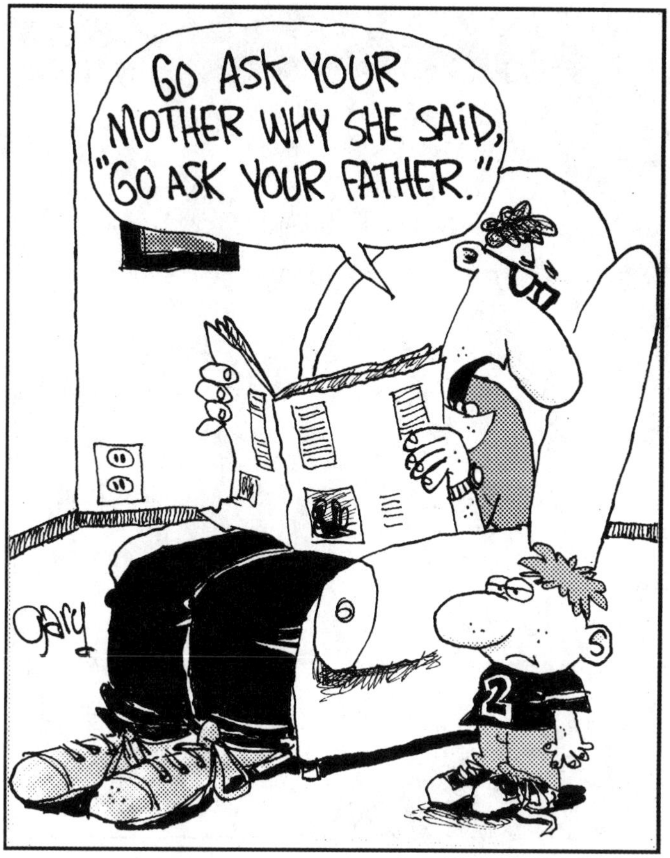
GO ASK YOUR MOTHER WHY SHE SAID, "GO ASK YOUR FATHER."
Gary

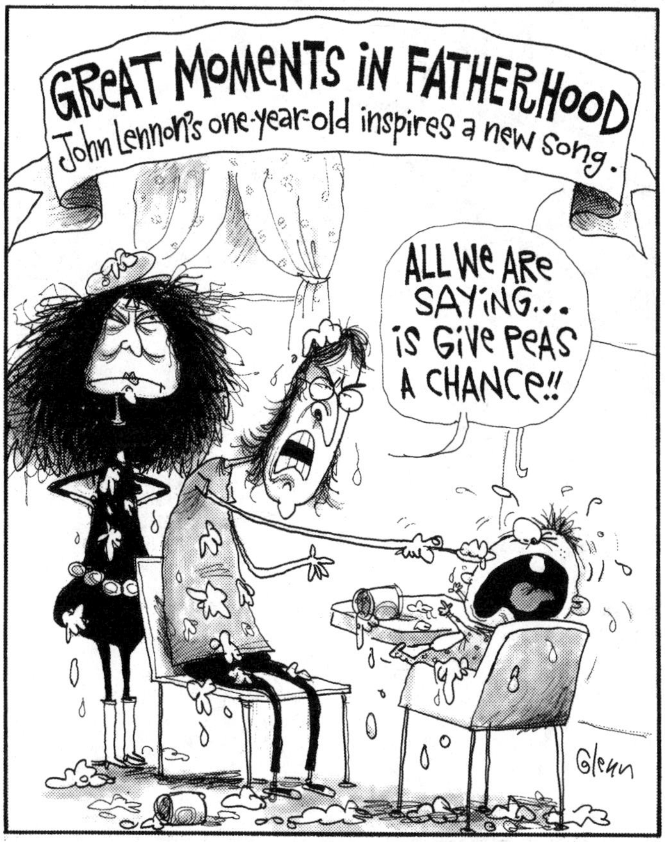
GREAT MOMENTS IN FATHERHOOD
John Lennon's one-year-old inspires a new song.
ALL WE ARE SAYING... IS GIVE PEAS A CHANCE!!
Glenn

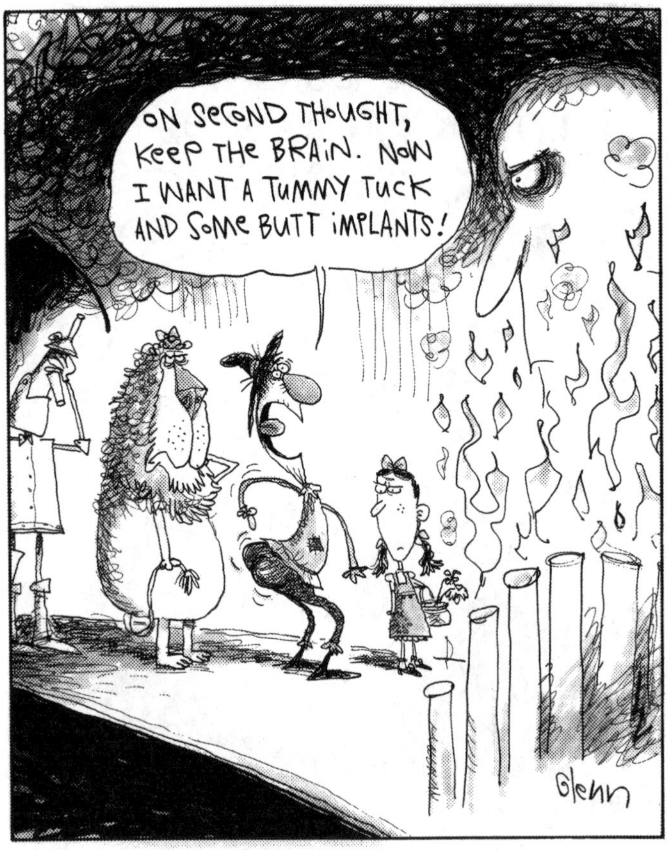
ON SECOND THOUGHT, KEEP THE BRAIN. NOW I WANT A TUMMY TUCK AND SOME BUTT IMPLANTS!
Glenn

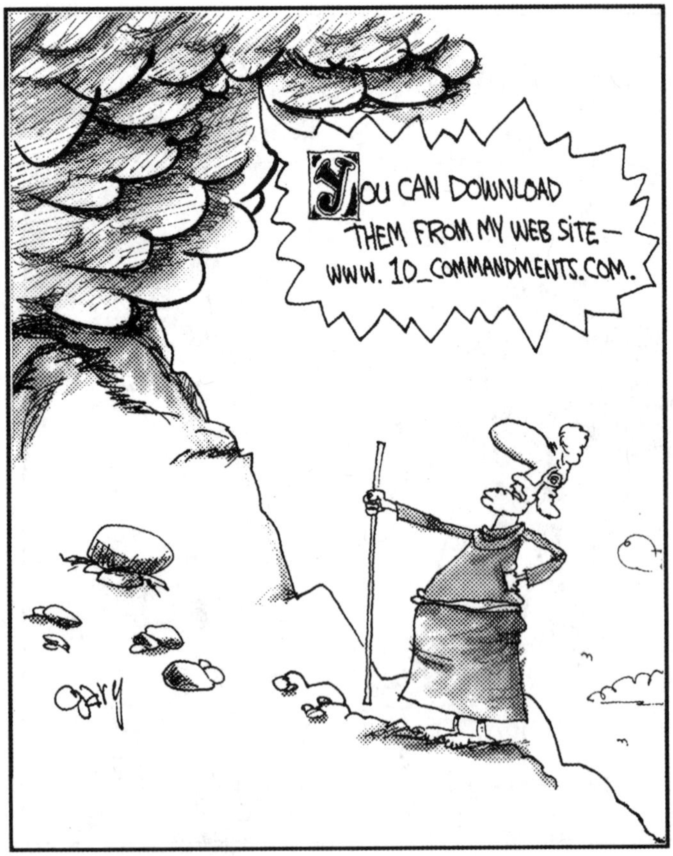
YOU CAN DOWNLOAD THEM FROM MY WEB SITE— WWW. 10_COMMANDMENTS.COM.
Gary

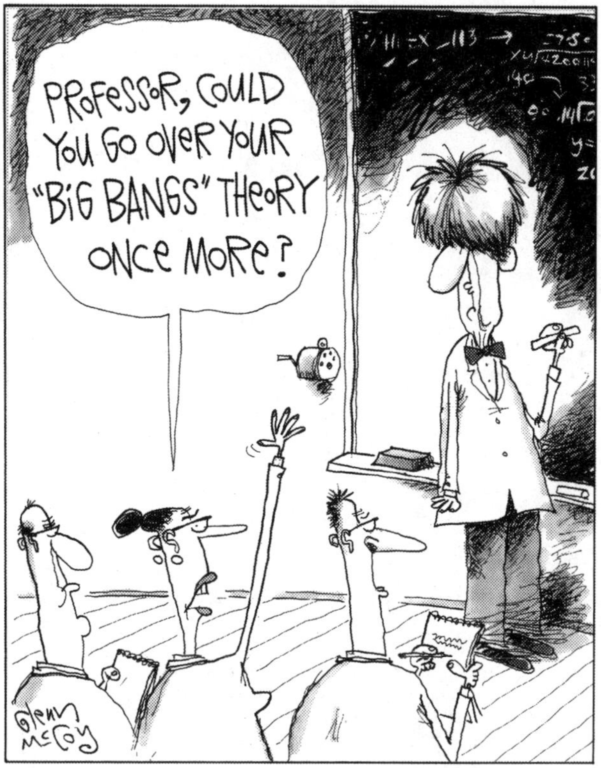
PROFESSOR, COULD YOU GO OVER YOUR "BIG BANGS" THEORY ONCE MORE?
Glenn McCoy

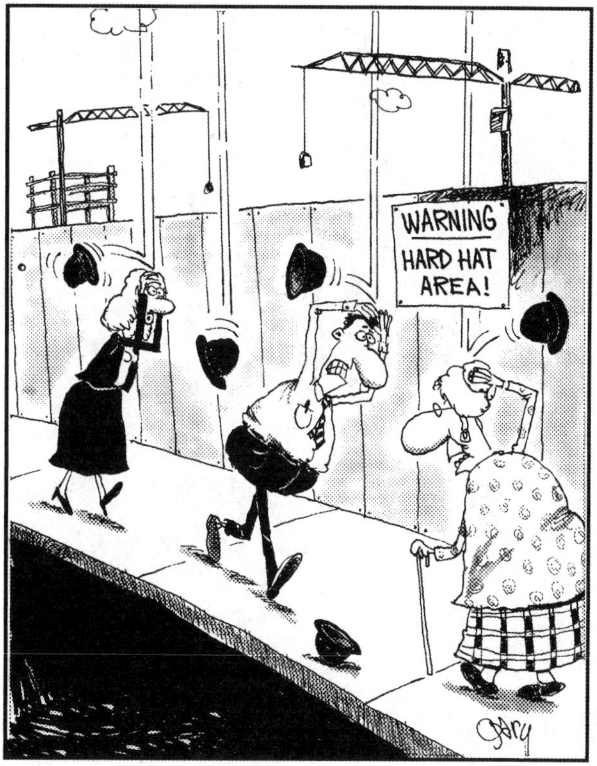
WARNING
HARD HAT AREA!
Gary

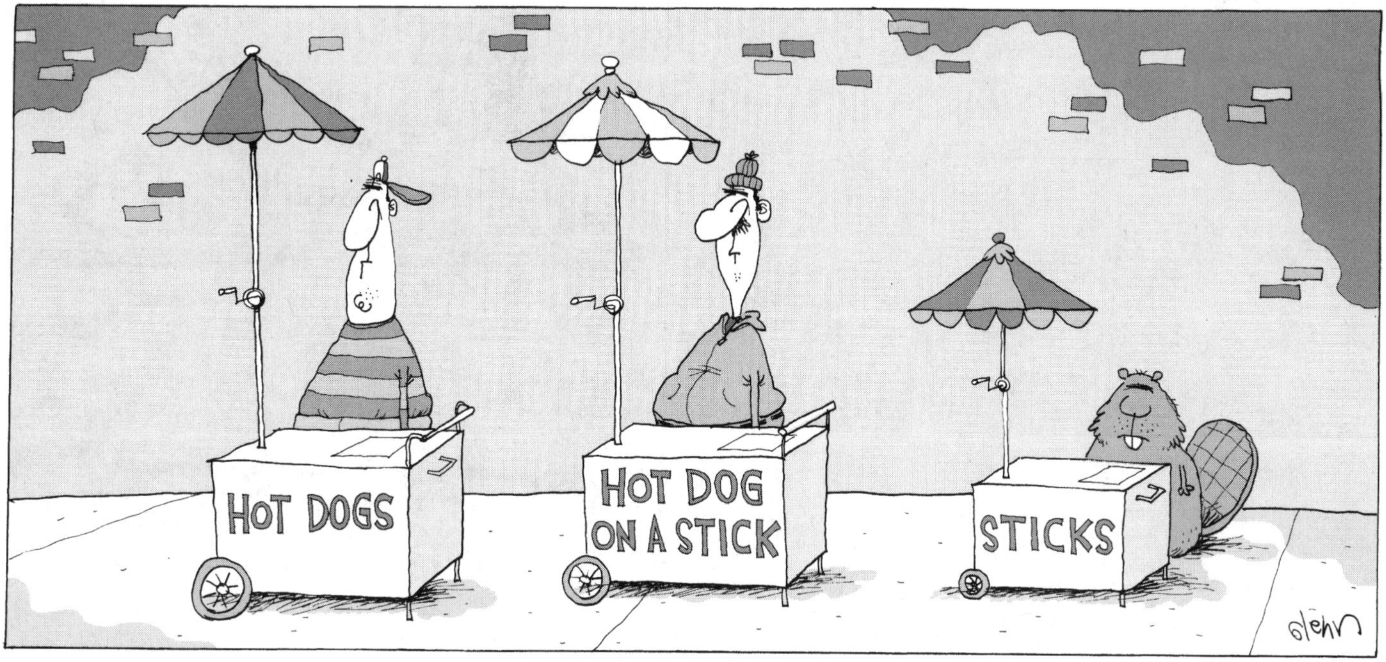
HOT DOGS
HOT DOG ON A STICK
STICKS
Glenn

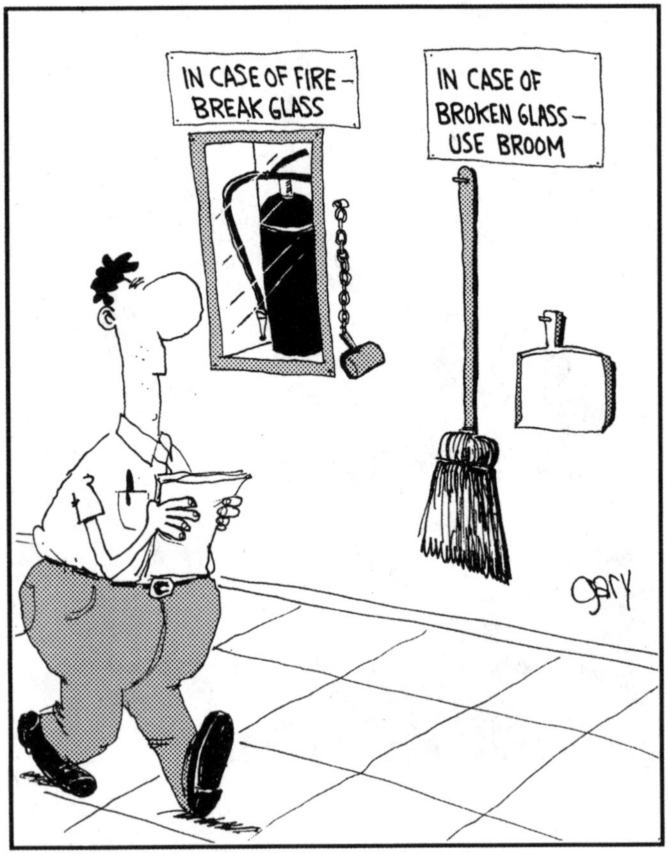
IN CASE OF FIRE – BREAK GLASS
IN CASE OF BROKEN GLASS – USE BROOM
gary

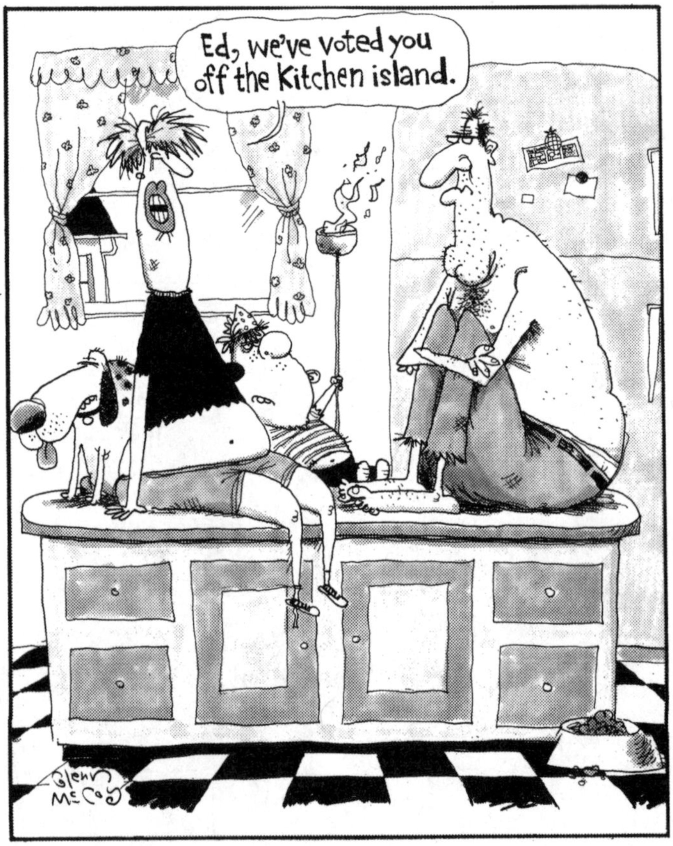
Ed, we've voted you off the Kitchen island.
Glenn McCoy

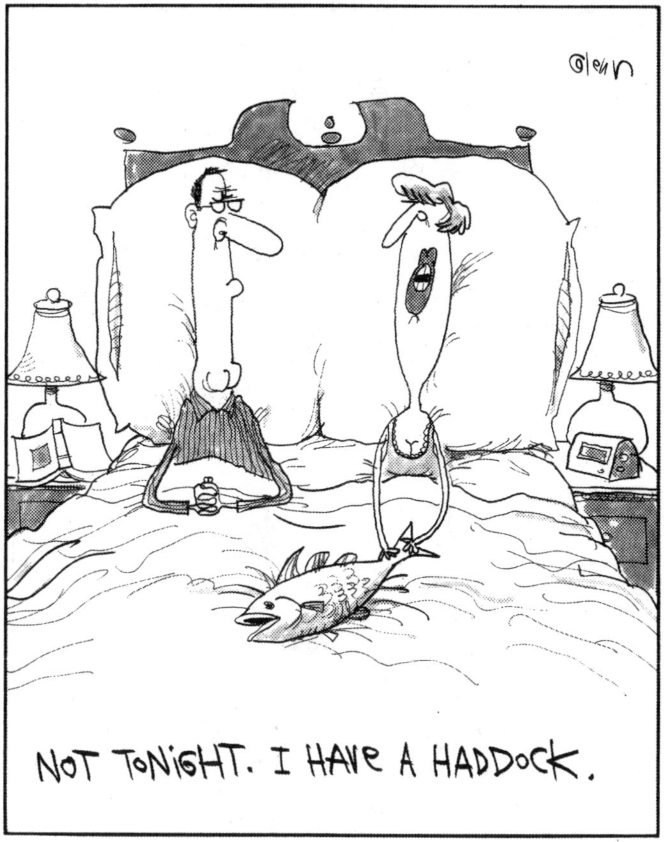
Glenn
NOT TONIGHT. I HAVE A HADDOCK.

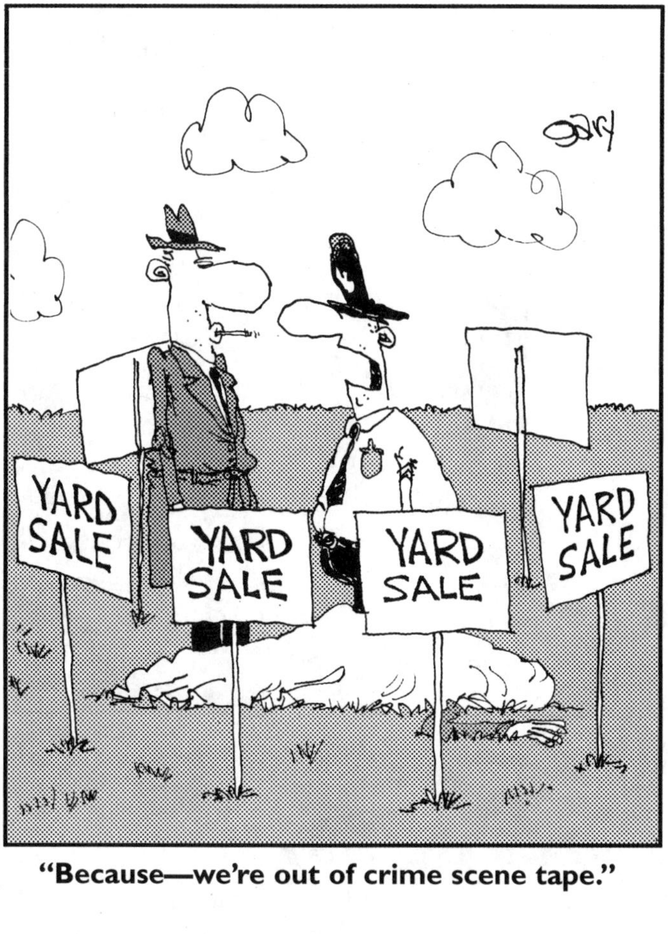
Gary
YARD SALE
YARD SALE
YARD SALE
YARD SALE

"Because—we're out of crime scene tape."

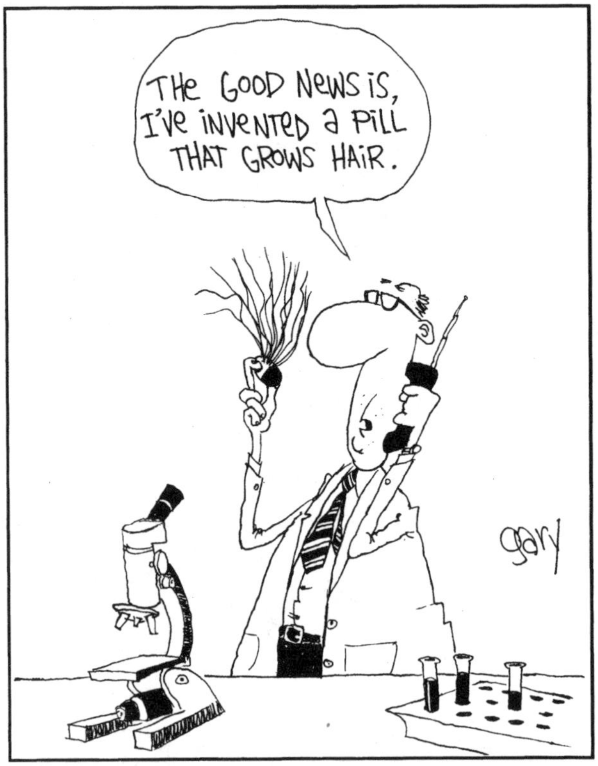
THE GOOD NEWS IS, I'VE INVENTED A PILL THAT GROWS HAIR.
gary

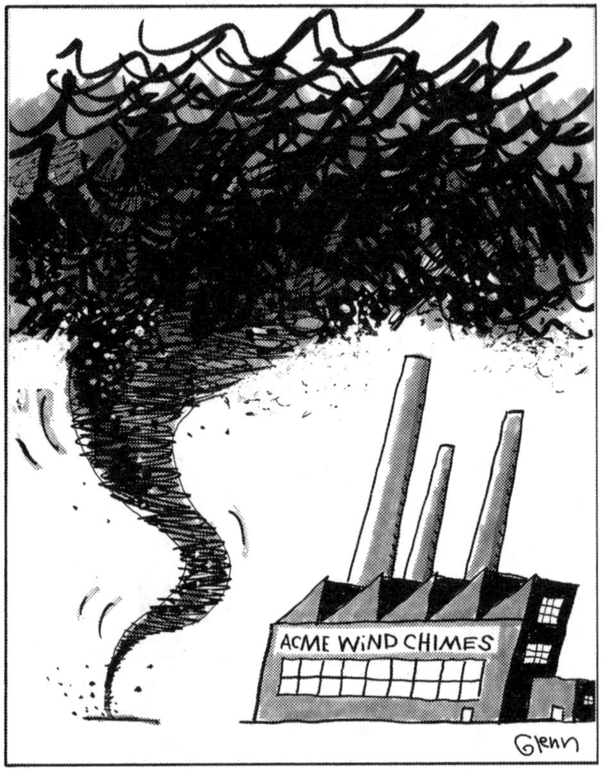
ACME WIND CHIMES
Glenn

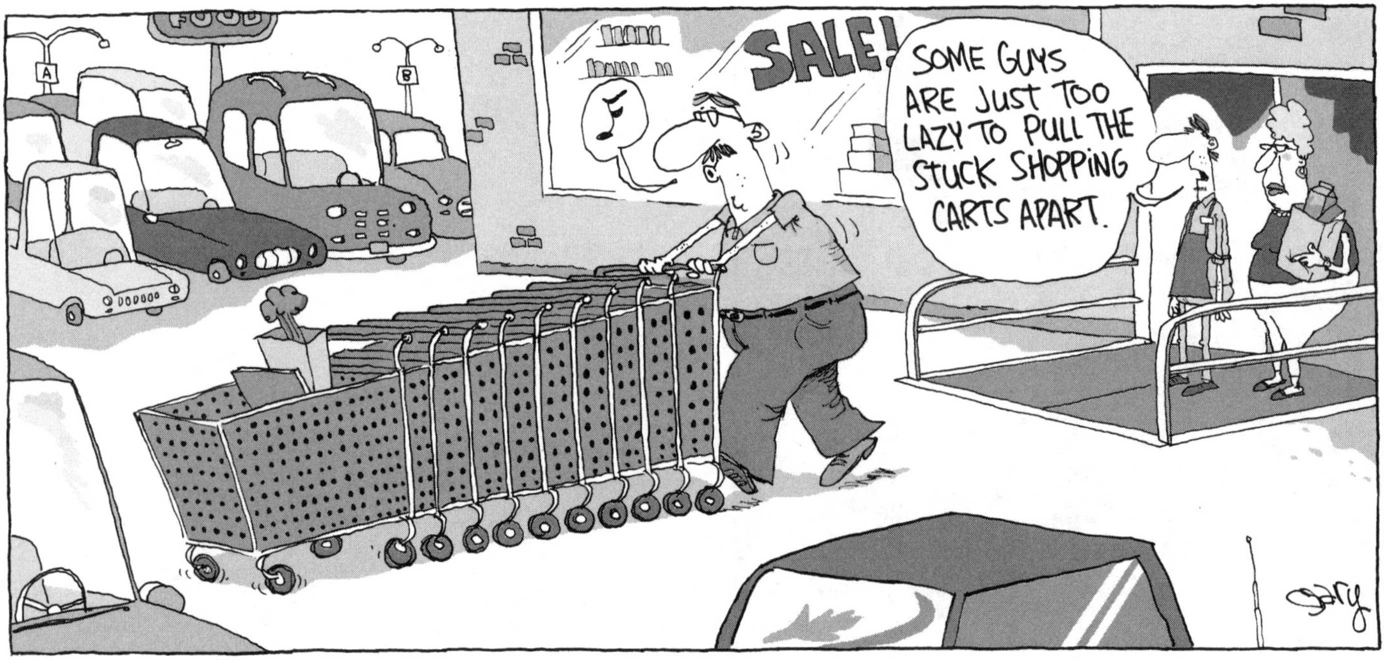
FOOD
A
B
SALE!
SOME GUYS ARE JUST TOO LAZY TO PULL THE STUCK SHOPPING CARTS APART.
gary

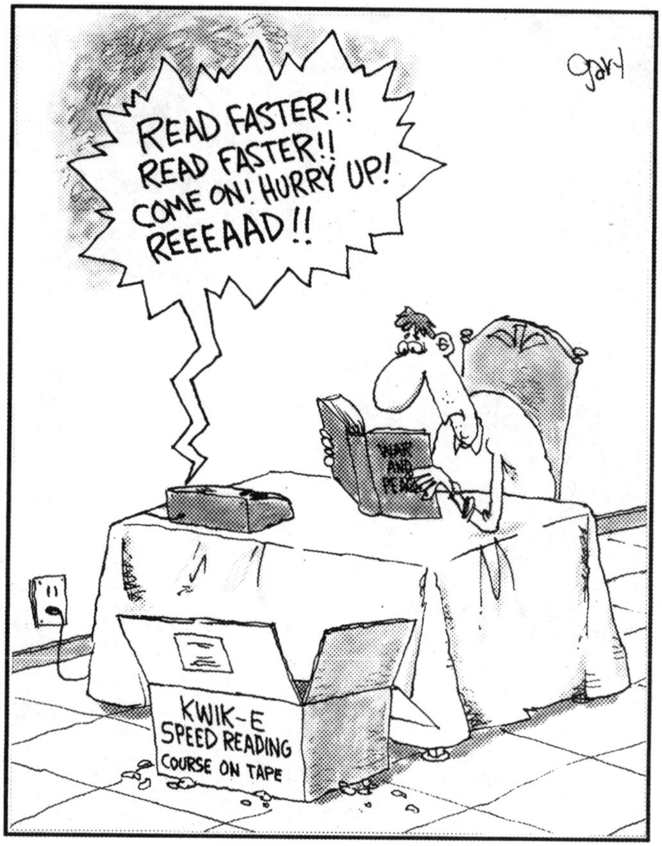
Gary
READ FASTER!!
READ FASTER!!
COME ON! HURRY UP!
REEEAAD!!
KWIK-E
SPEED READING
COURSE ON TAPE

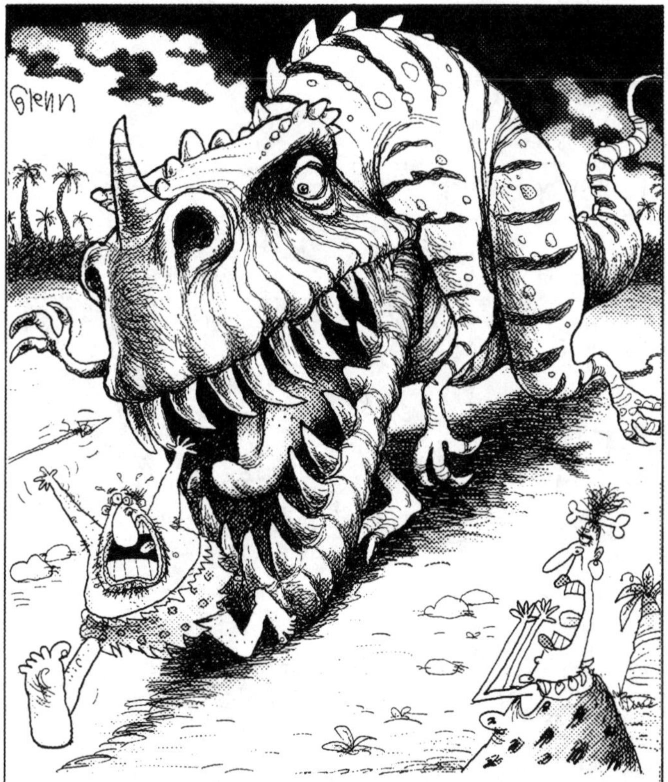
Glenn
"LET ME KNOW WHEN I SHOULD START THE POTATOES."

NOTHING MUCH. JUST SITTING DOWN IN THE BAT CAVE ON THE BAT COUCH MUNCHING ON SOME BATCHIPS.
Glenn

NURSERY
PLEASE HELP- HAVEN'T EATEN IN 2 HOURS
Gary

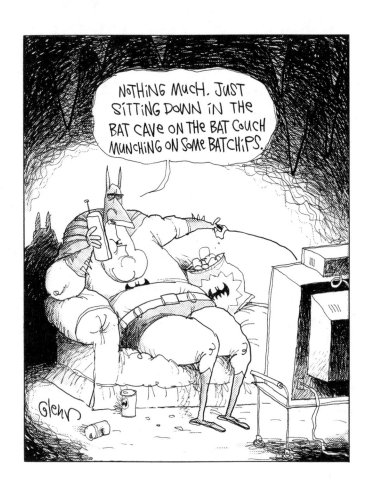

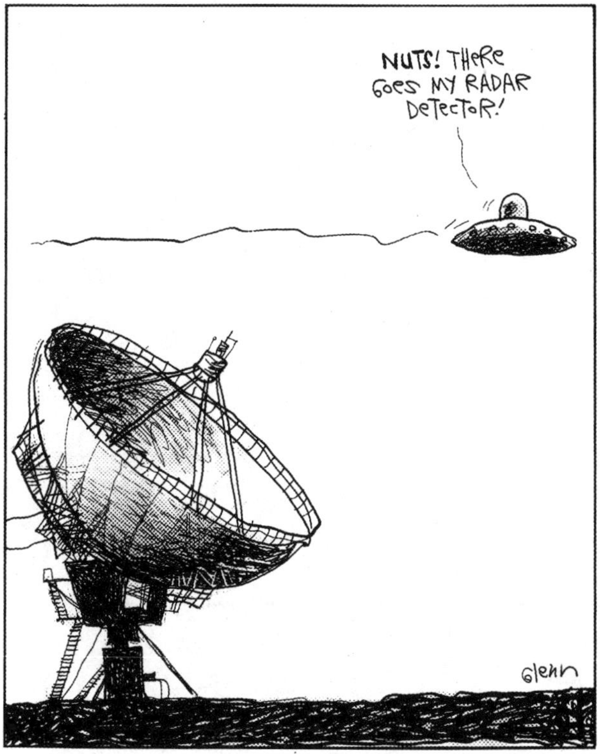
NUTS! THERE GOES MY RADAR DETECTOR!
Glenn

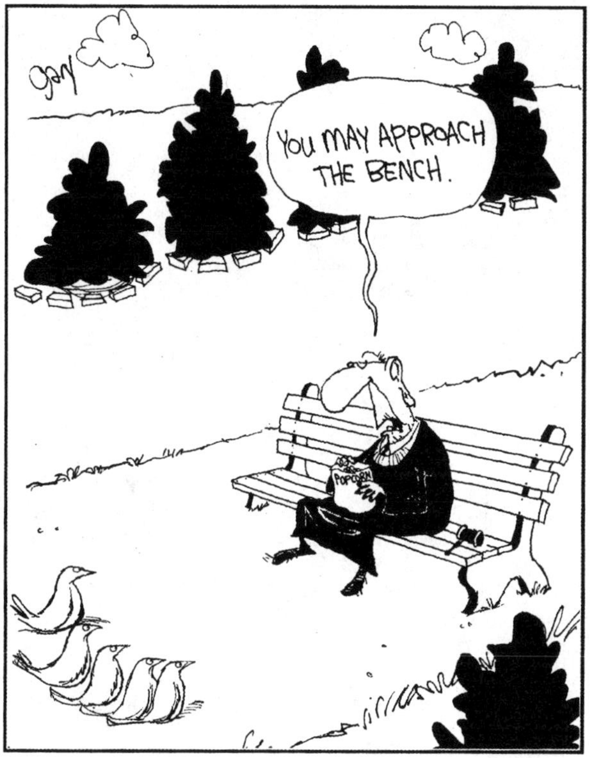
Gary
YOU MAY APPROACH THE BENCH.
POPCORN

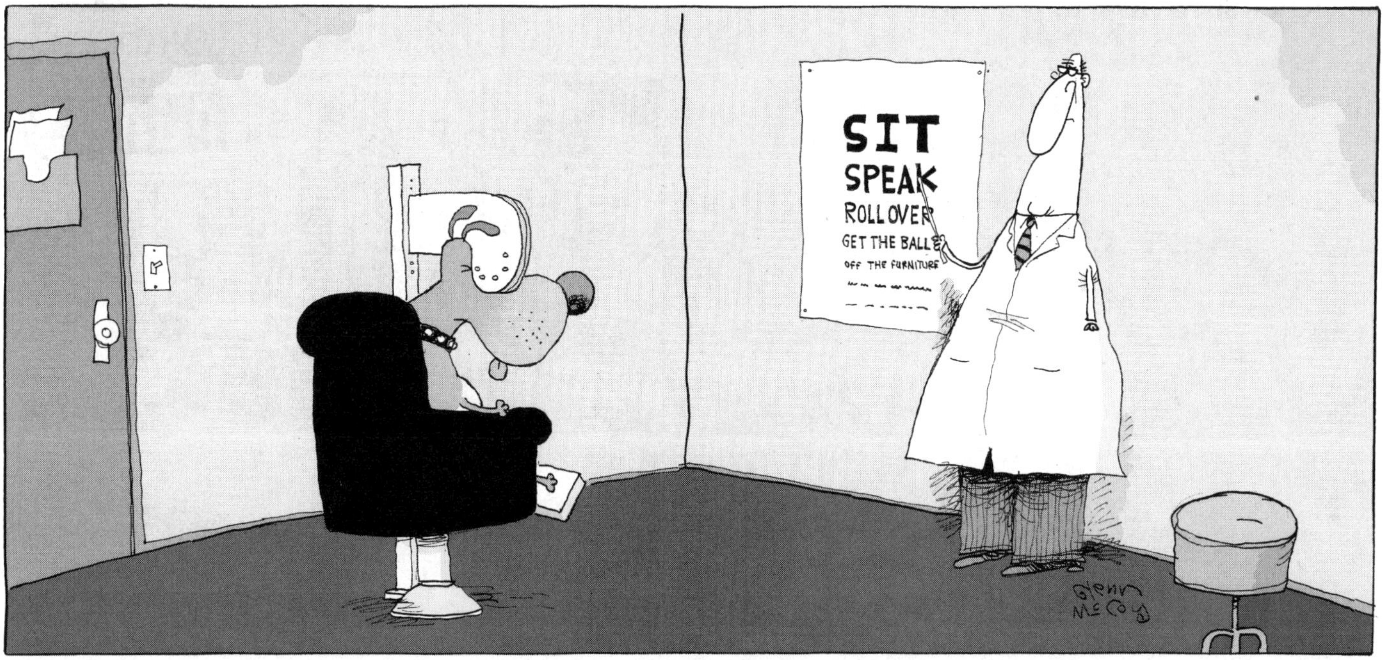
SIT
SPEAK
ROLL OVER
GET THE BALL
OFF THE FURNITURE
Glenn McCoy

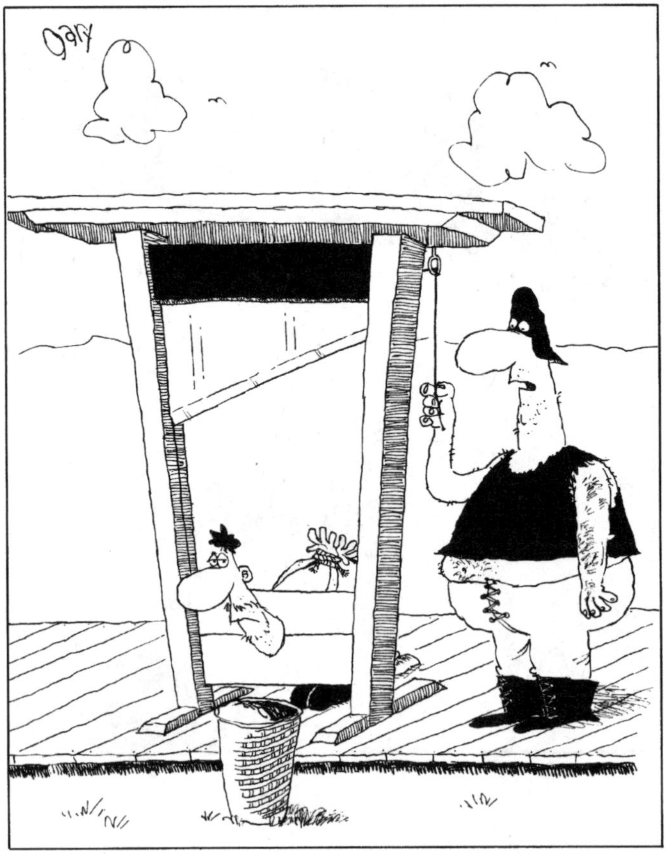
Gary

"OK, you're going to feel a little sting."

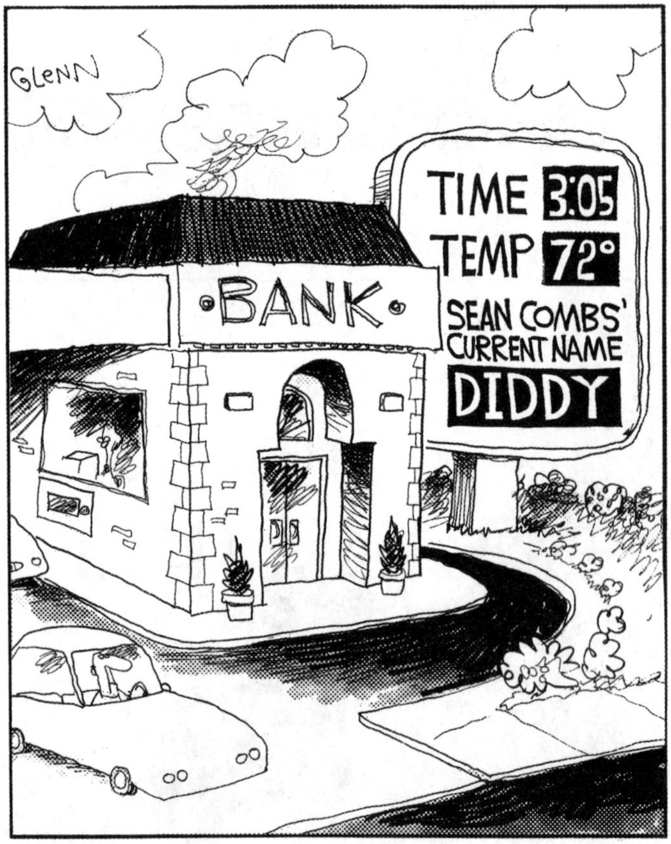
GLENN
BANK
TIME 3:05
TEMP 72°
SEAN COMBS' CURRENT NAME
DIDDY

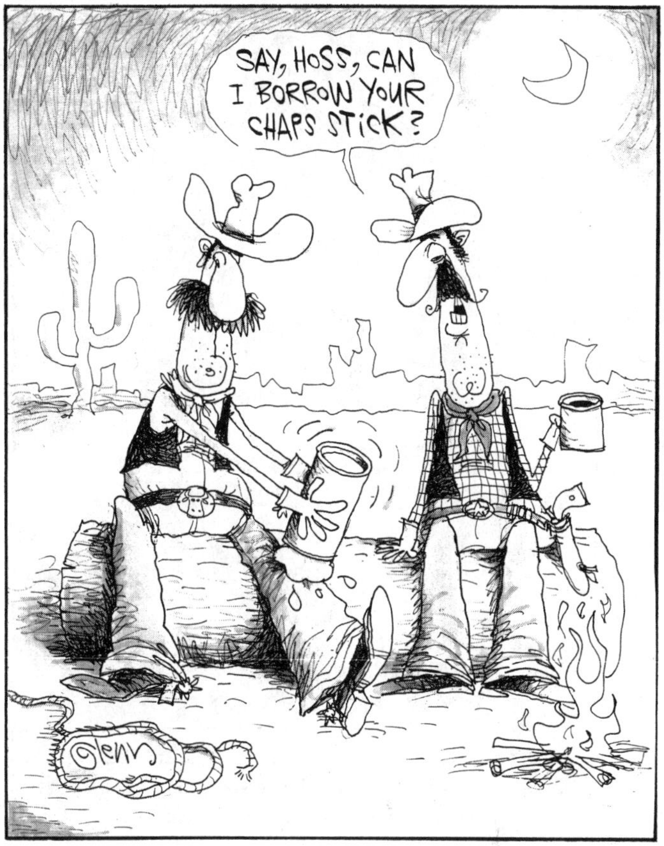
SAY, HOSS, CAN I BORROW YOUR CHAPS STICK?
Glenn

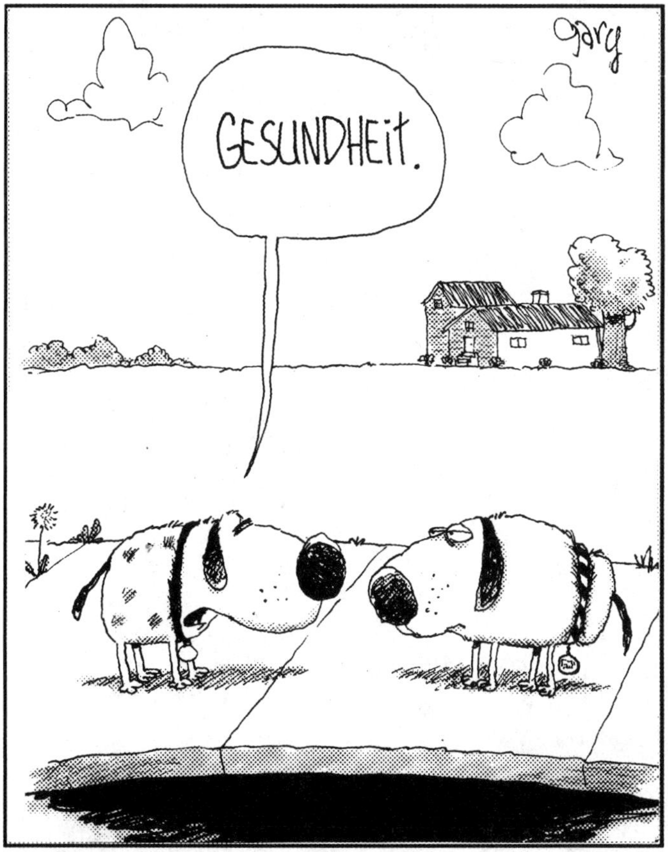
Gary
GESUNDHEIT.

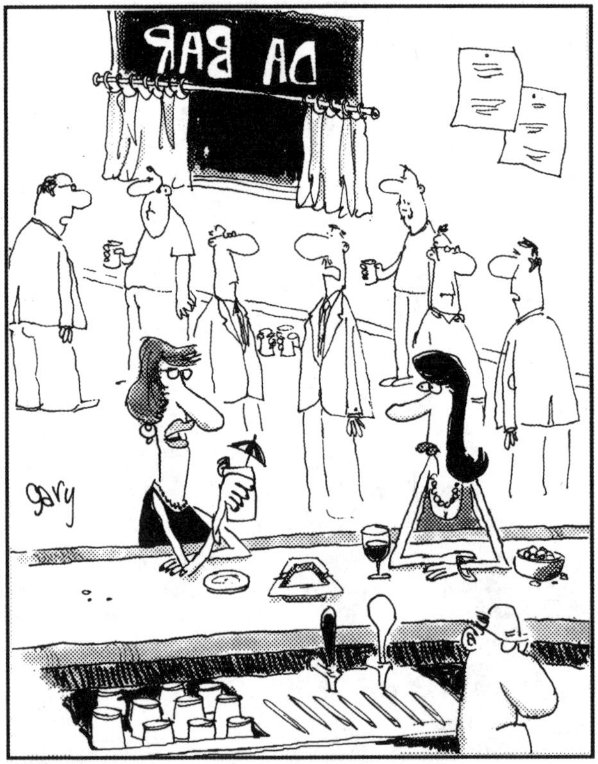
DA BAR

"Are you the type of girl who sees the guy as 'half empty-headed' or 'half full of it'?"

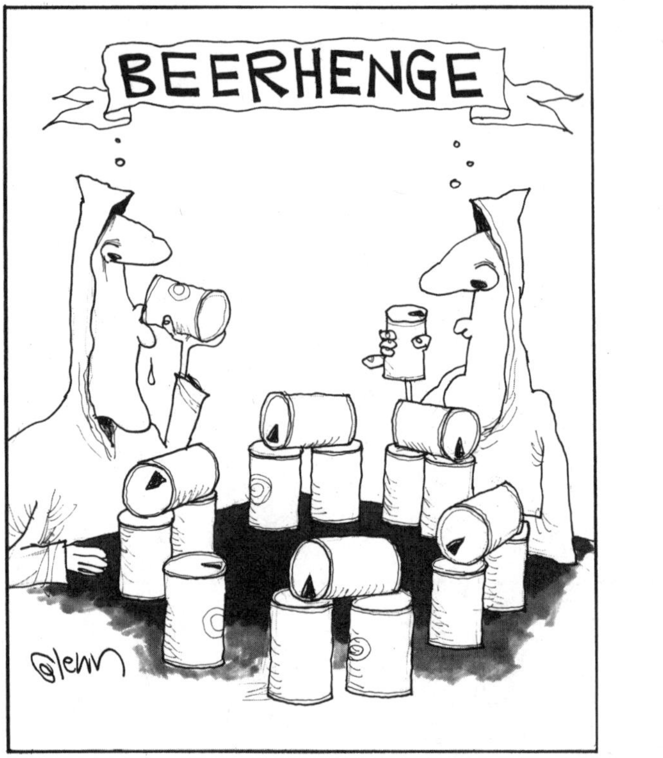
BEERHENGE

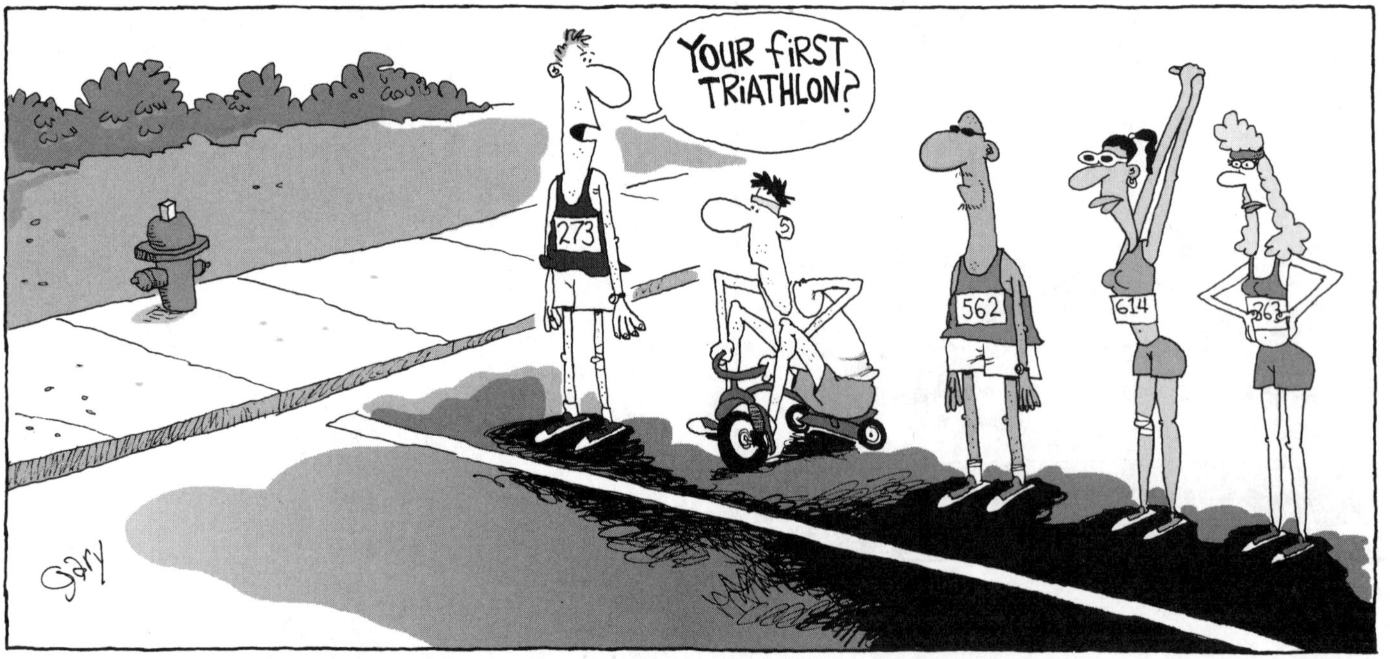
YOUR FIRST TRIATHLON?
273
562
614
363

YELLOW BRICK ROAD CREW
FALLING HOUSES
NEXT TWO MILES
MUNCHKIN LOCAL 220
Glenn

LEMONADE
$20,000
Per cup
garg

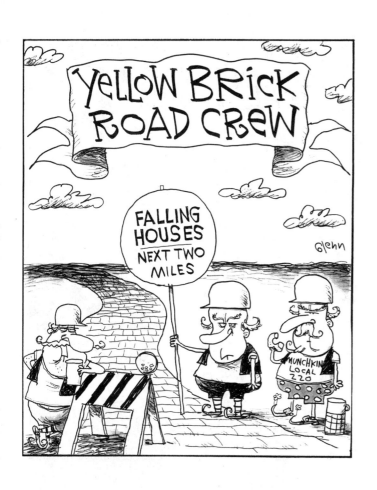

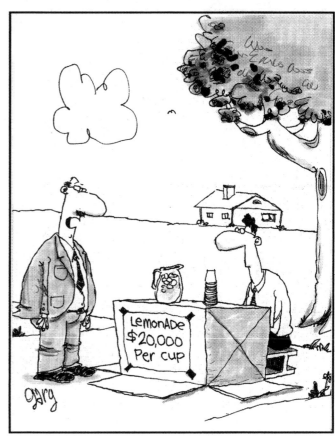

"Haskins, I'd like you to come back and work for me."

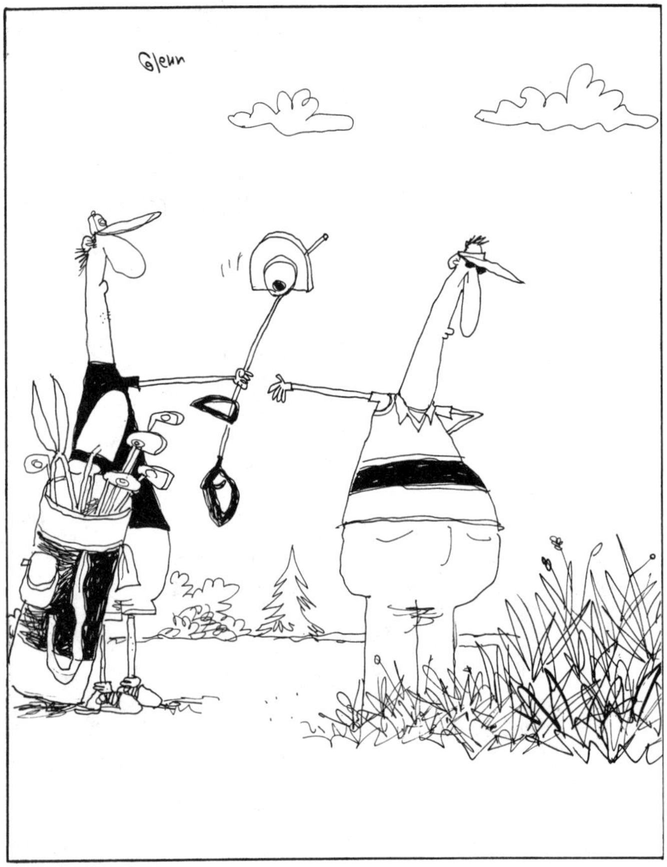

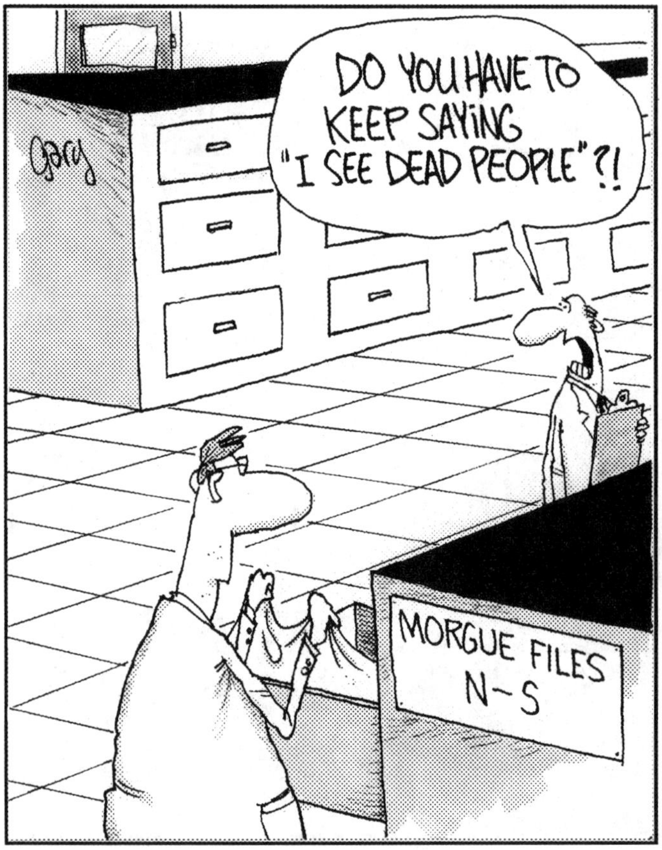
DO YOU HAVE TO KEEP SAYING "I SEE DEAD PEOPLE"?!
MORGUE FILES N–S

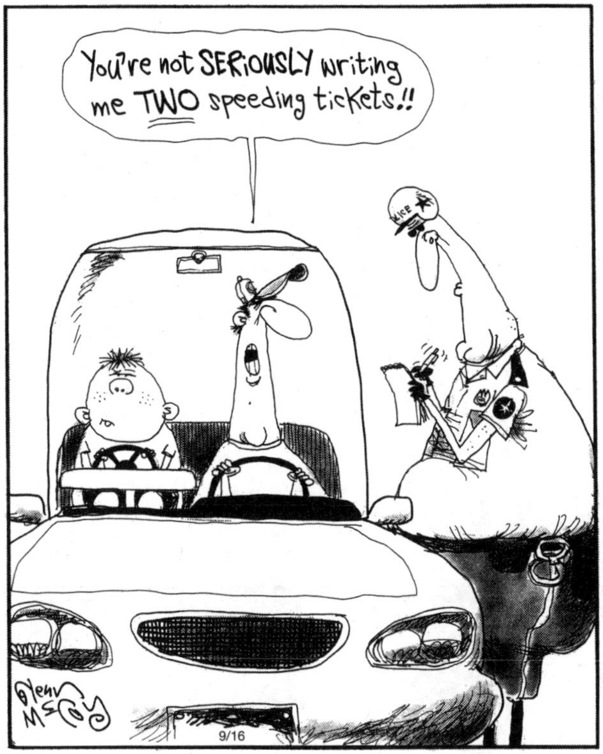
You're not SERIOUSLY writing me TWO speeding tickets!!
Glenn McCoy
9/16

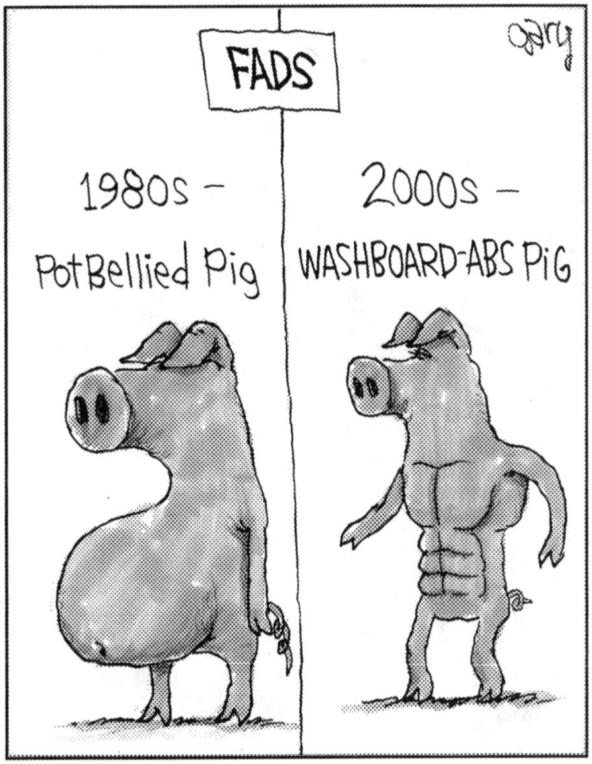
Gary
FADS
1980s - PotBellied Pig
2000s - WASHBOARD-ABS PiG

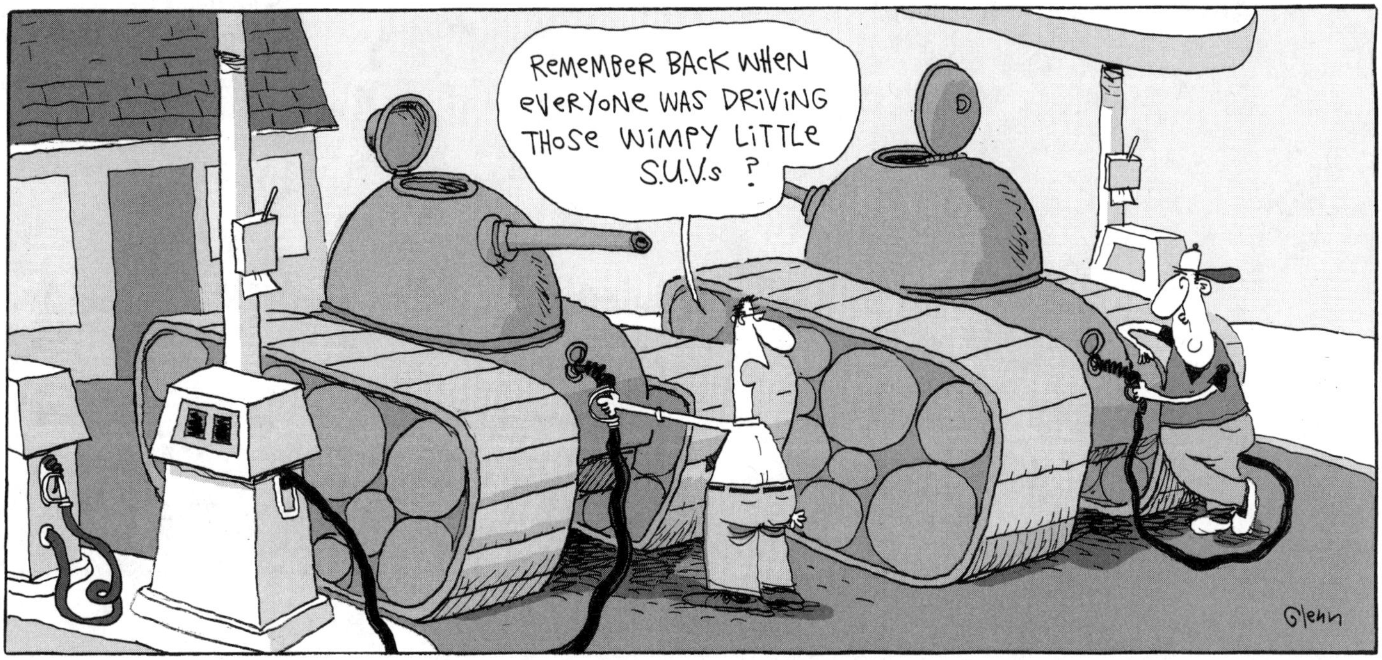
REMEMBER BACK WHEN EVERYONE WAS DRIVING THOSE WIMPY LITTLE S.U.V.s ?
Glenn

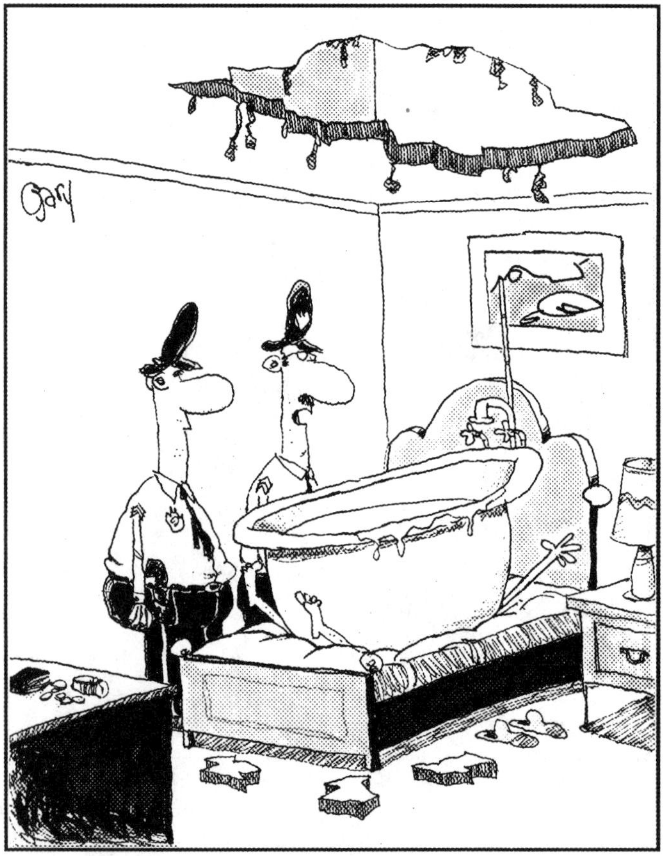
Gary

"At least he died in his sleep."

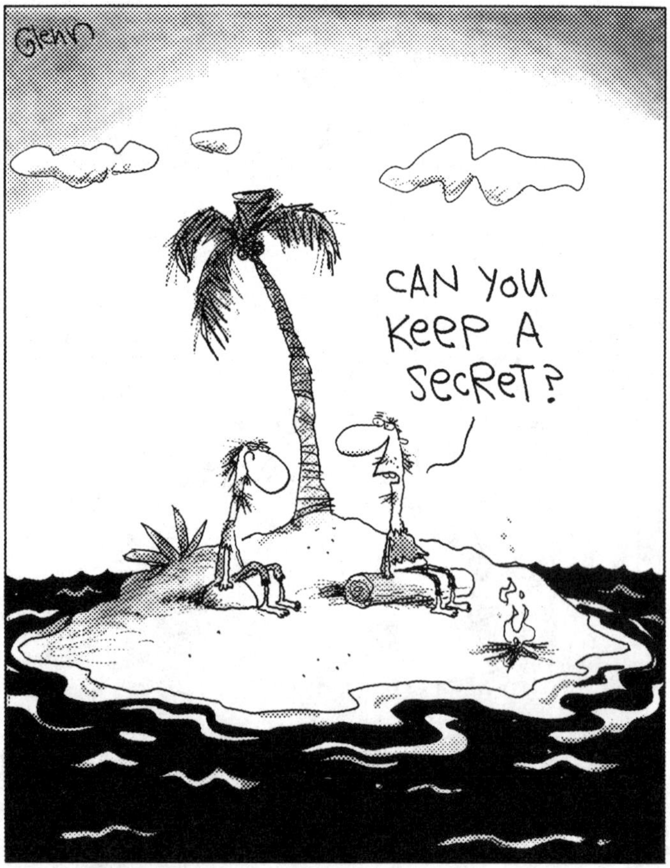
Glenn
CAN YOU KEEP A SECRET?

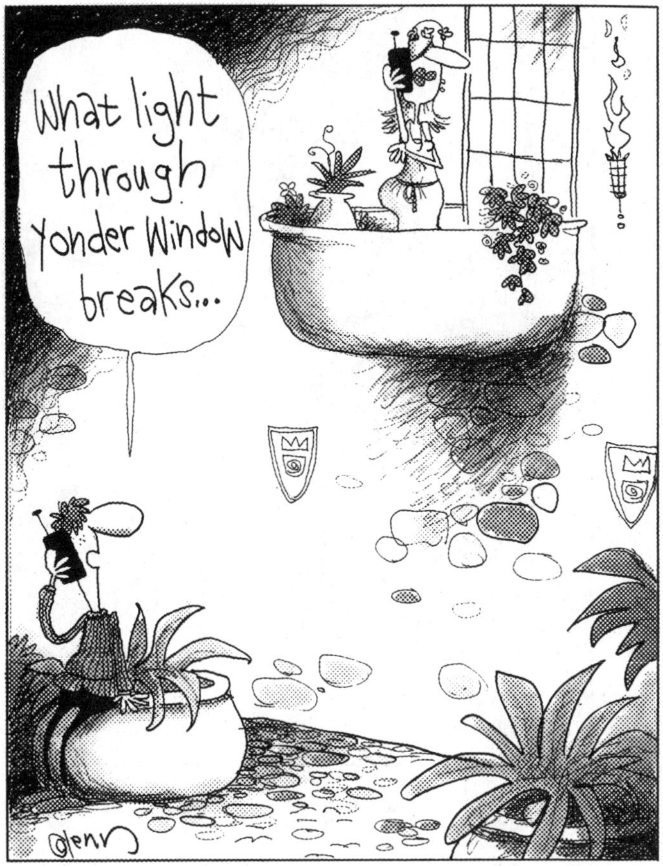
What light through Yonder Window breaks...
Glenn

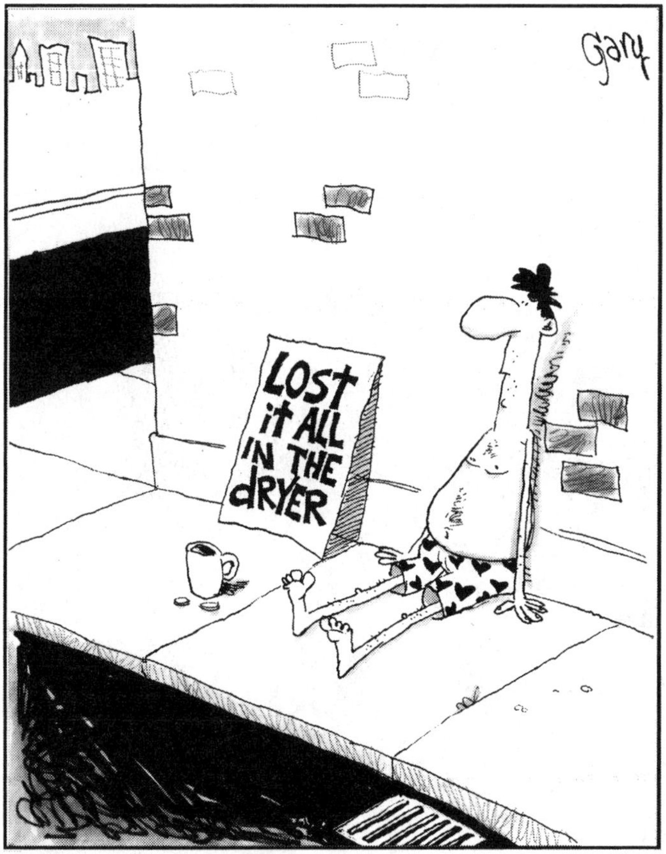
Gary
LOST it ALL IN THE dRYER

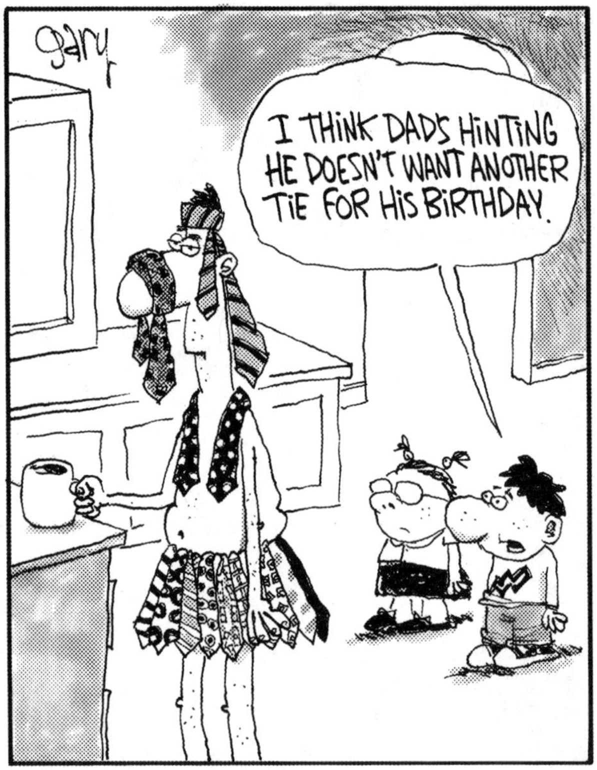
Gary
I THINK DAD'S HINTING HE DOESN'T WANT ANOTHER TIE FOR HIS BIRTHDAY.

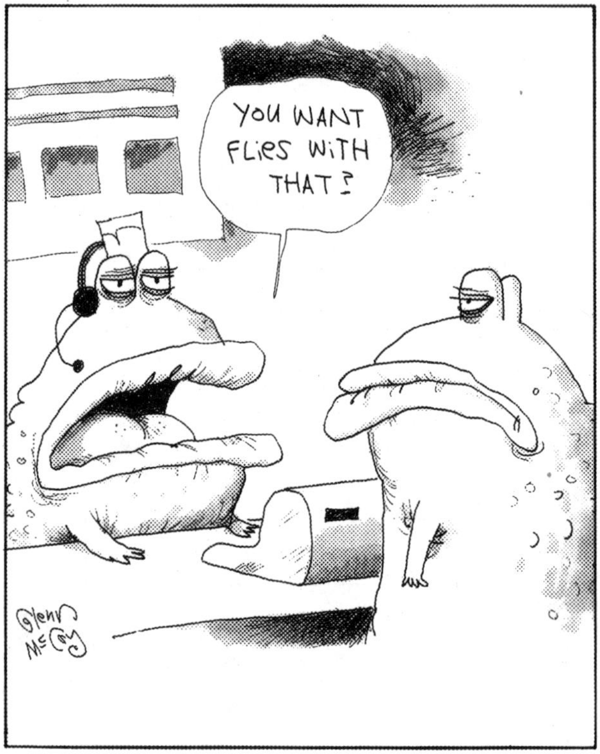
YOU WANT FLIES WITH THAT?
Glenn McCoy

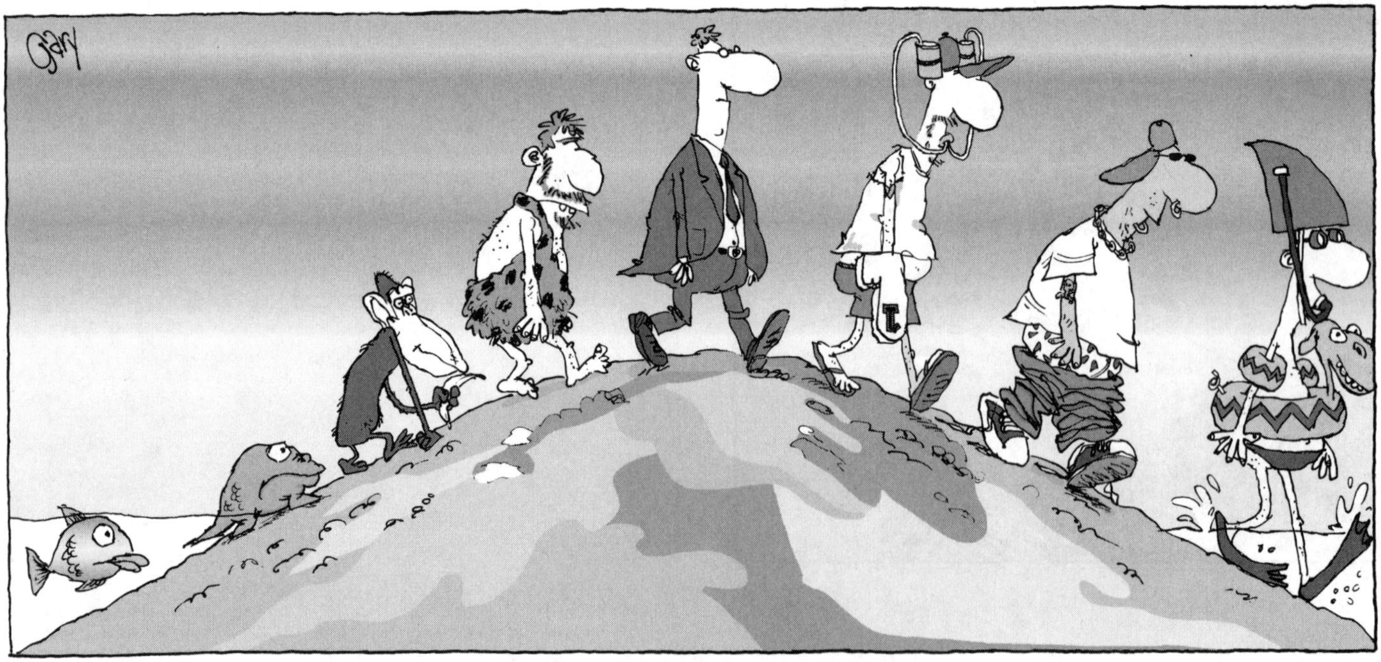
Gary

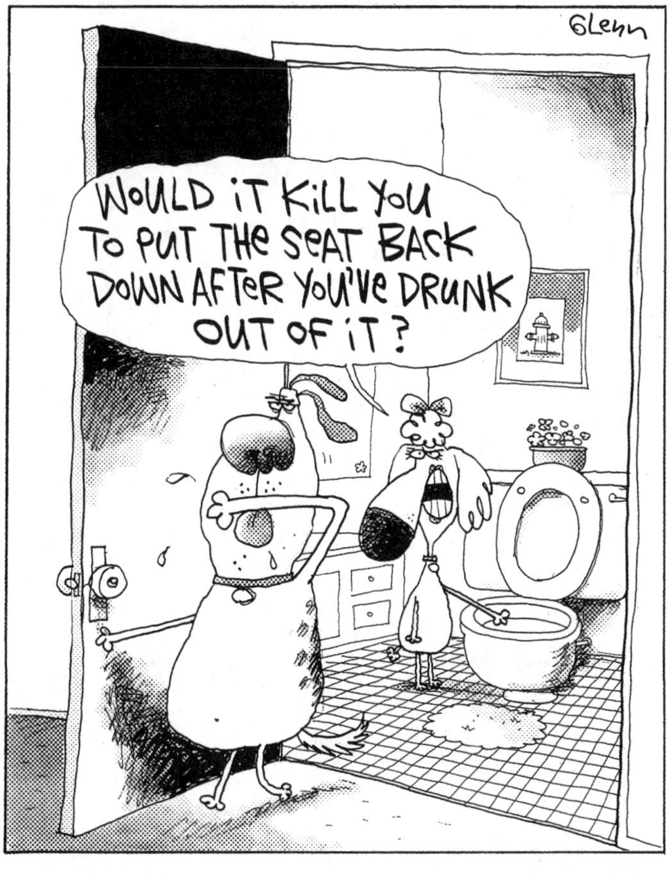
Glenn
WOULD iT KiLL YOU TO PUT THE SEAT BACK DOWN AFTER YOU'VE DRUNK OUT OF iT?

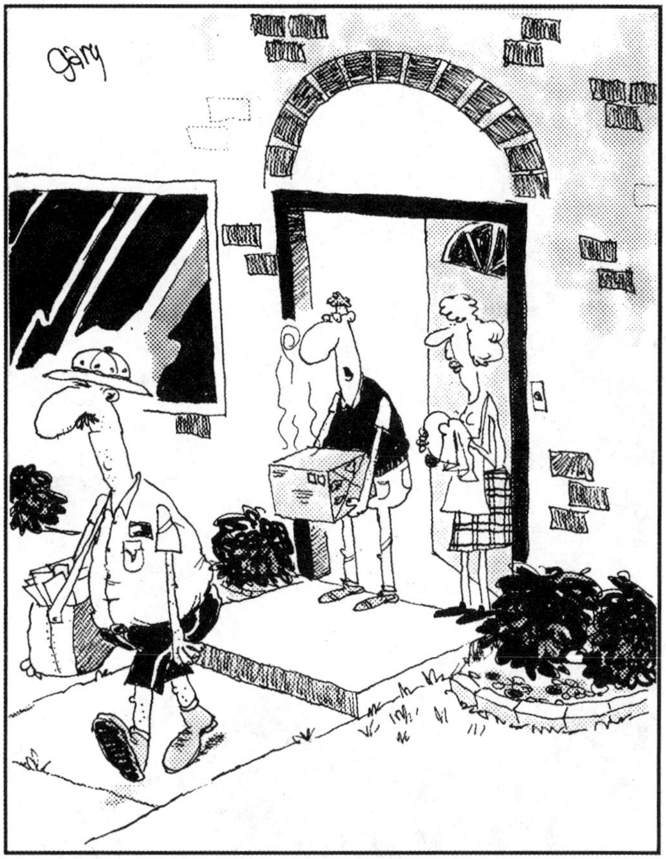
Gary

"This solves the riddle of which came first, the chicken or the egg. It's the chicken—and with postage due."

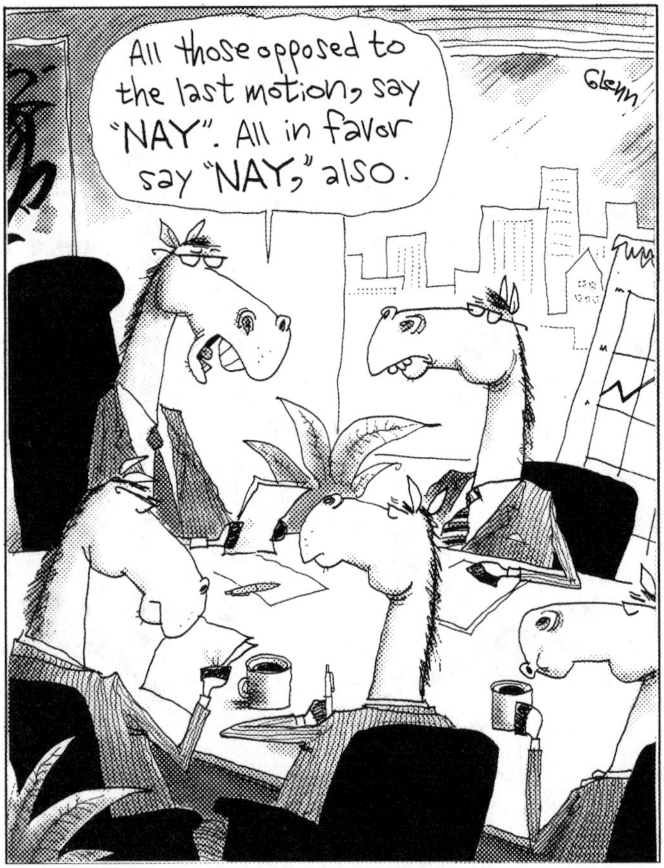
All those opposed to the last motion, say "NAY". All in favor say "NAY," also.
Glenn

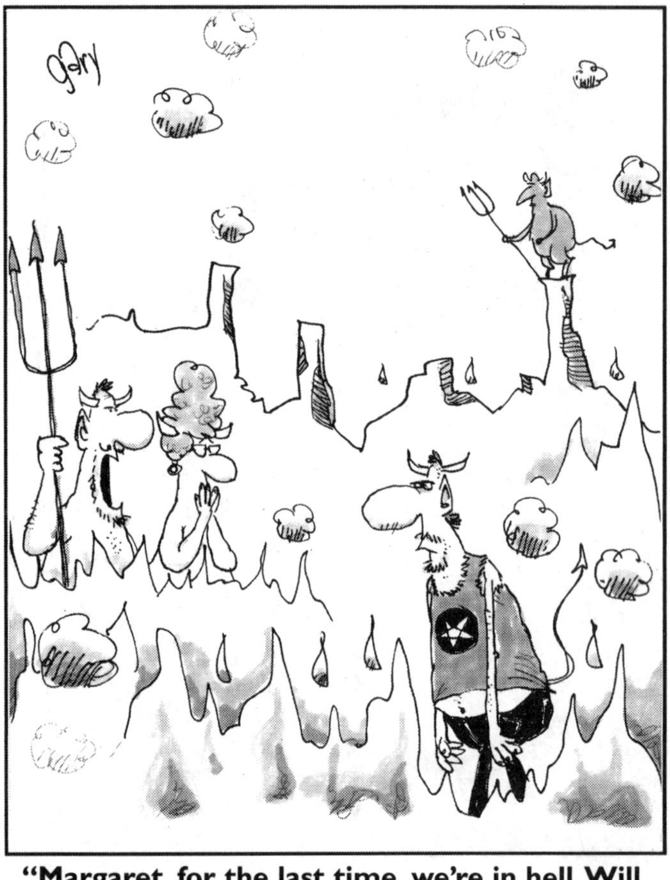
Gary

"Margaret, for the last time, we're in hell. Will you quit fretting that our son joined a satanic cult?!"

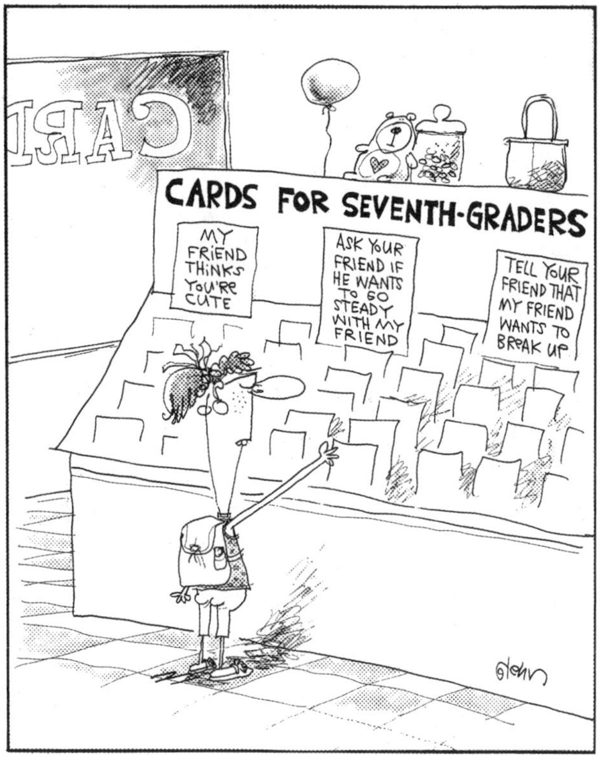
CARDS FOR SEVENTH-GRADERS
MY FRIEND THINKS YOU'RE CUTE
ASK YOUR FRIEND IF HE WANTS TO GO STEADY WITH MY FRIEND
TELL YOUR FRIEND THAT MY FRIEND WANTS TO BREAK UP
Glenn

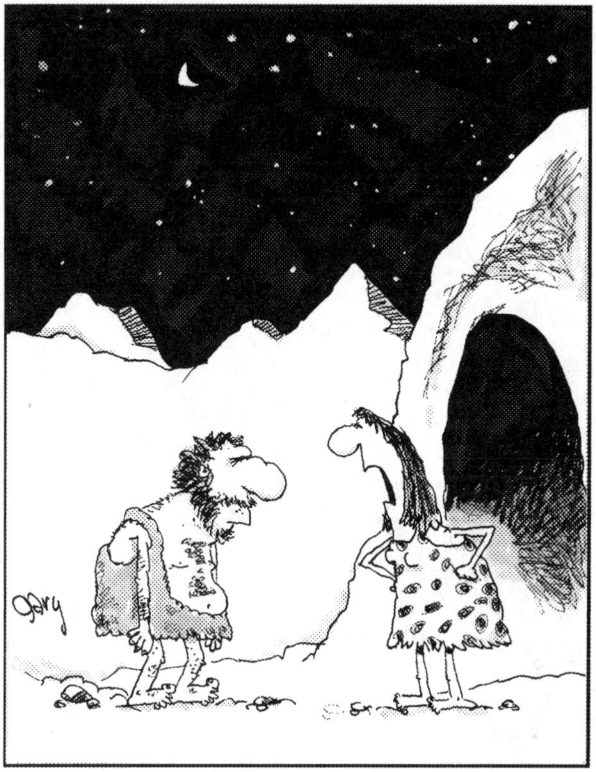
Gary

"'Early man' my foot. It's 9:35!"

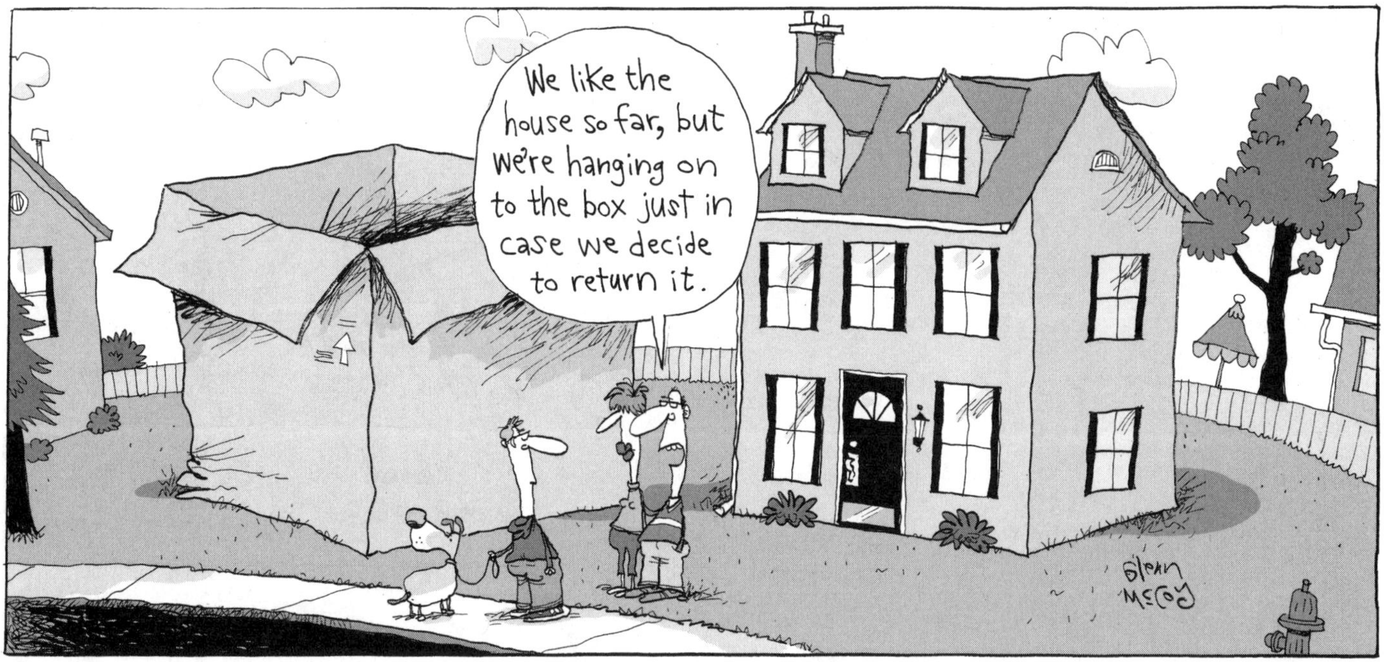
We like the house so far, but we're hanging on to the box just in case we decide to return it.
Glenn McCoy

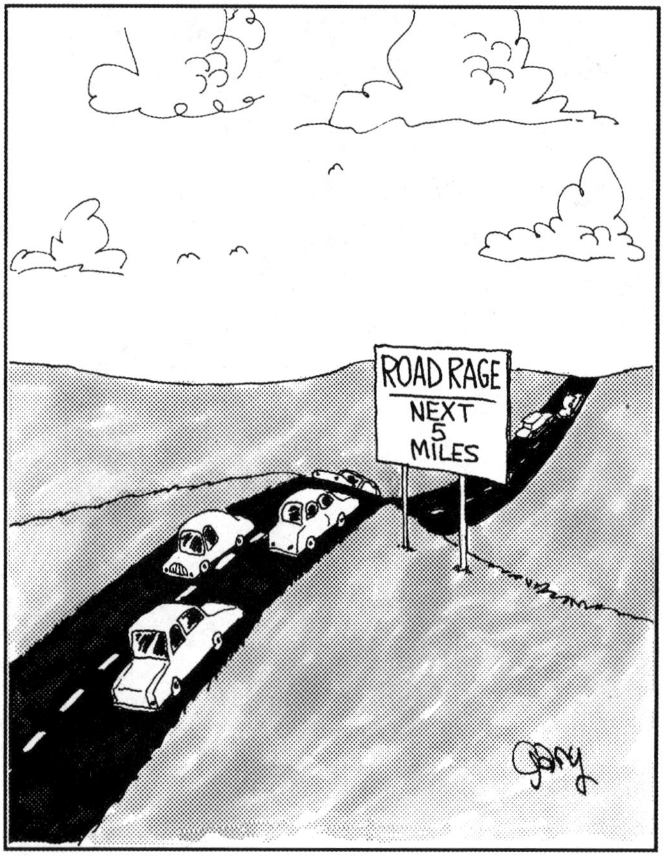
ROAD RAGE
NEXT
5
MILES

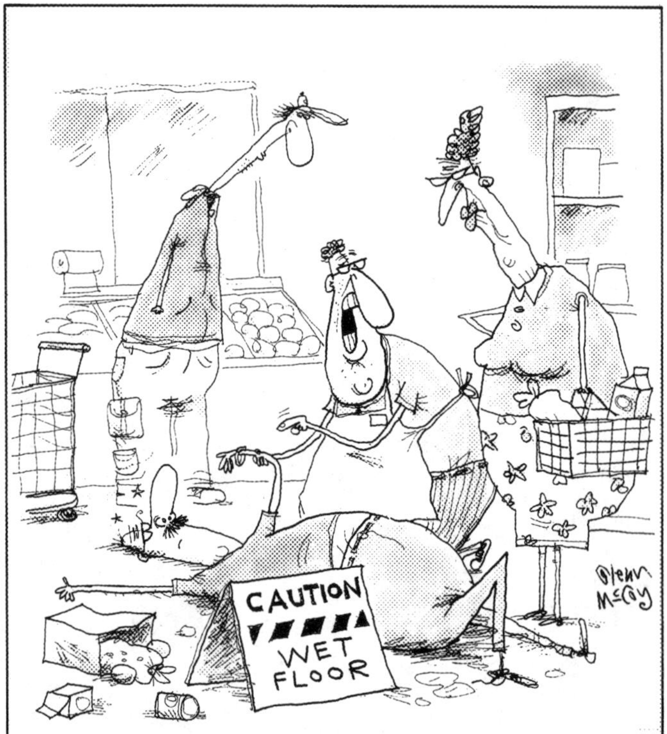
CAUTION
WET
FLOOR

YeAH. HeRe We GO. He's WeARiNG A LAWYeR-ALeRT BRACeLeT.

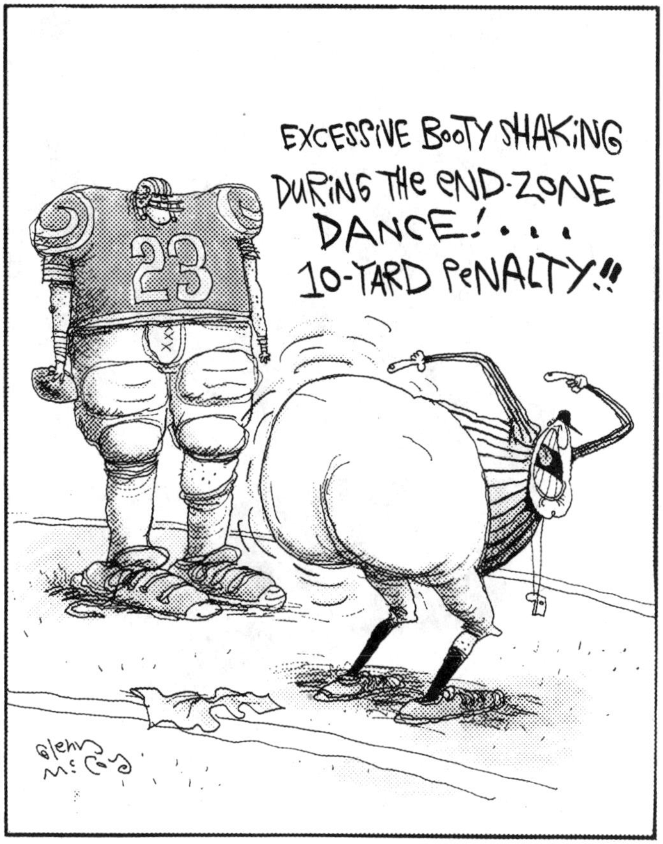
EXCESSIVE BOOTY SHAKING DURING THE END-ZONE DANCE!... 10-YARD PENALTY!!
Glenn McCoy

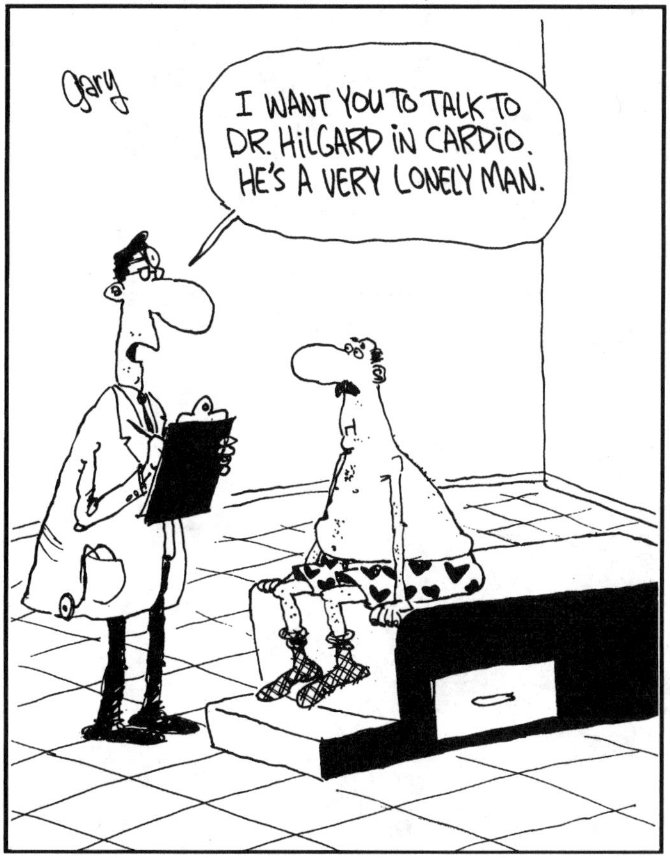
Gary
I WANT YOU TO TALK TO DR. HILGARD IN CARDIO. HE'S A VERY LONELY MAN.

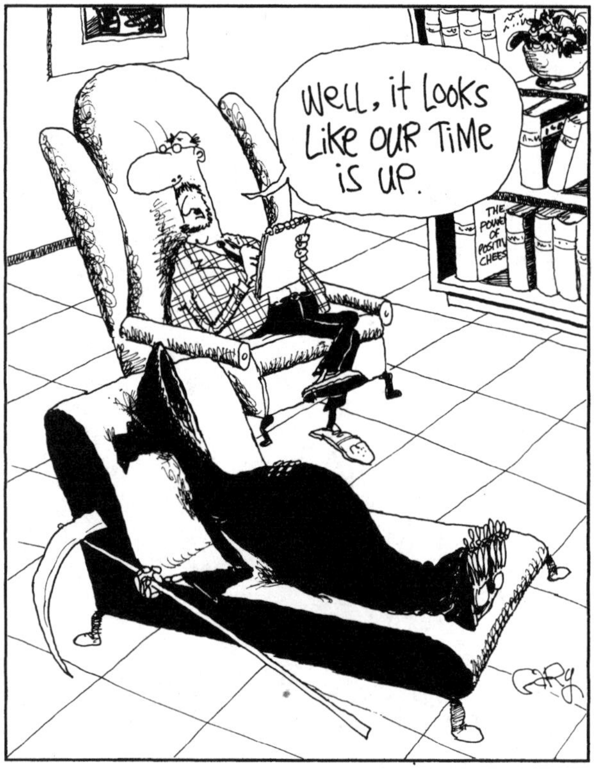
WELL, it LOOKS LIKE OUR TIME iS UP.
THE POWER OF POSITIVE CHEES

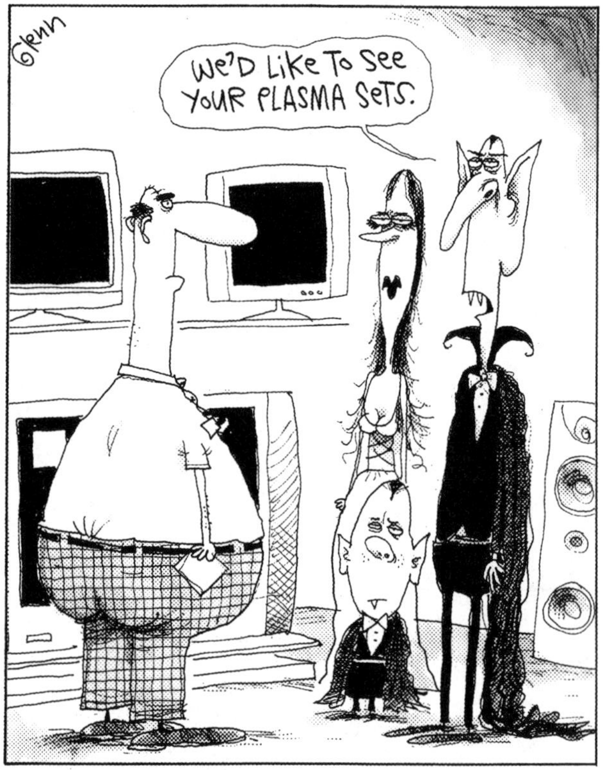
WE'D LIKE TO SEE YOUR PLASMA SETS.

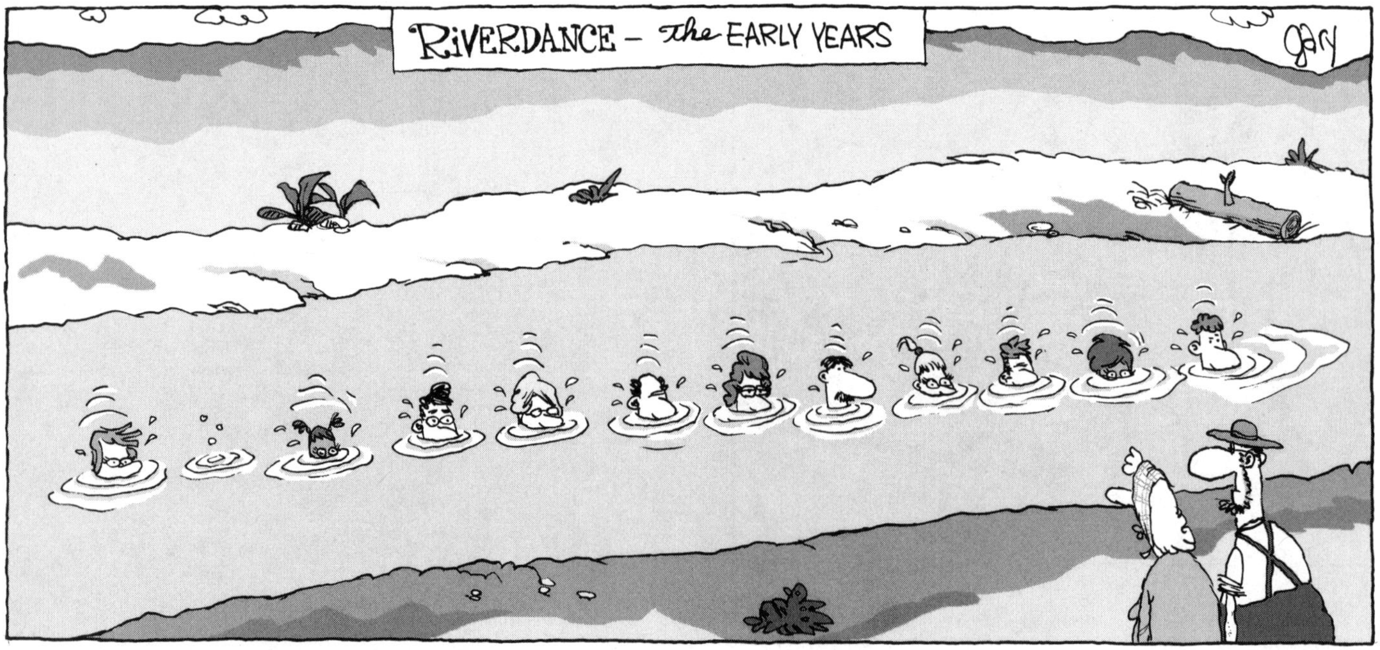
RiVERDANCE – the EARLY YEARS

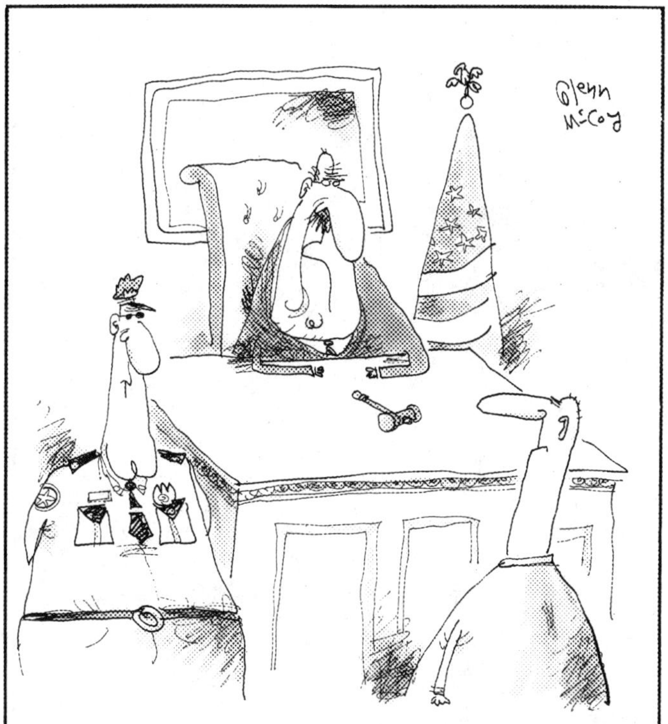
Glenn McCoy

WE'RE RUNNING SHORT ON THOSE ANKLE-MONITORING BRACELETS, SO I'M JUST GOING TO STICK YOU IN THAT "BIG BROTHER" HOUSE FOR A FEW MONTHS.

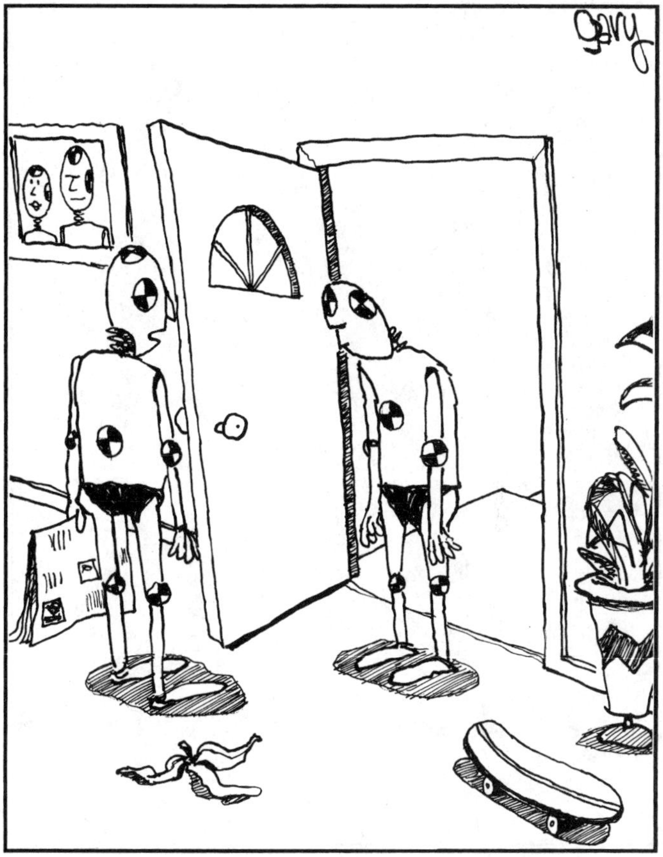
Gary

"Son, I'm ashamed of you. This is the third time this week that you didn't wreck the car."

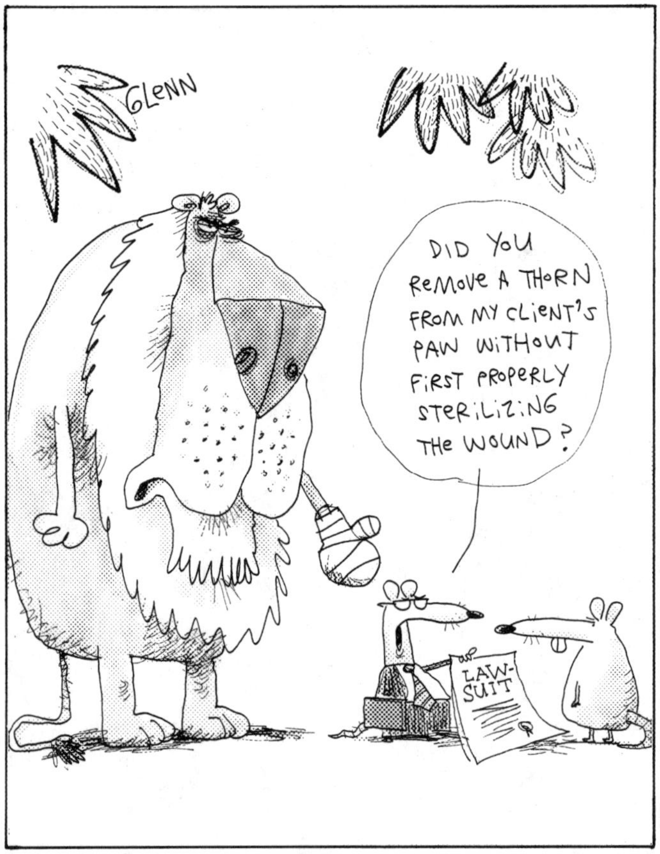
GLENN
DID YOU REMOVE A THORN FROM MY CLIENT'S PAW WITHOUT FIRST PROPERLY STERILIZING THE WOUND?
LAW-SUIT

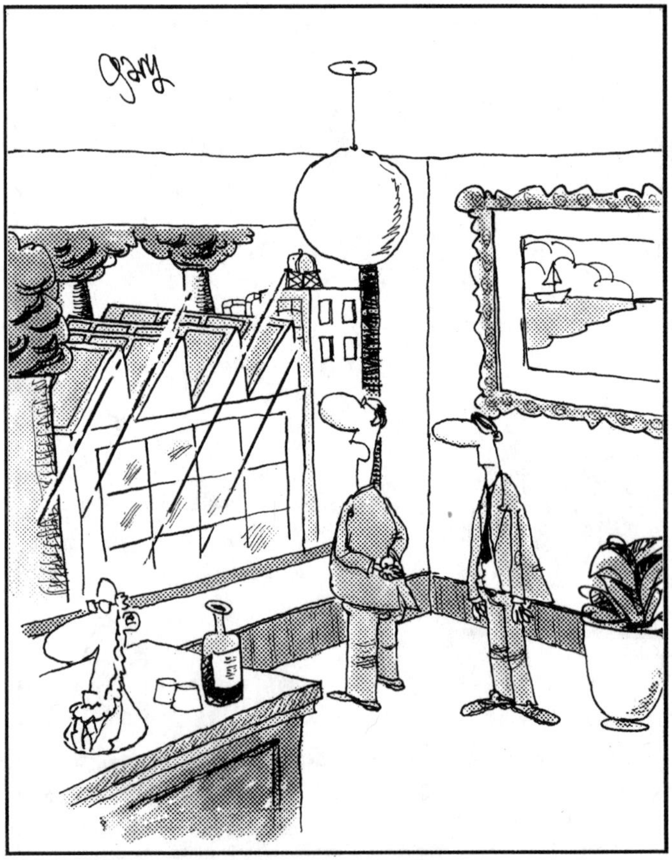
Gary

"Someday, son, this will be all yours. This window, that is."

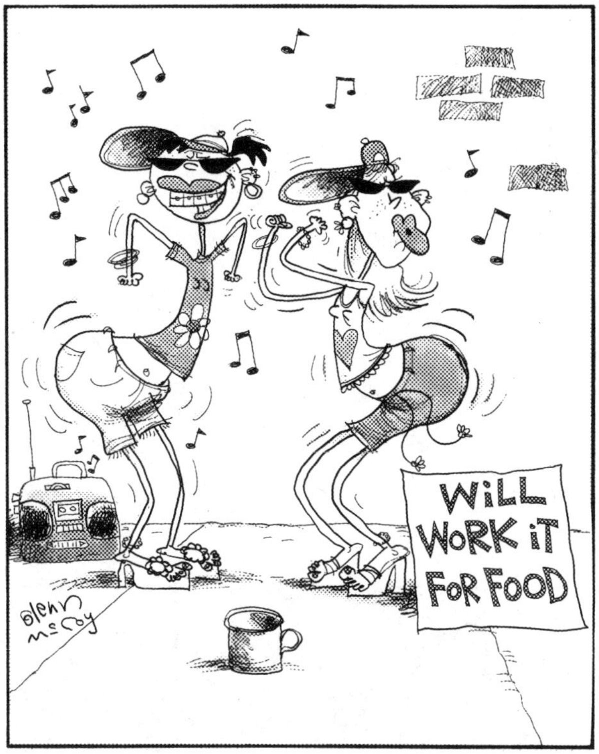
WiLL WORK iT FOR FOOD

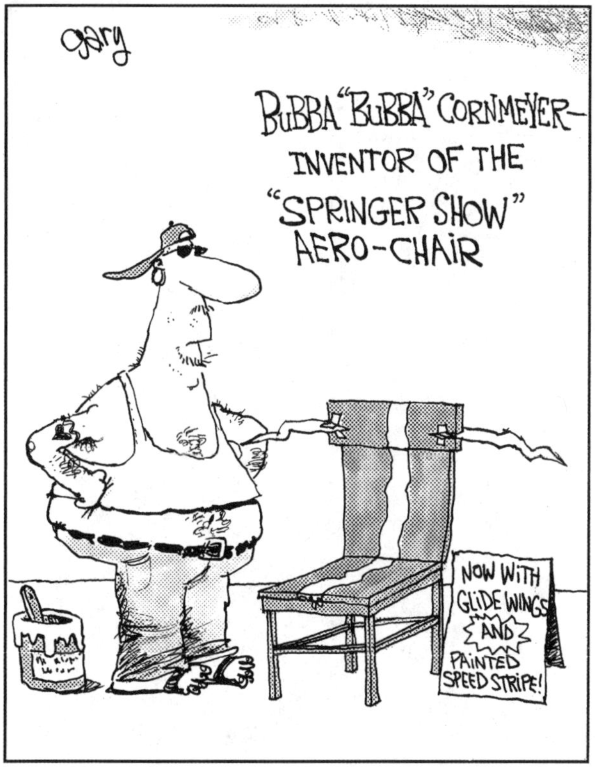
BUBBA "BUBBA" CORNMEYER–
INVENTOR OF THE
"SPRINGER SHOW"
AERO-CHAIR
NOW WiTH GLIDE WINGS AND PAINTED SPEED STRIPE!

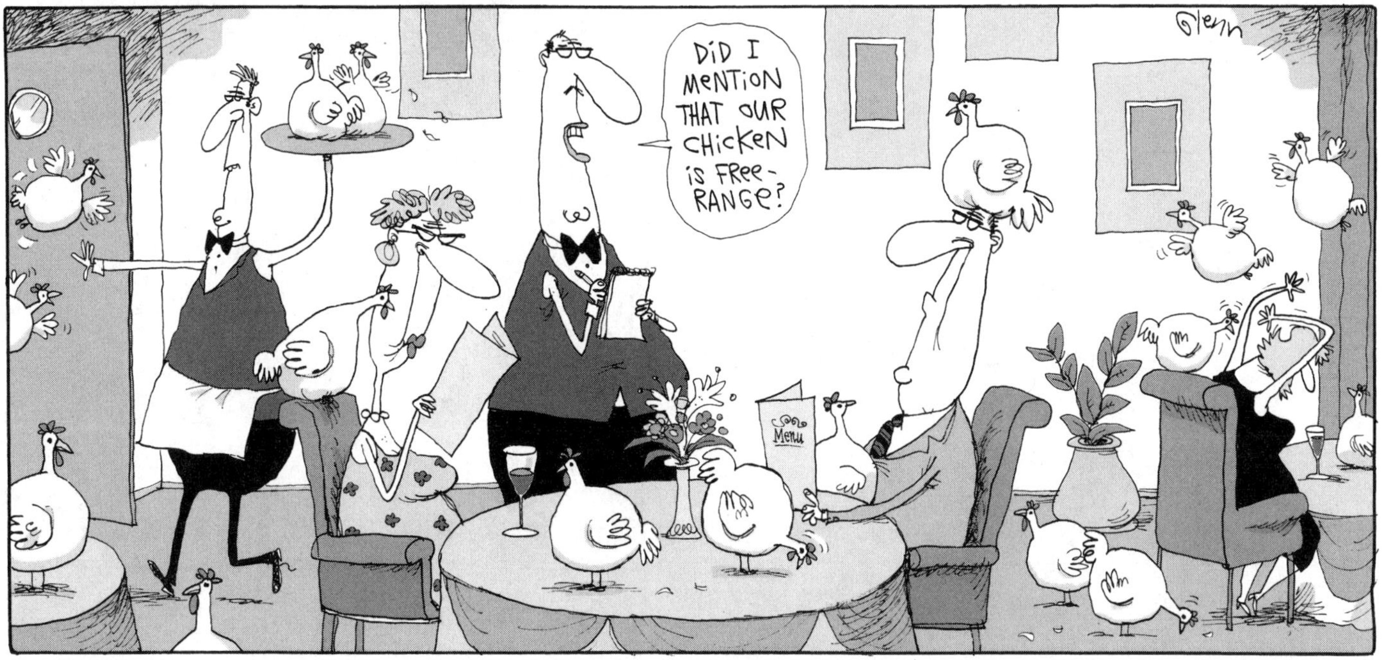
DiD I MENTION THAT OUR CHICKEN is FREE-RANGE?
Menu

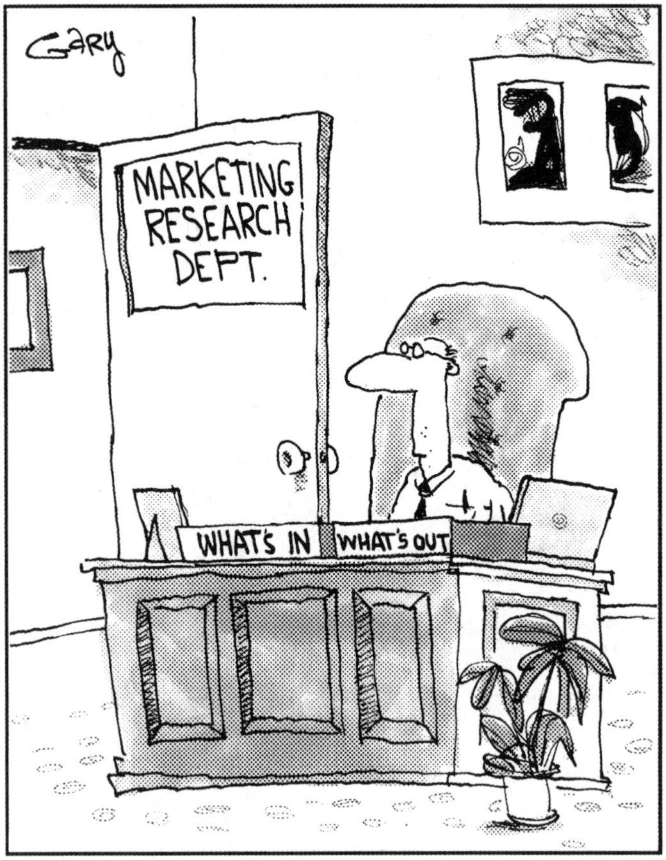
GARY
MARKETING RESEARCH DEPT.
WHAT'S IN
WHAT'S OUT

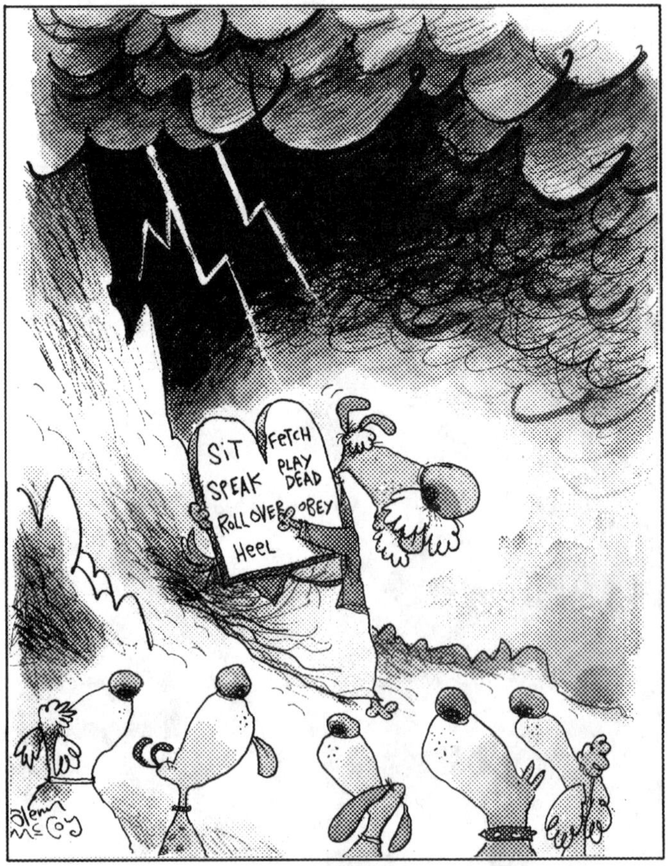
SIT
SPEAK
ROLL OVER
HEEL
FETCH
PLAY DEAD
OBEY
Glenn McCoy

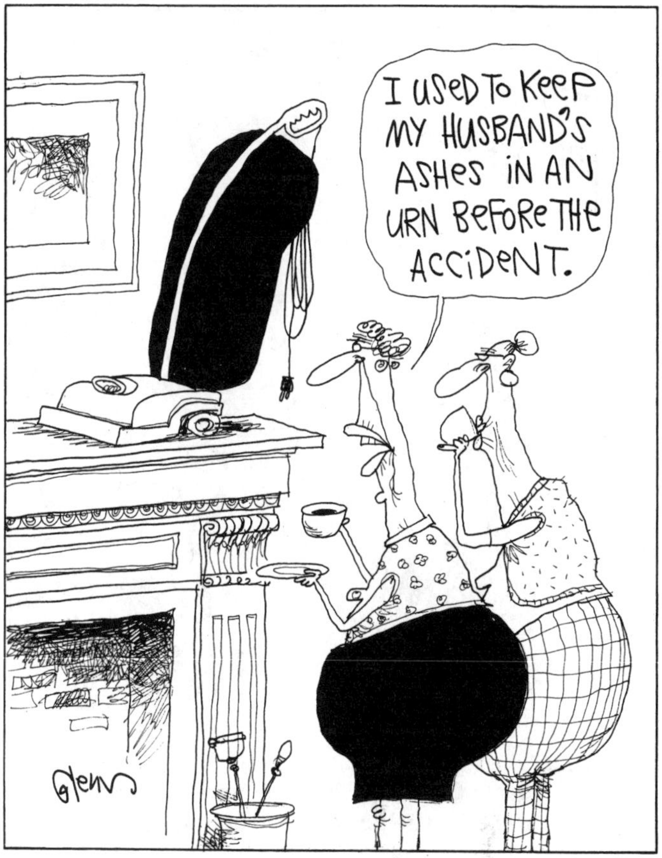
I USED TO KEEP MY HUSBAND'S ASHES IN AN URN BEFORE THE ACCIDENT.
Glenn

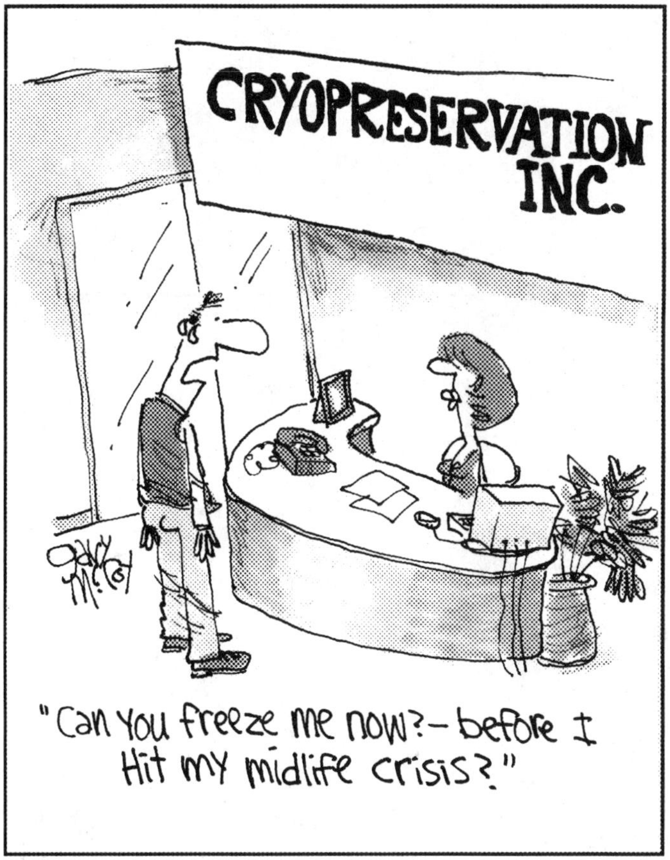
CRYOPRESERVATION INC.
"Can you freeze me now?– before I Hit my midlife crisis?"

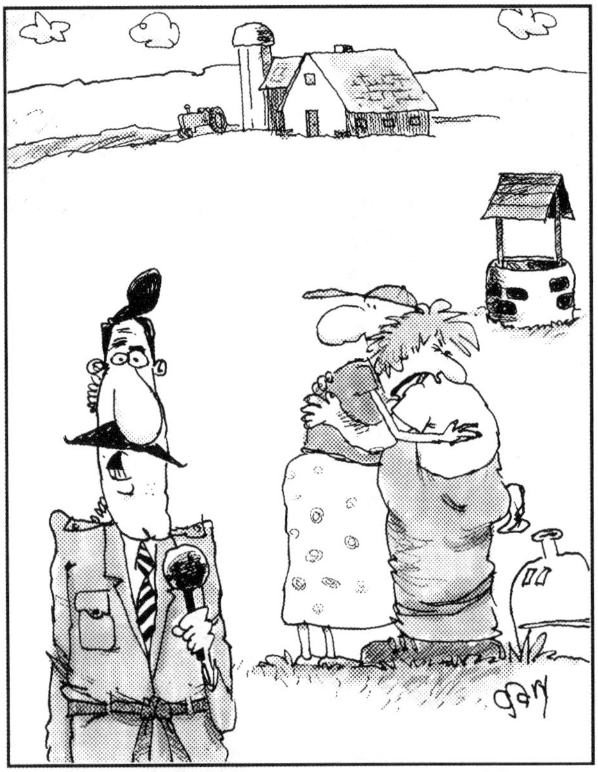
gary

"Sadly, Bob and Ellen Peterson—parents of little Billy, the boy trapped in a well for two weeks—are running very low on bottled water."

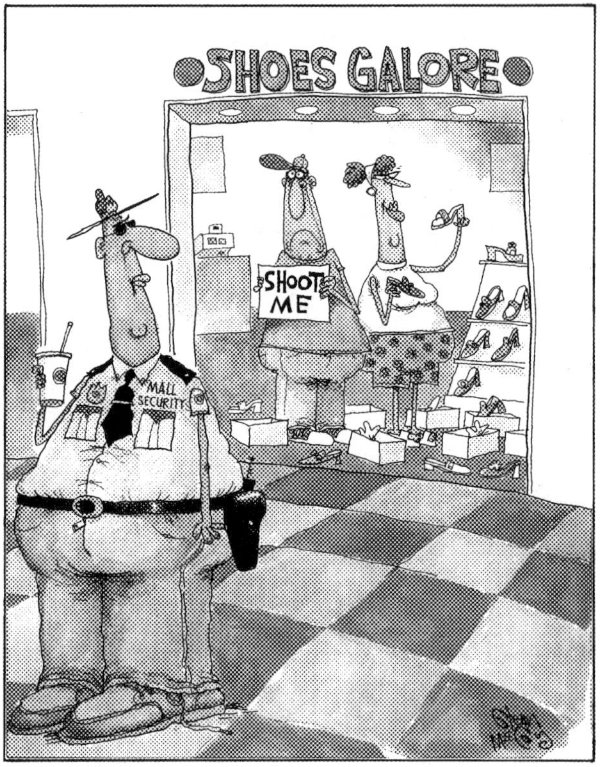
SHOES GALORE
SHOOT ME
MALL SECURITY

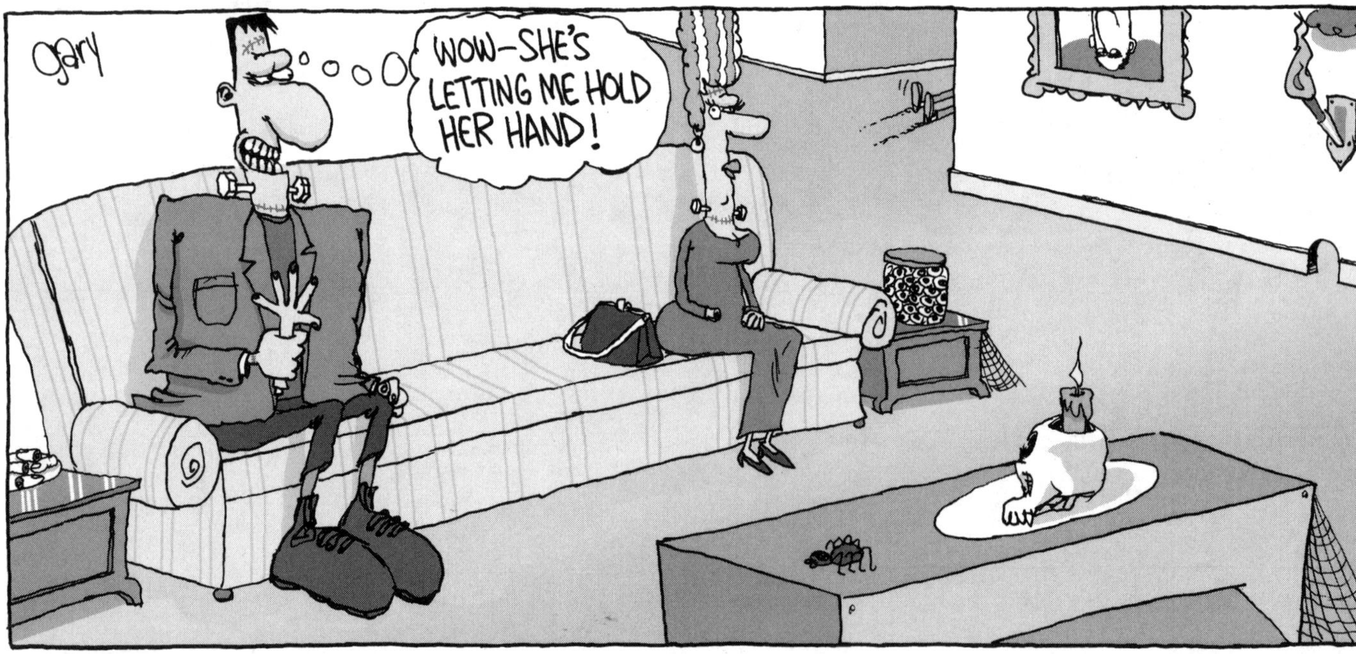
gary
WOW-SHE'S LETTING ME HOLD HER HAND!

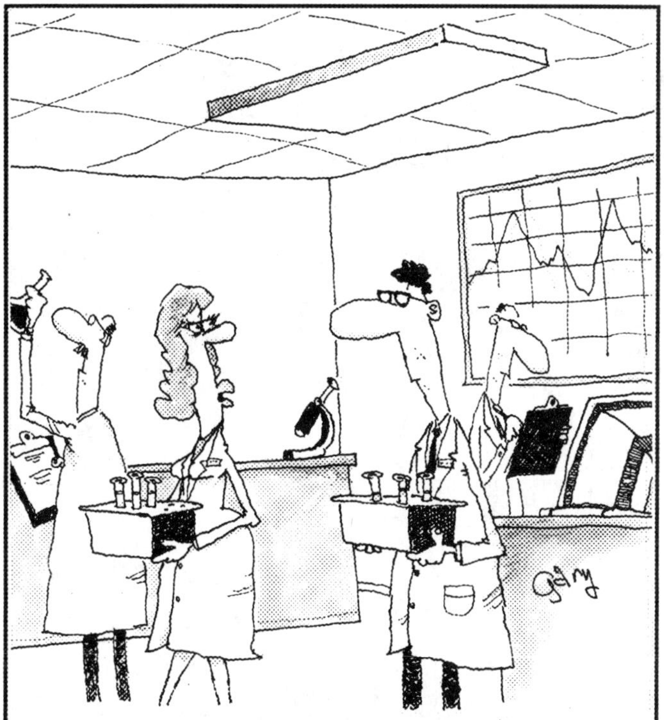

"Yes, Dr. Bloom, I'll run these saliva samples down to the lab. But please stop telling the other doctors we often swap spit."

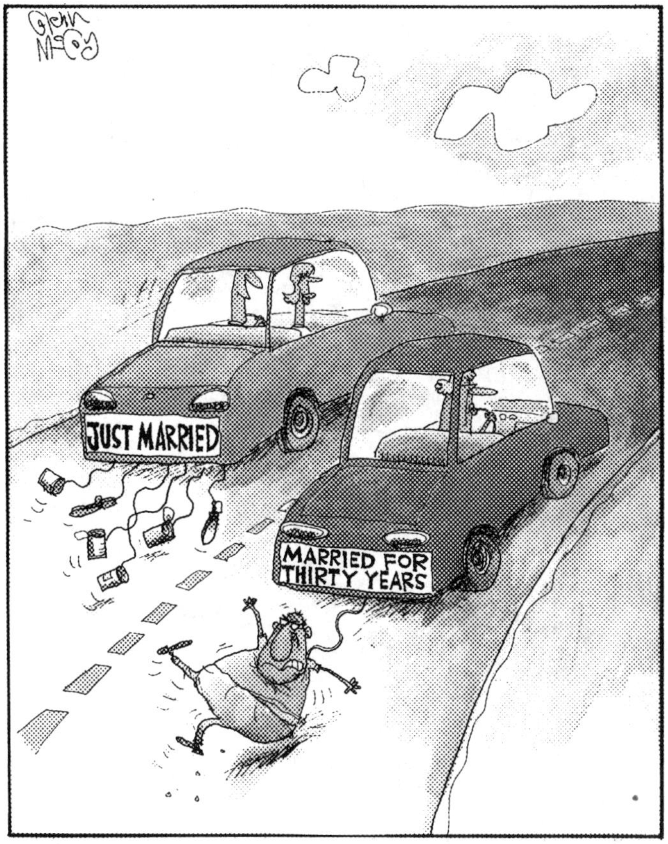
JUST MARRIED
MARRIED FOR THIRTY YEARS

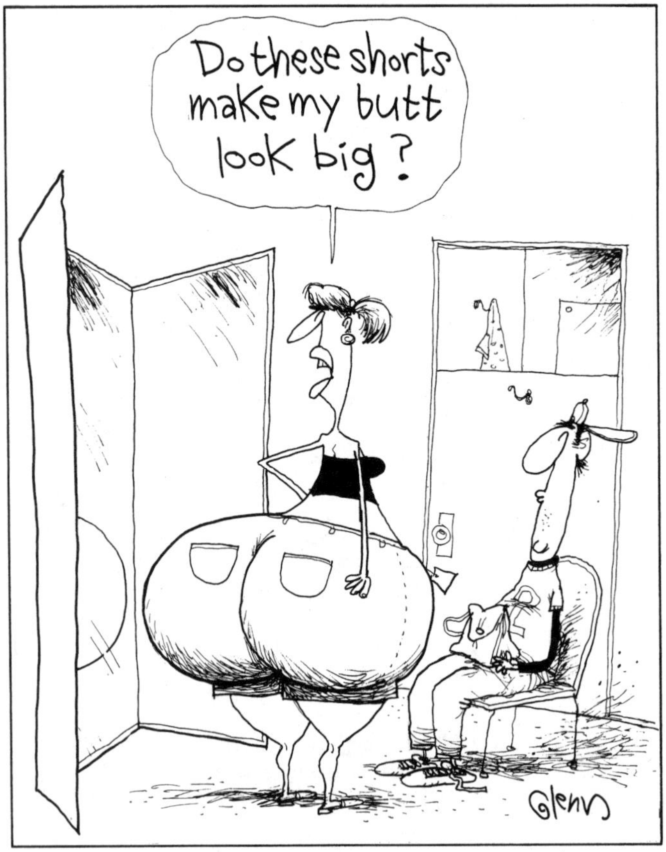
Do these shorts make my butt look big ?
Glenn

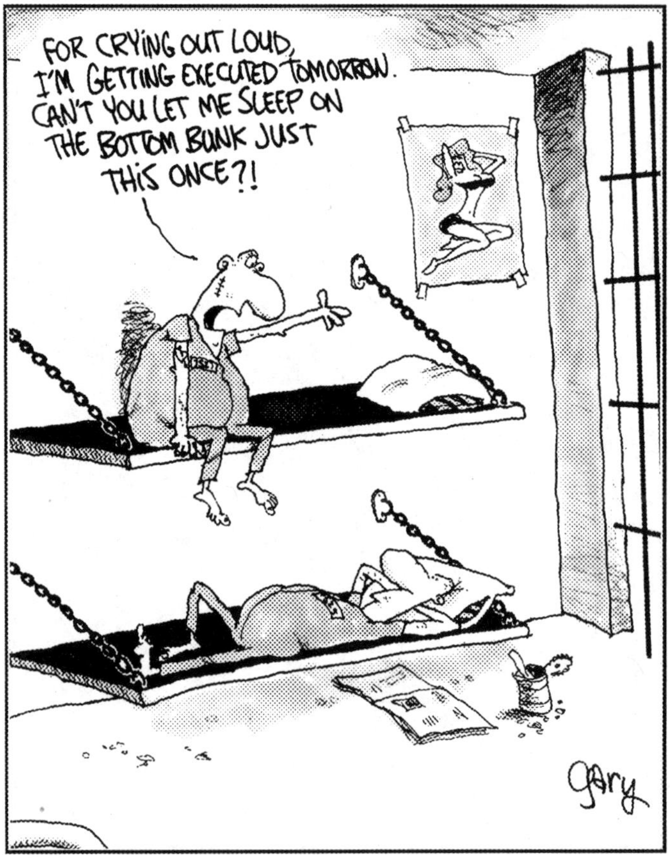
FOR CRYING OUT LOUD, I'M GETTING EXECUTED TOMORROW. CAN'T YOU LET ME SLEEP ON THE BOTTOM BUNK JUST THIS ONCE?!
Gary

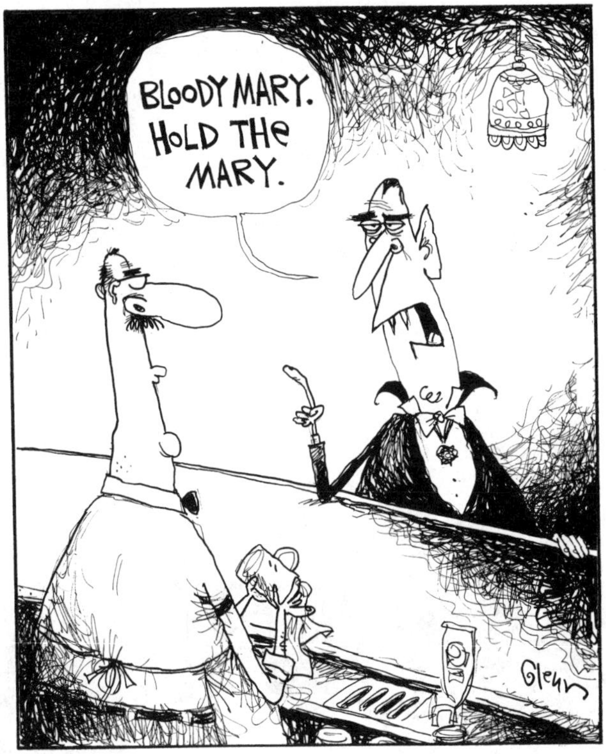
BLOODY MARY. HOLD THE MARY.
Glenn

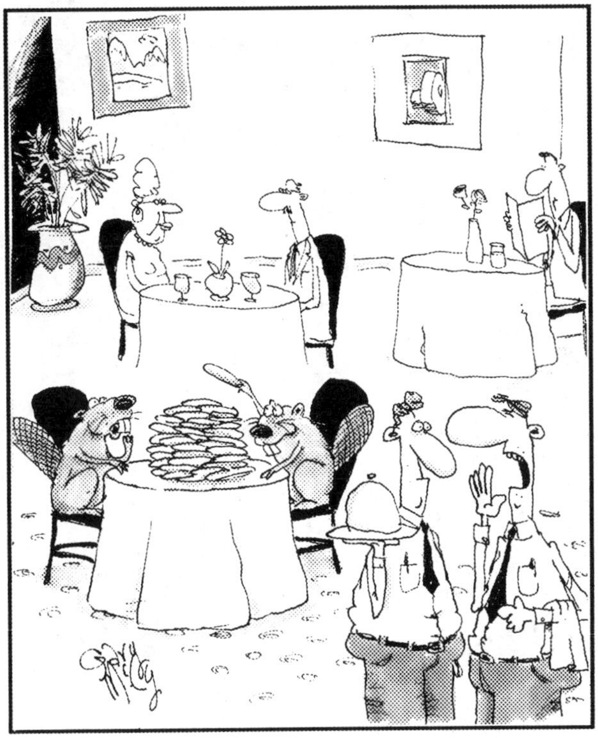

"No more breadsticks for table seven."

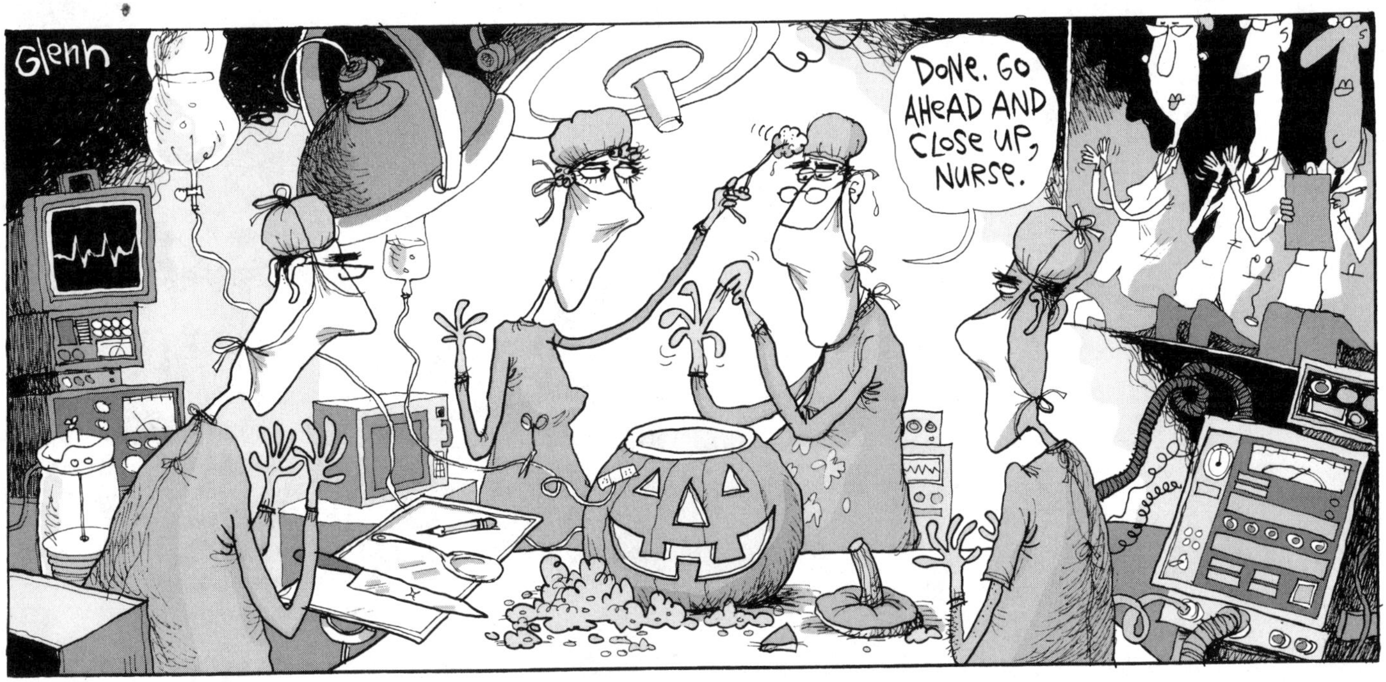
Glenn
DONE. GO AHEAD AND CLOSE UP, NURSE.

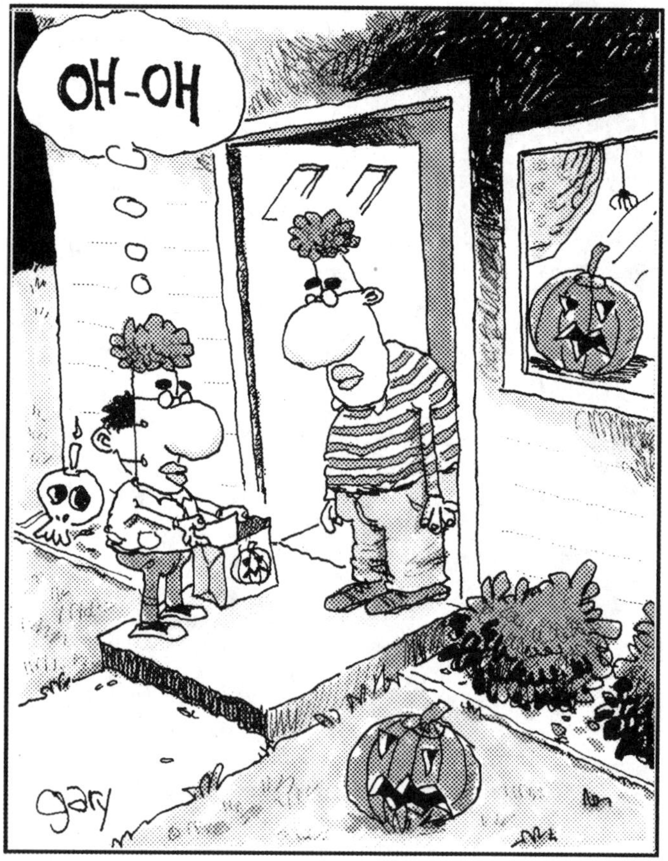
OH-OH
gary

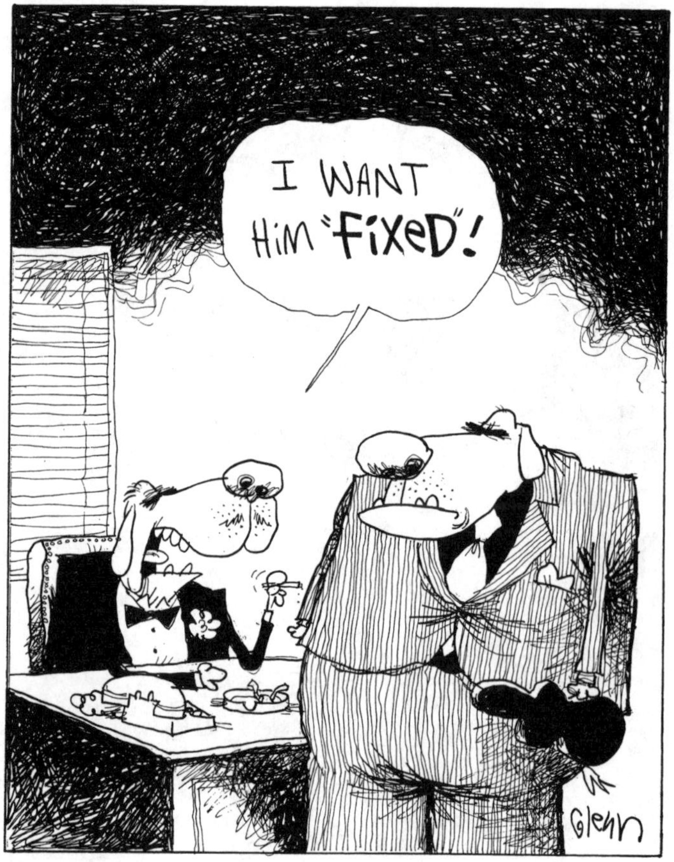
I WANT Him "FixeD"!
Glenn

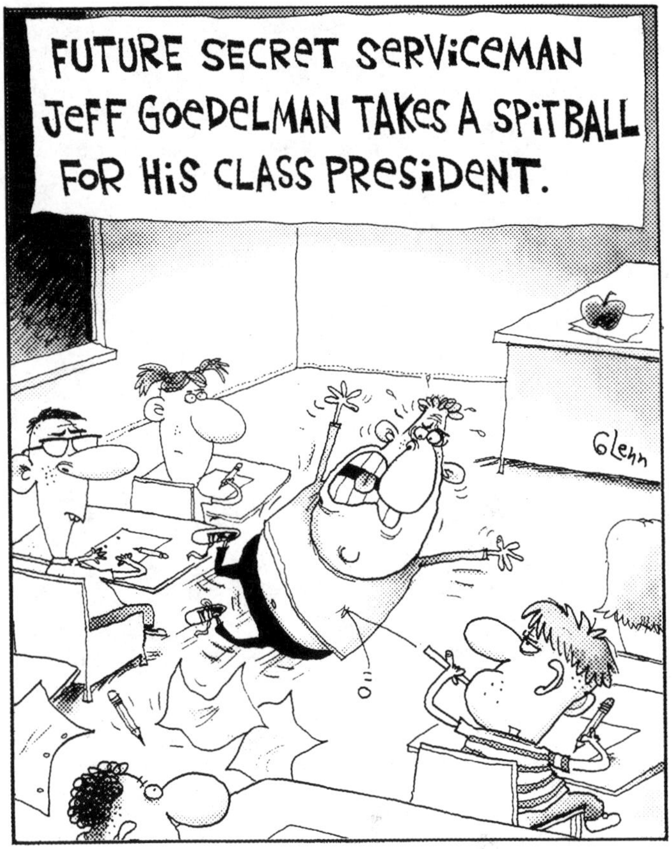
FUTURE SECRET SERVICEMAN JEFF GOEDELMAN TAKES A SPITBALL FOR HIS CLASS PRESIDENT.
Glenn

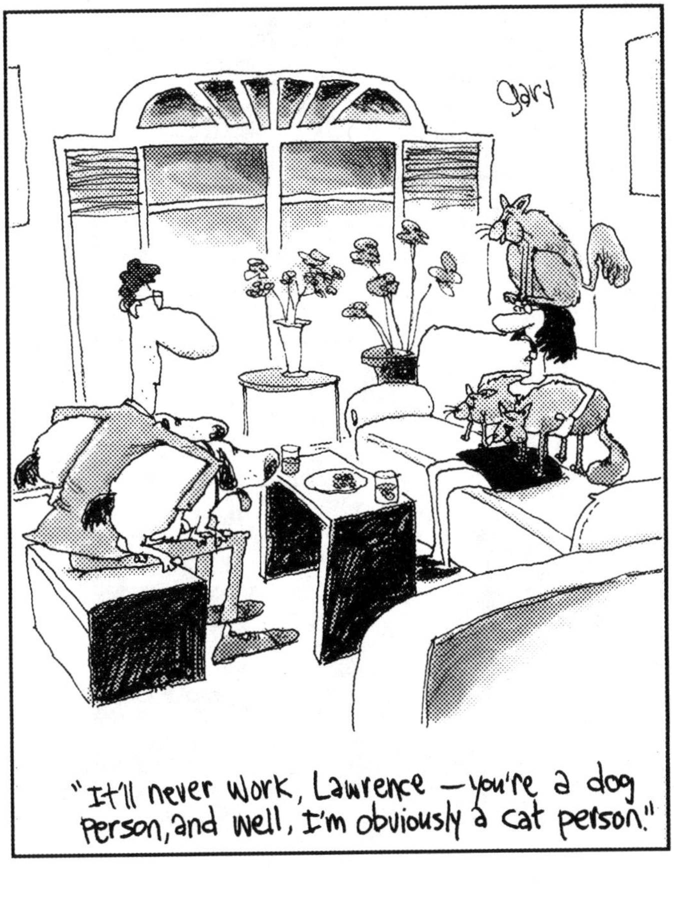
Gary

"It'll never work, Lawrence—you're a dog person, and well, I'm obviously a cat person."

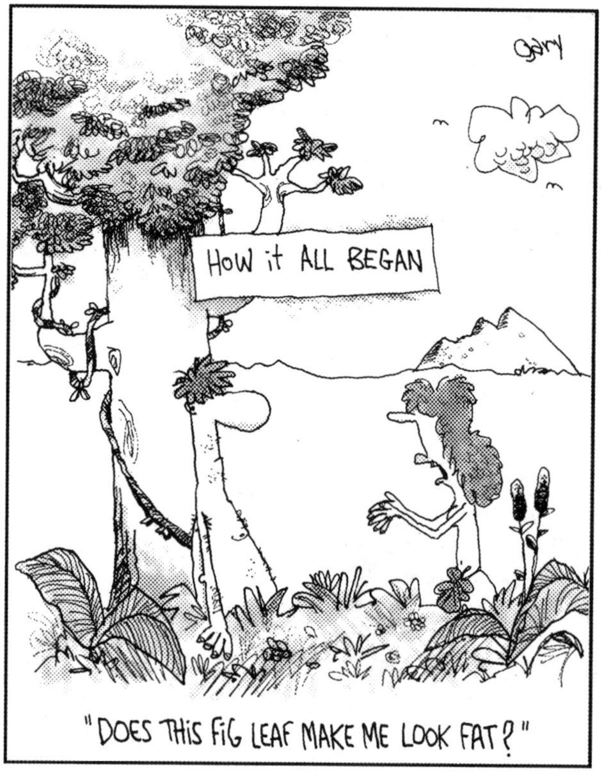
gary
How it ALL BEGAN
"DOES THIS FIG LEAF MAKE ME LOOK FAT?"

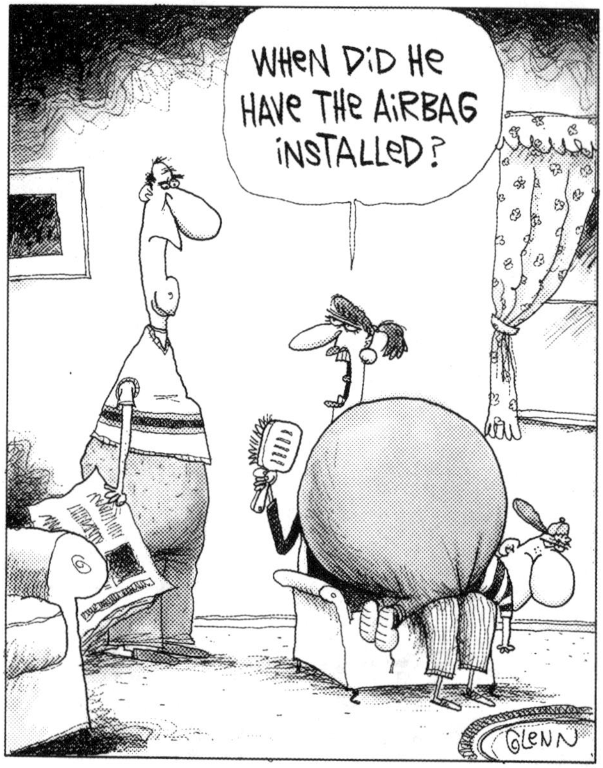
WHEN DID HE HAVE THE AIRBAG INSTALLED?
GLENN

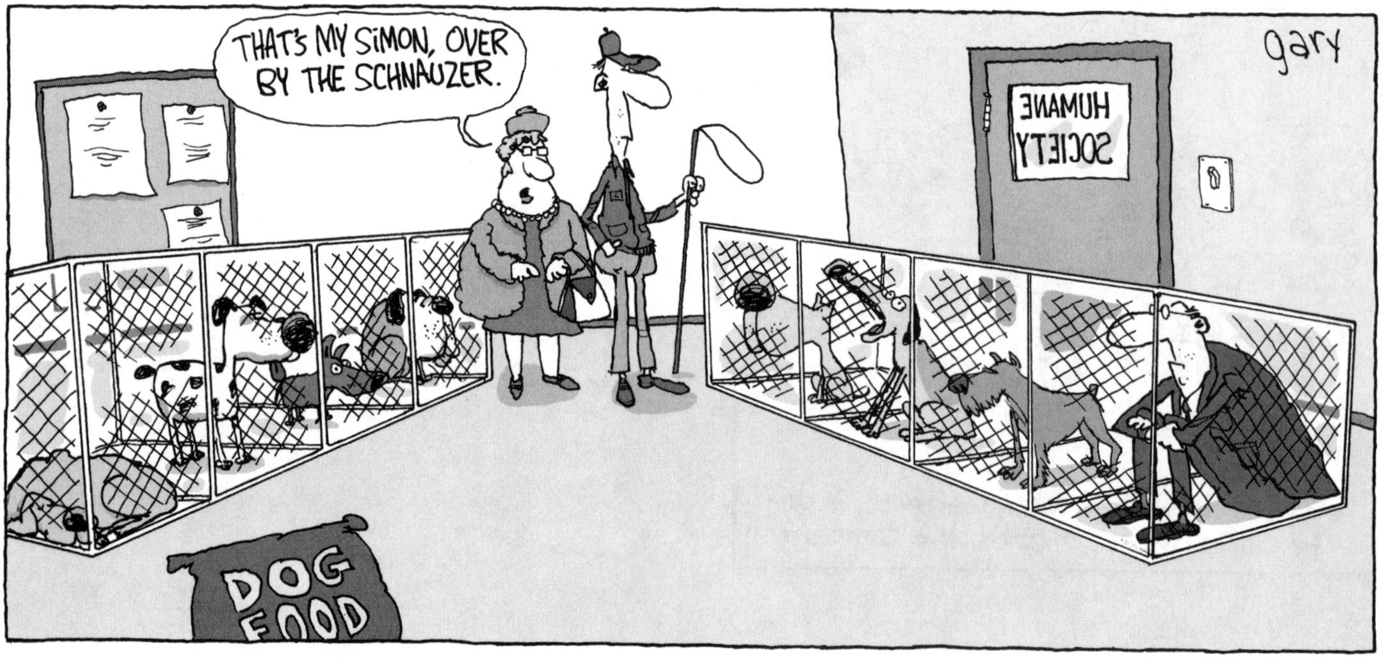
THAT'S MY SIMON, OVER BY THE SCHNAUZER.
gary
HUMANE SOCIETY
DOG FOOD

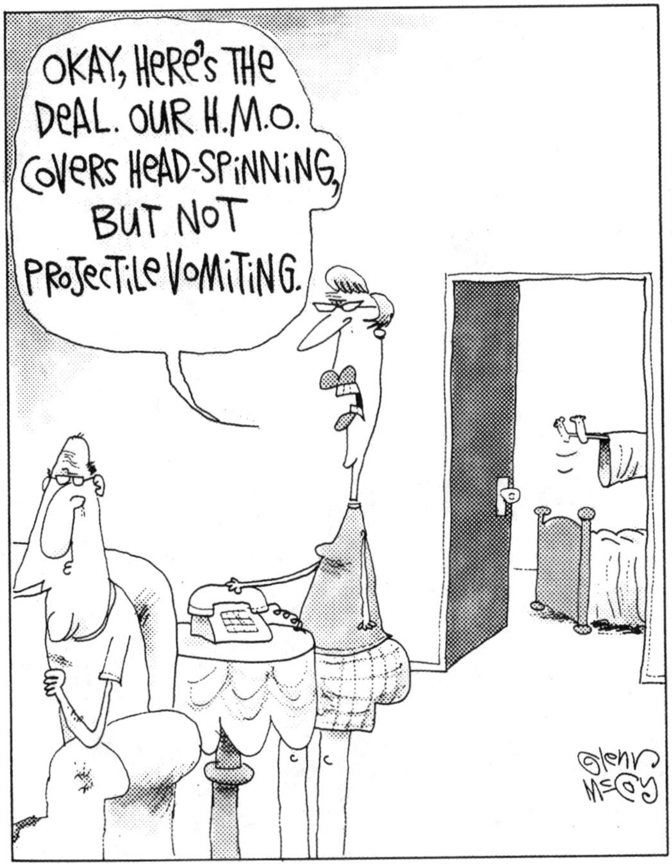
OKAY, HERE'S THE DEAL. OUR H.M.O. COVERS HEAD-SPINNING, BUT NOT PROJECTILE VOMITING.
Glenn McCoy

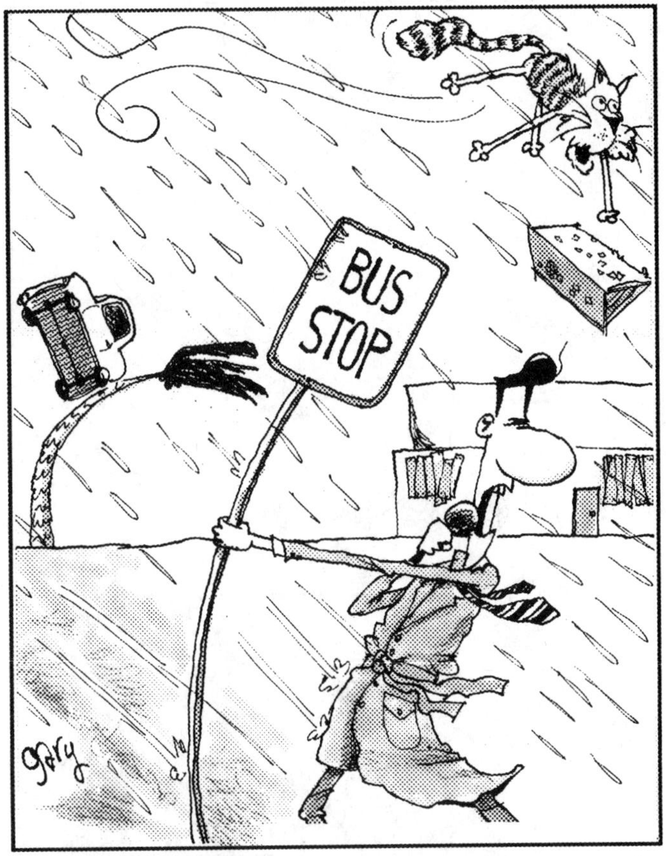
BUS STOP
Gary

"Michelle, the winds have increased from tropical storm to hurricane force, as can be seen by the fact that my hair is starting to move."

"...And for your chronic pain, I'm prescribing for you to go see the 'feel-good movie of the year.'"

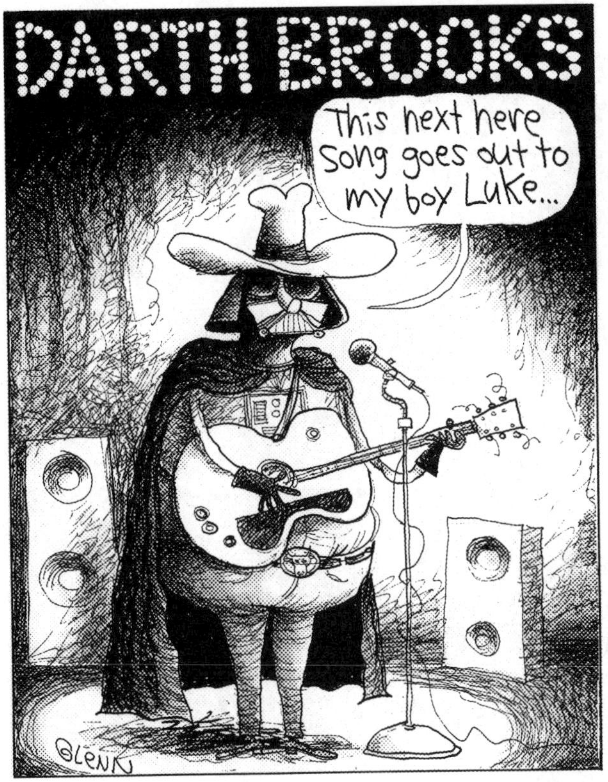
DARTH BROOKS
This next here song goes out to my boy Luke...
GLENN

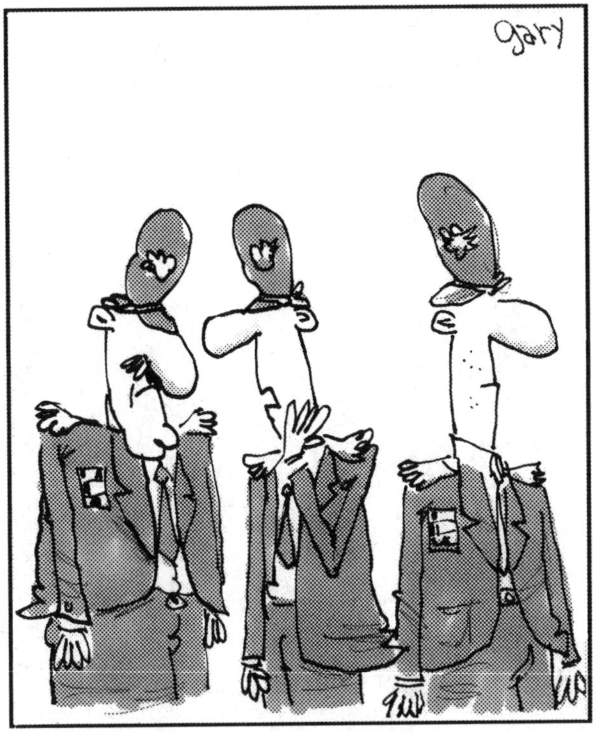
gary

"I was just as surprised as you to learn that five-star generals are allowed to wear their hats sideways."

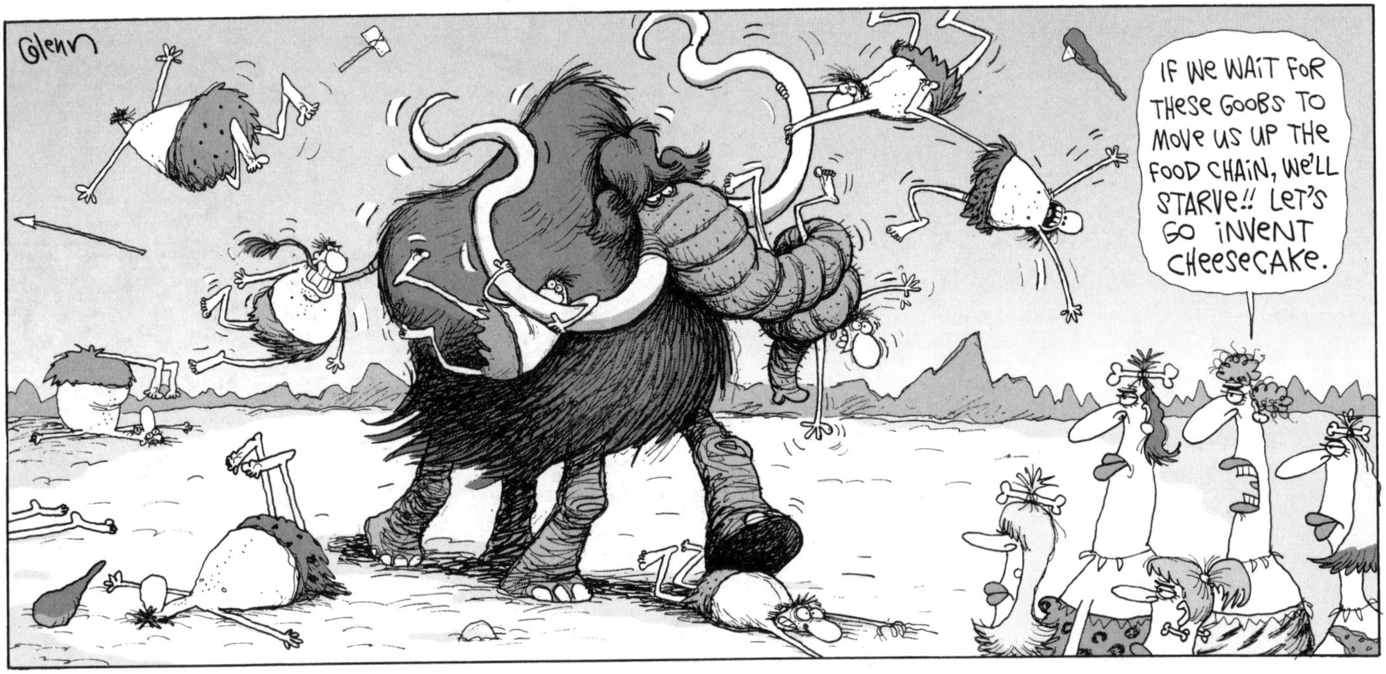
Glenn
IF WE WAIT FOR THESE GOOBS TO MOVE US UP THE FOOD CHAIN, WE'LL STARVE!! LET'S GO INVENT CHEESECAKE.

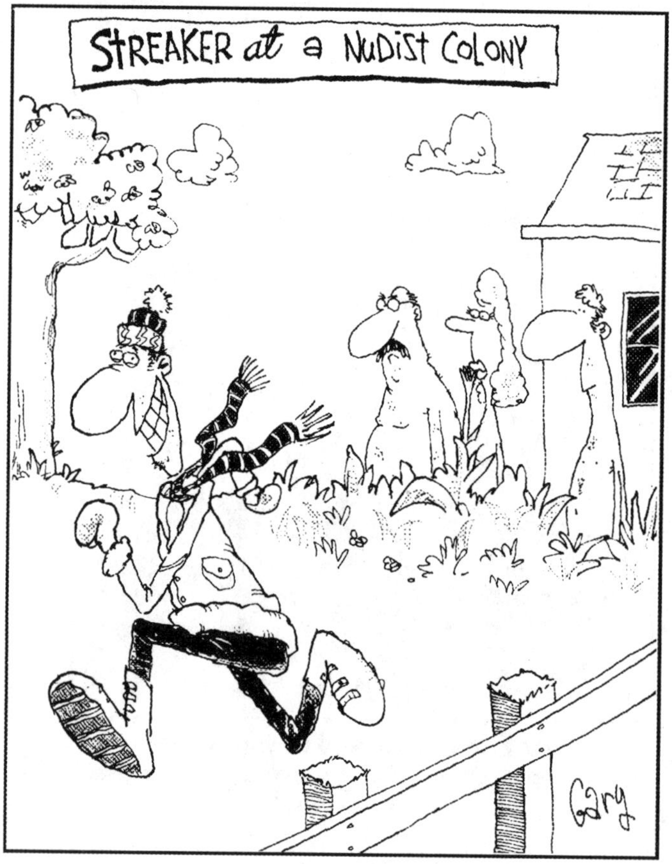
STREAKER at a NUDIST COLONY
Gary

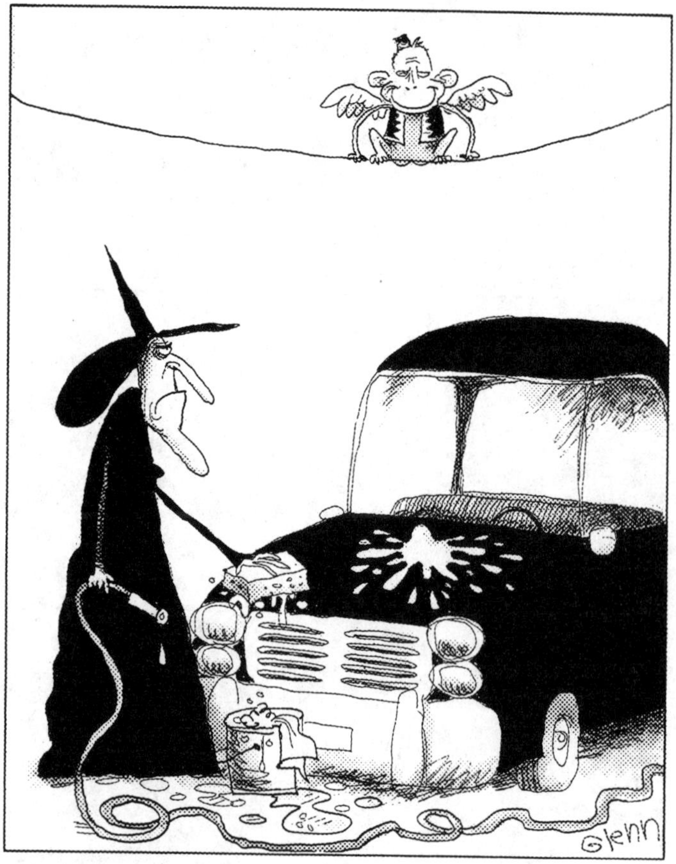
Glenn

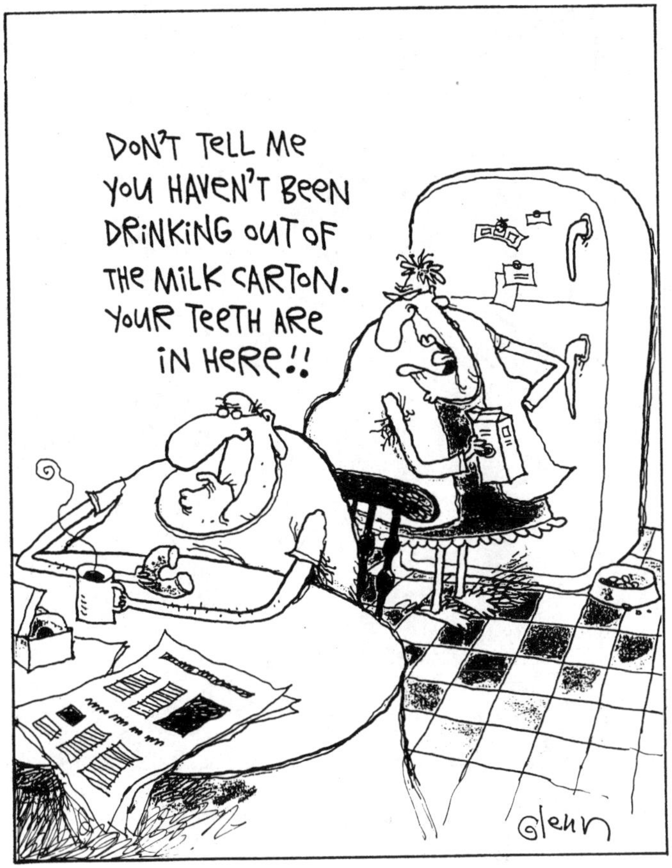
DON'T TELL ME YOU HAVEN'T BEEN DRINKING OUT OF THE MILK CARTON. YOUR TEETH ARE IN HERE!!
Glenn

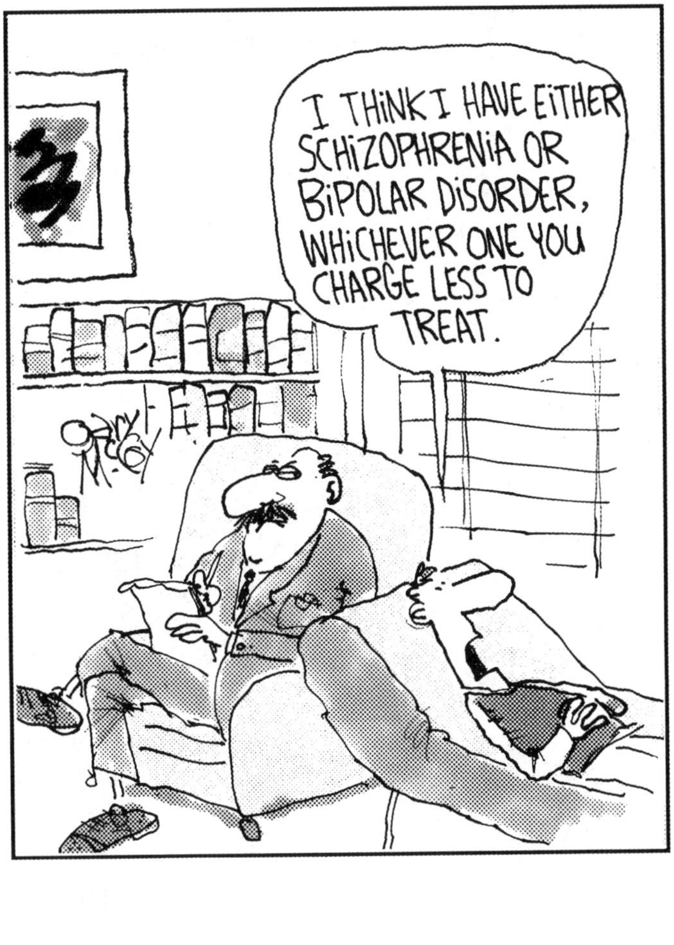
I THINK I HAVE EITHER SCHIZOPHRENIA OR BIPOLAR DISORDER, WHICHEVER ONE YOU CHARGE LESS TO TREAT.

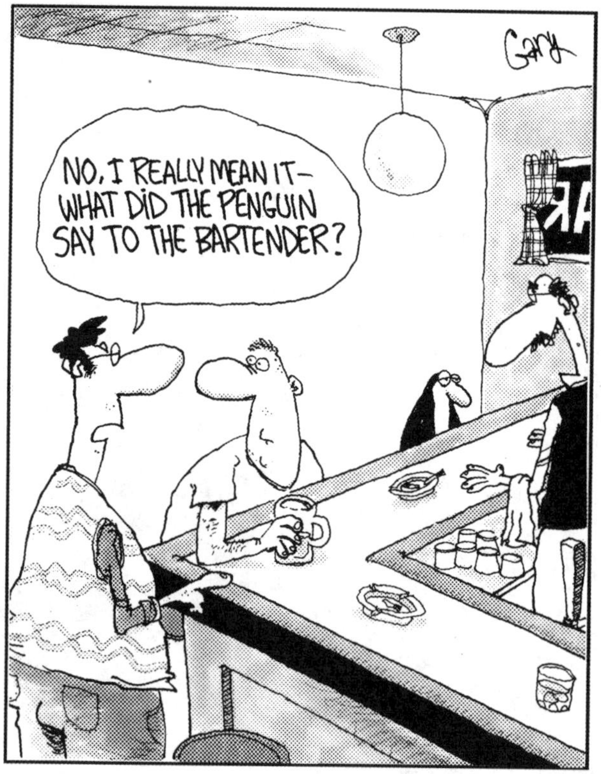
Gary
NO, I REALLY MEAN IT— WHAT DID THE PENGUIN SAY TO THE BARTENDER?

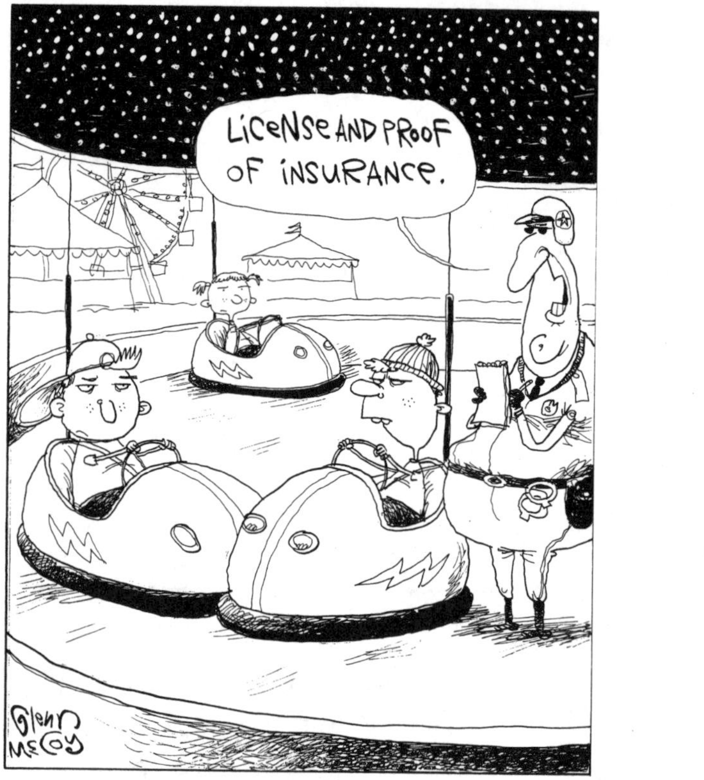
LICENSE AND PROOF OF INSURANCE.
Glenn McCoy

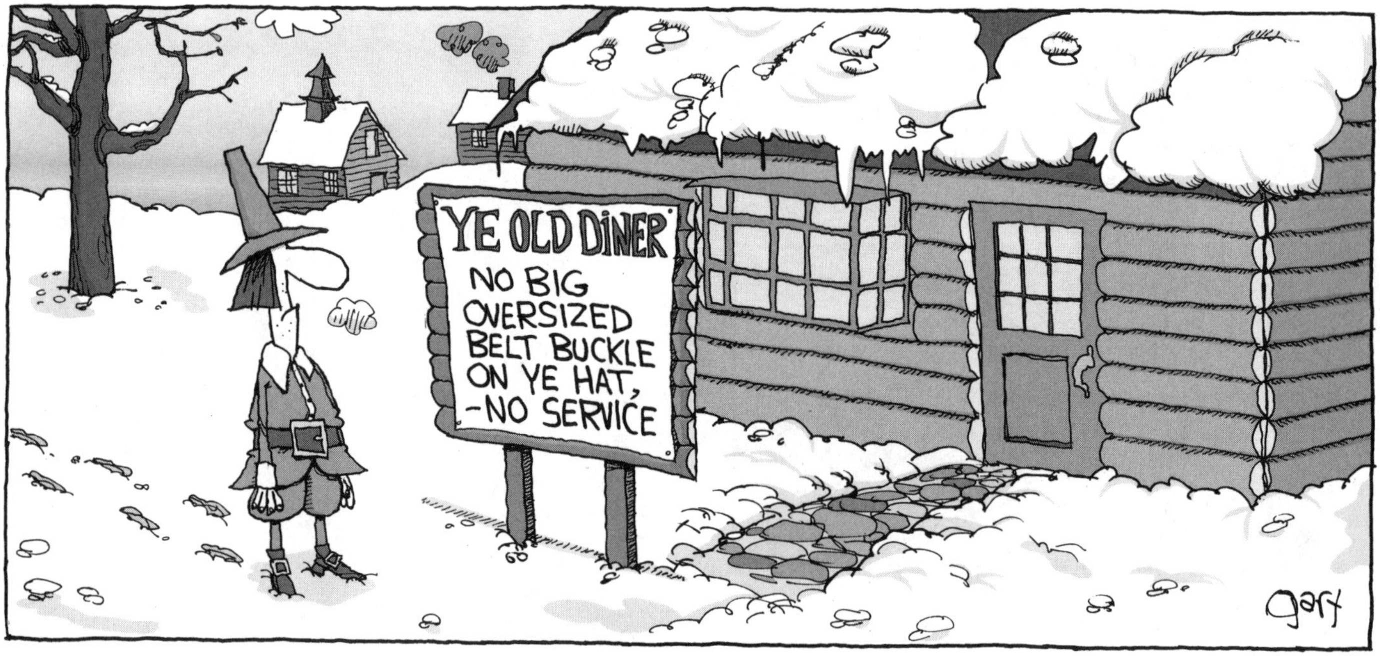
YE OLD DINER
NO BIG OVERSIZED BELT BUCKLE ON YE HAT, -NO SERVICE
gary

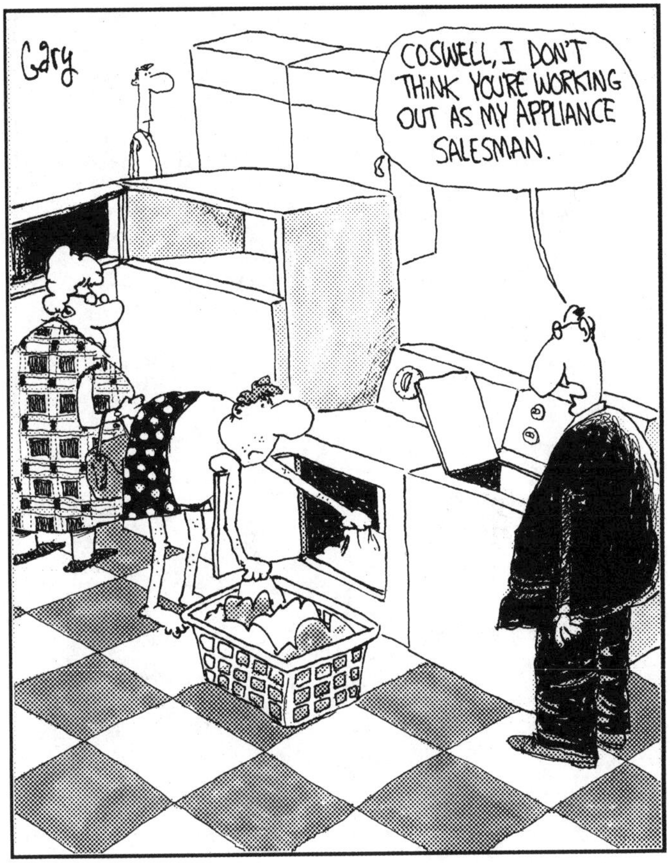
Gary
COSWELL, I DON'T THINK YOU'RE WORKING OUT AS MY APPLIANCE SALESMAN.

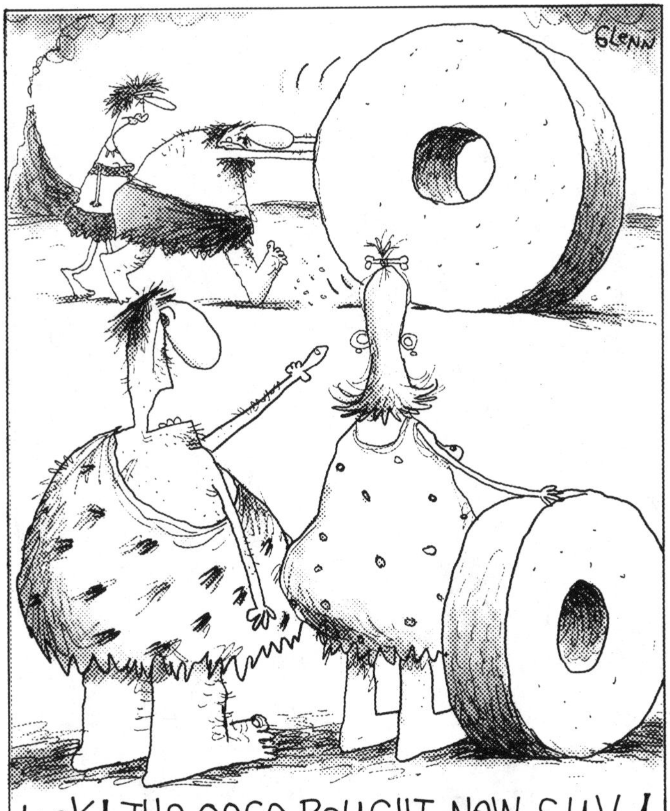
GLENN
LOOK! THE OOGS BOUGHT NEW S.U.V.!

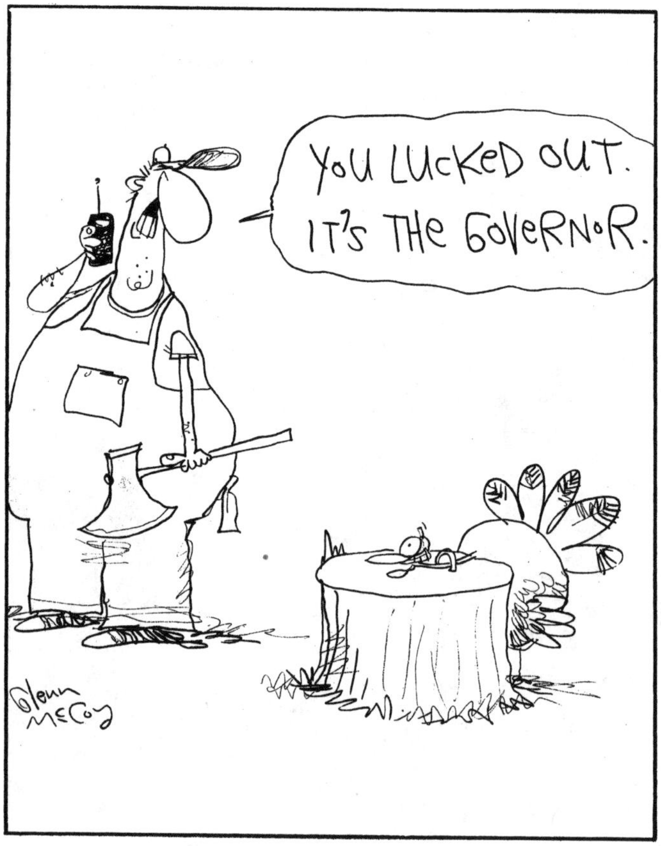
YOU LUCKED OUT.
IT'S THE GOVERNOR.
Glenn McCoy

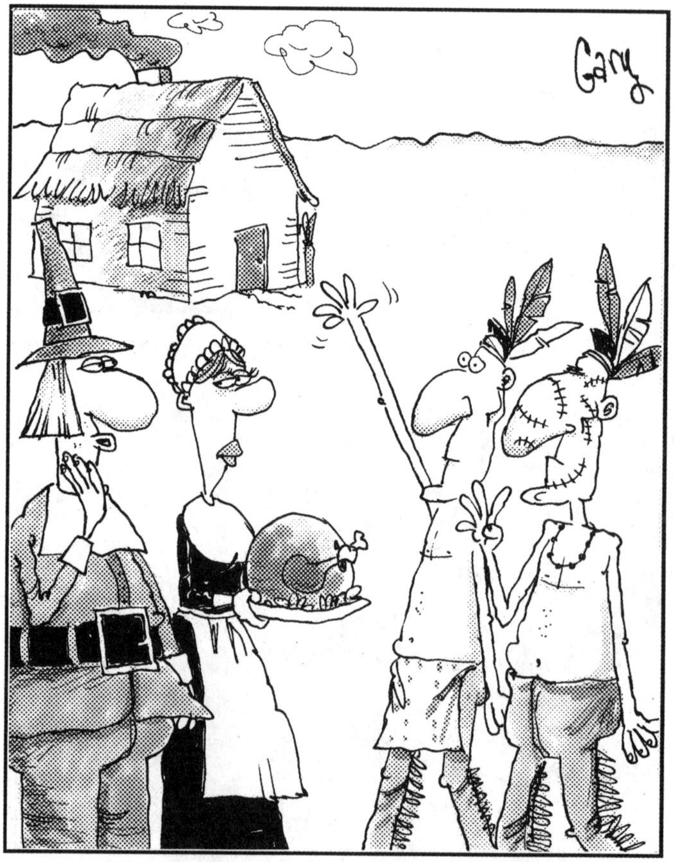
Gary

"Psst . . . tell me again—which one is Chief Mauled-by-Bear?"

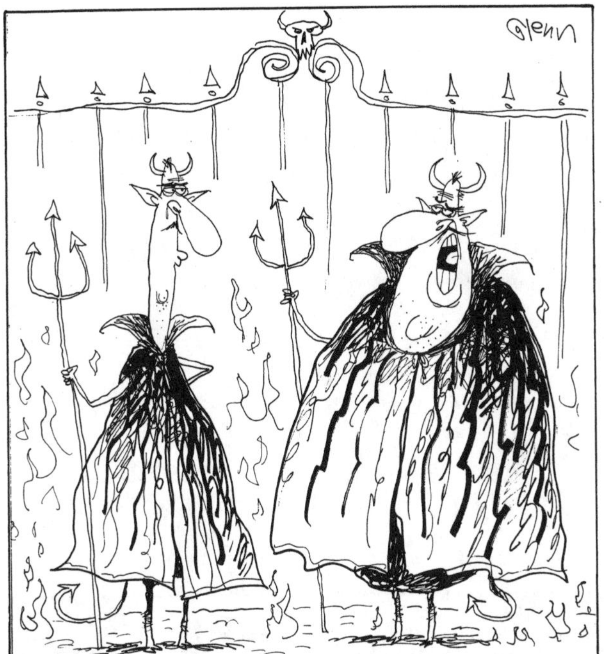
Glenn

LOOK, FOR THE LAST TIME, WE'RE UNHOLY DEMONS OF THE FIERY NETHERWORLD. STOP SAYING H-E-DOUBLE-HOCKEY-STICKS!!

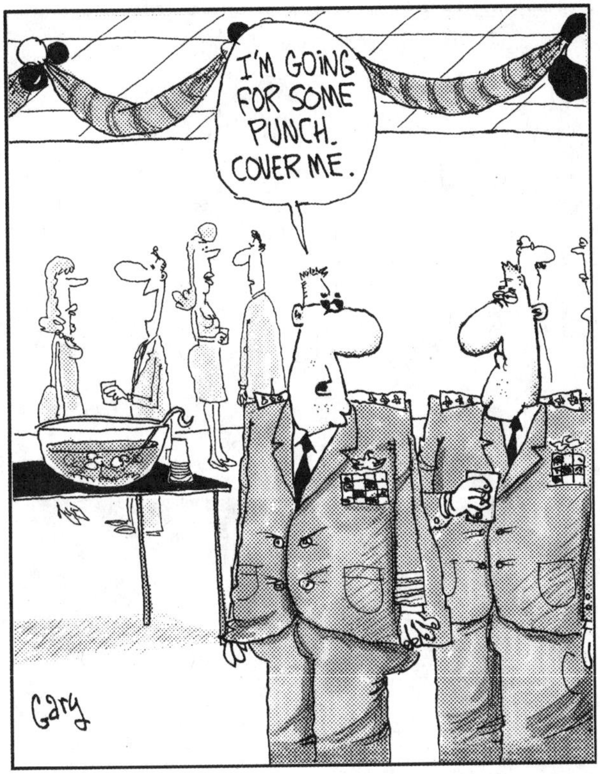
I'M GOING FOR SOME PUNCH. COVER ME.
Gary

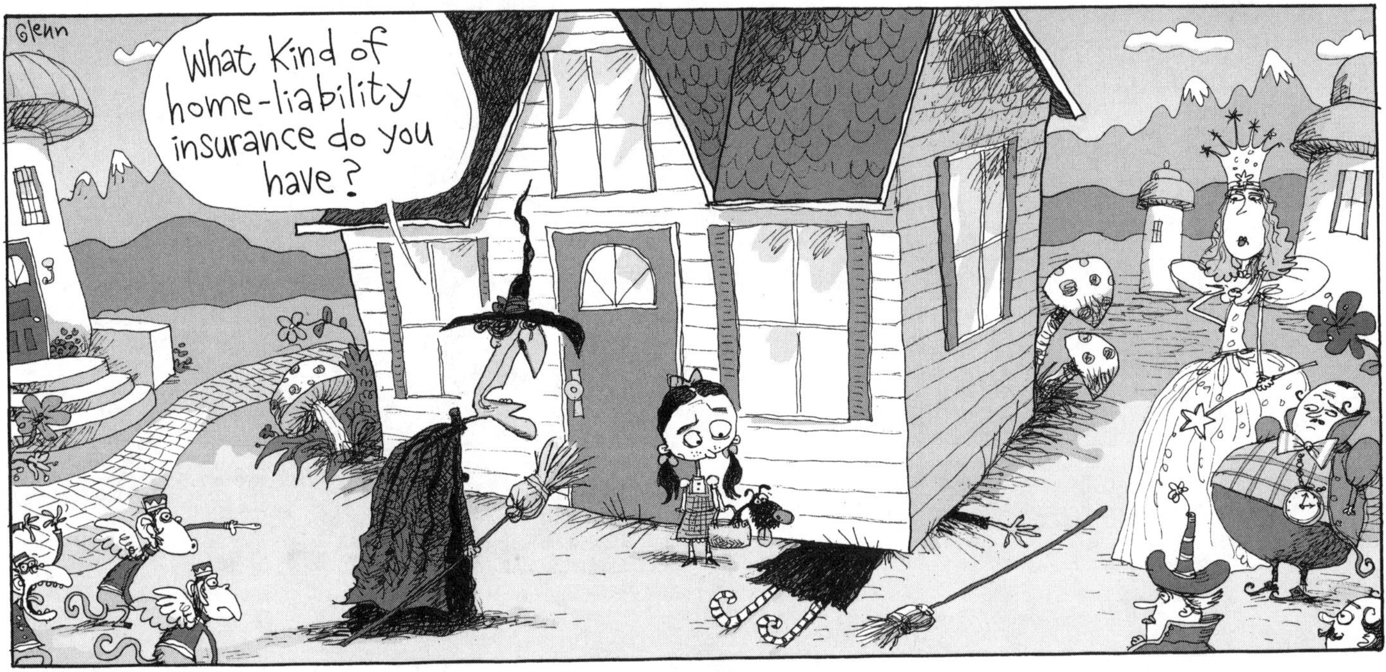
Glenn
What kind of home-liability insurance do you have?

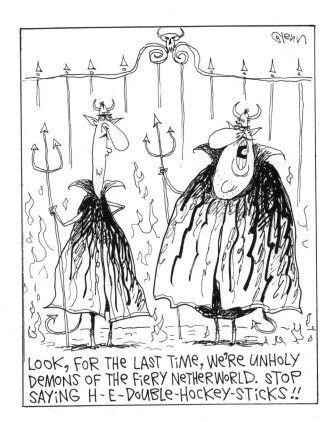

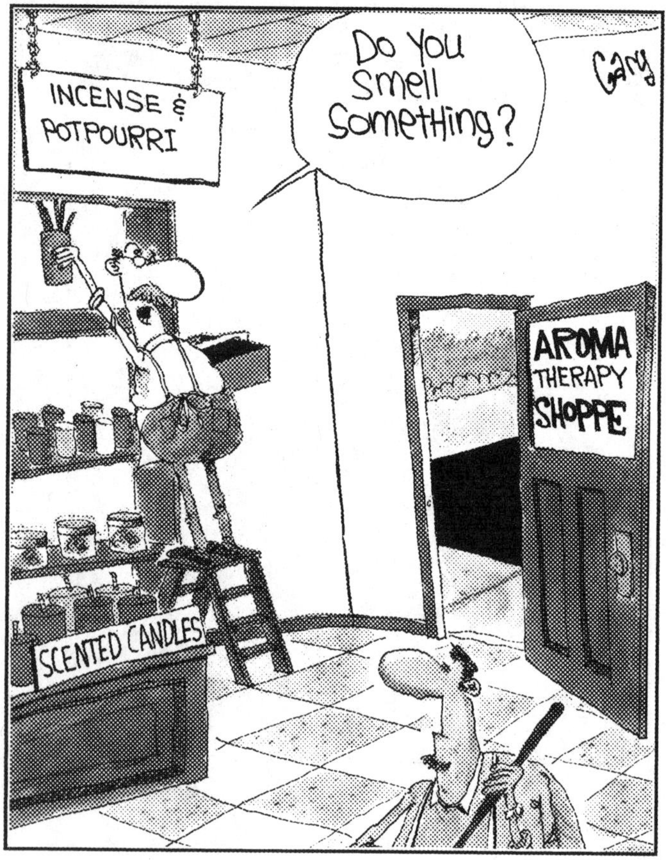
INCENSE & POTPOURRI
Do You Smell Something?
Gary
AROMA THERAPY SHOPPE
SCENTED CANDLES

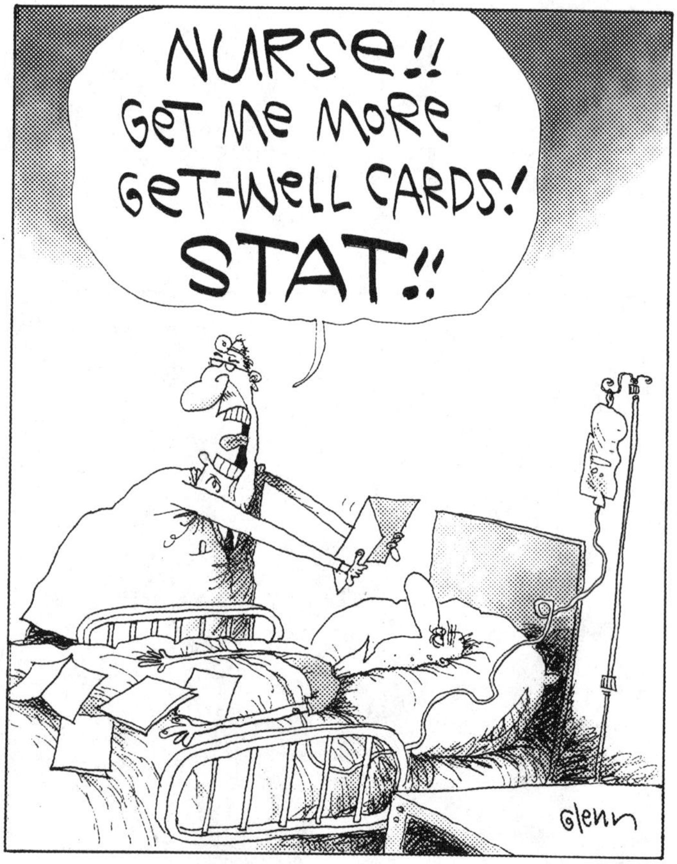
NURSE!! GET ME MORE GET-WELL CARDS! STAT!!
Glenn

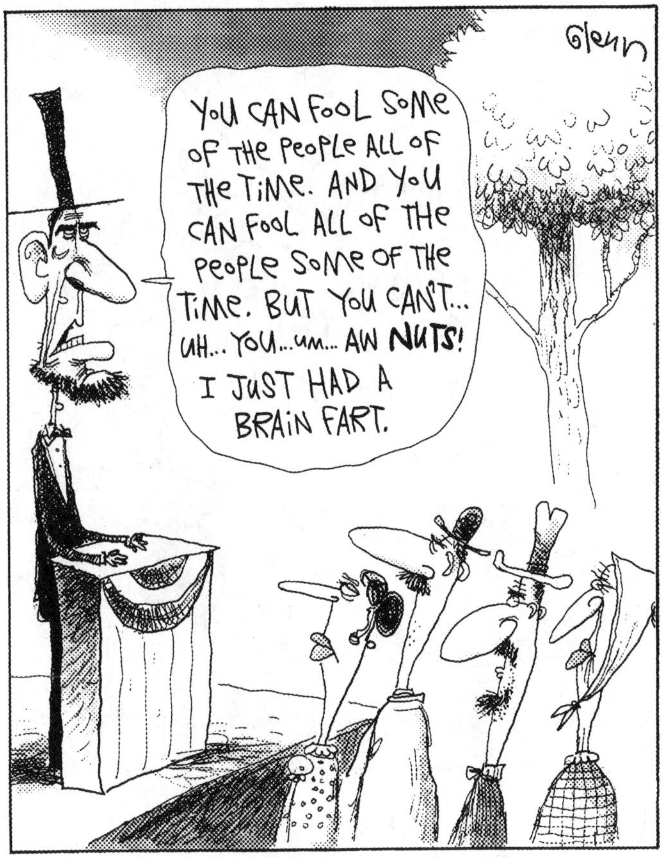
Glenn
YOU CAN FOOL SOME OF THE PEOPLE ALL OF THE TIME. AND YOU CAN FOOL ALL OF THE PEOPLE SOME OF THE TIME. BUT YOU CAN'T... UH... YOU... UM... AW NUTS! I JUST HAD A BRAIN FART.

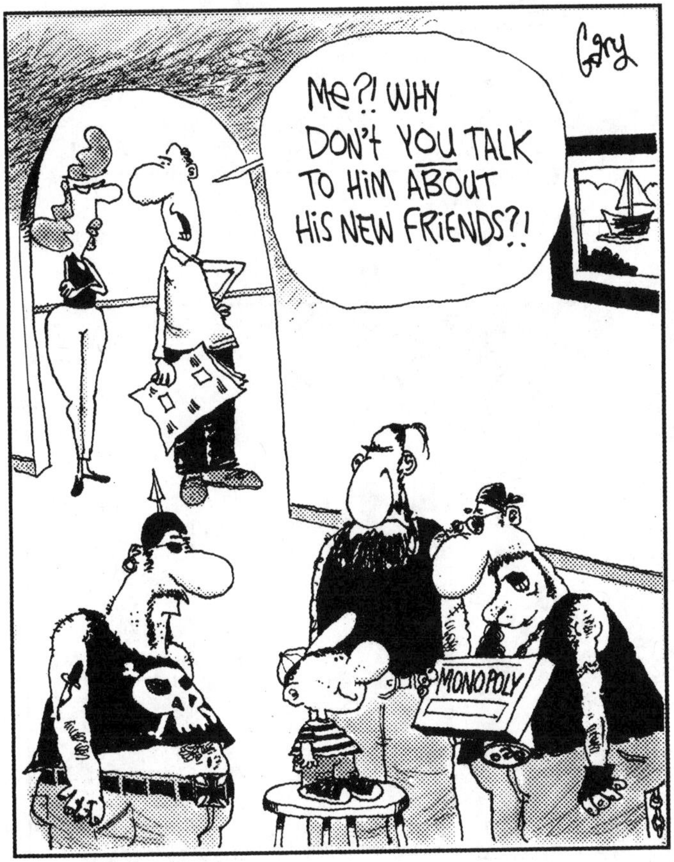
Gary
ME?! WHY DON'T YOU TALK TO HIM ABOUT HIS NEW FRIENDS?!
MONOPOLY

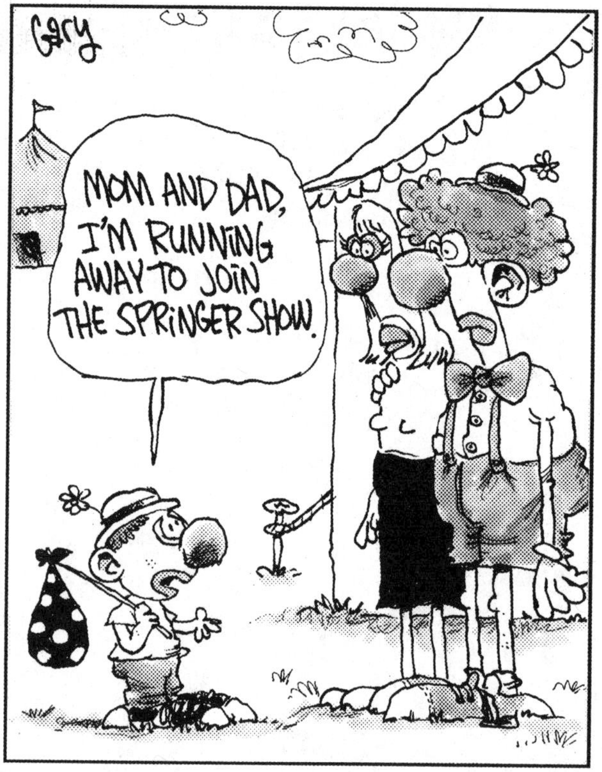
Gary
MOM AND DAD, I'M RUNNING AWAY TO JOIN THE SPRINGER SHOW.

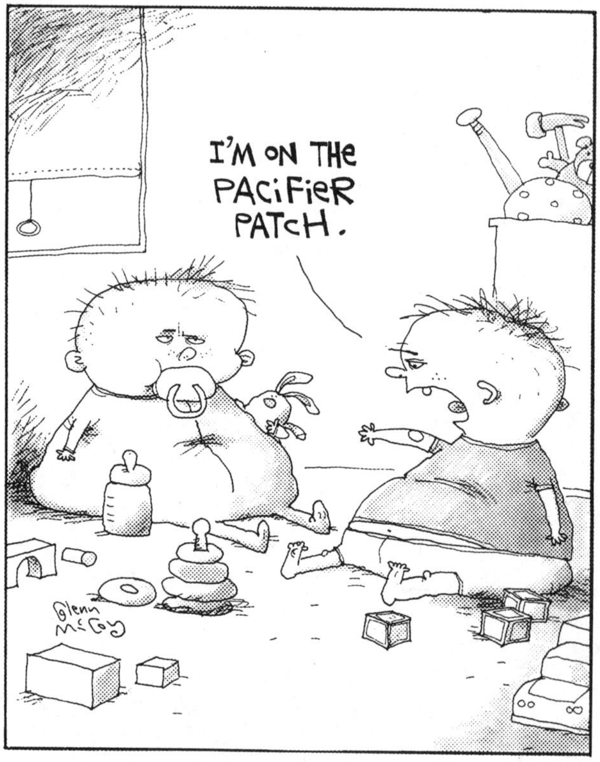
I'M ON THE PACIFIER PATCH.
Glenn McCoy

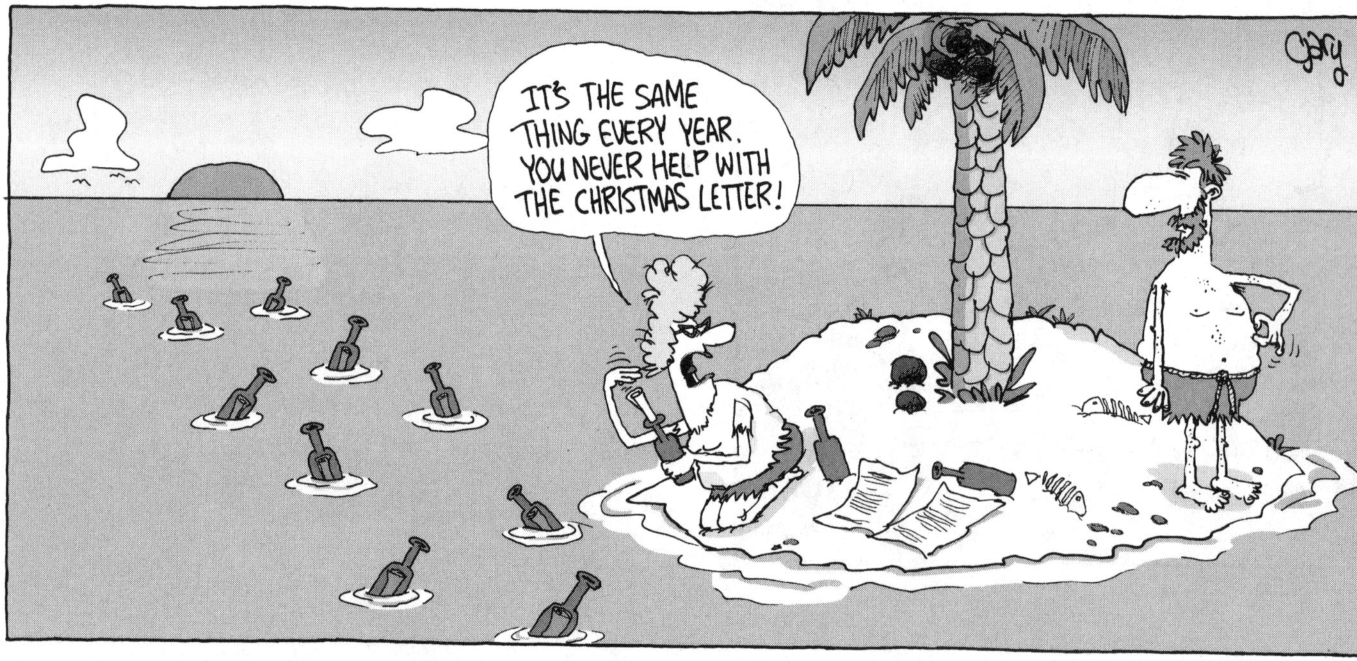
Gary
IT'S THE SAME THING EVERY YEAR. YOU NEVER HELP WITH THE CHRISTMAS LETTER!

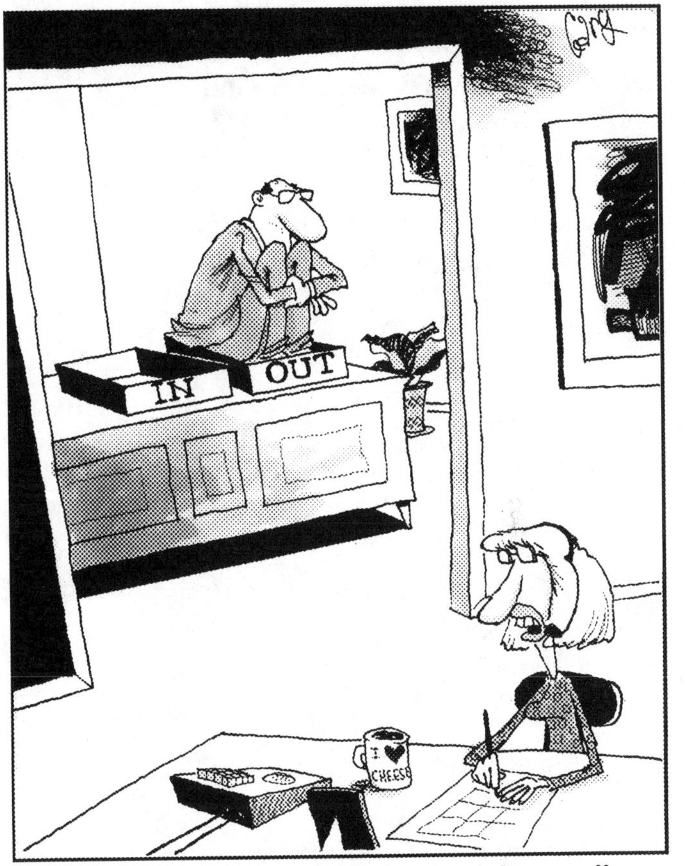
IN
OUT
I ♥ CHEESE
"I'm sorry, Mr. Schaab isn't in right now."

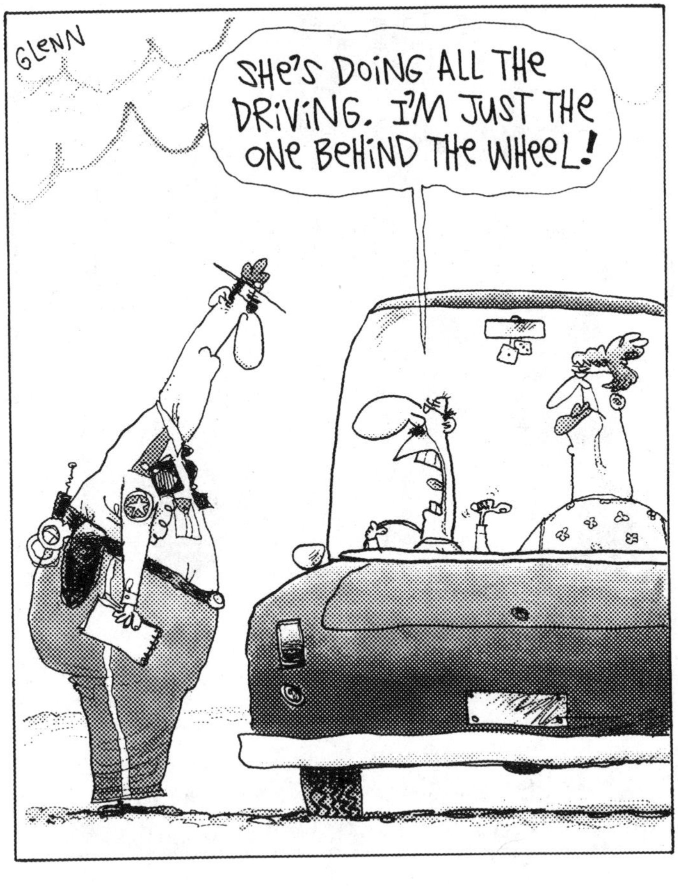
GLENN
SHE'S DOING ALL THE DRIVING. I'M JUST THE ONE BEHIND THE WHEEL!

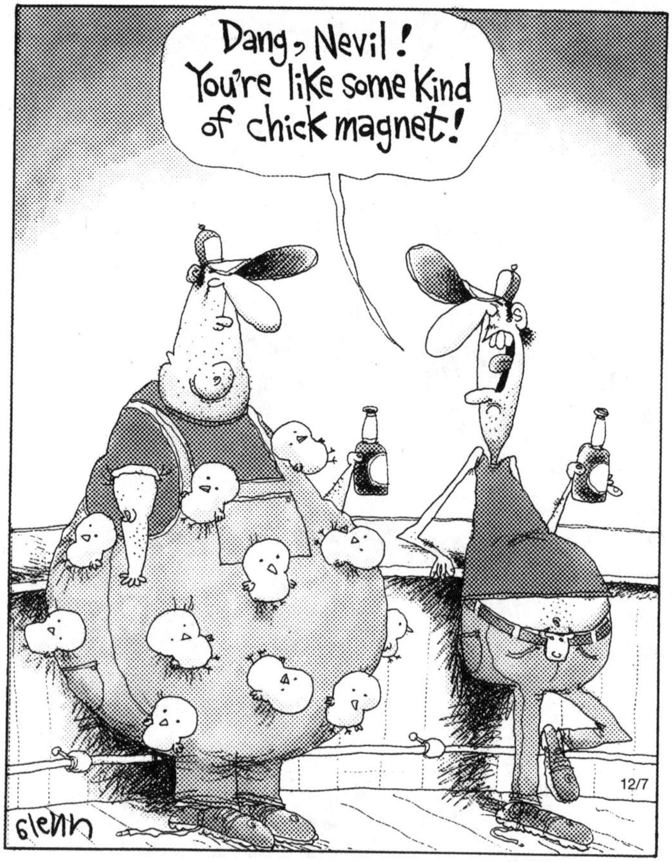
Dang, Nevil! You're like some Kind of chick magnet!
12/7
Glenn

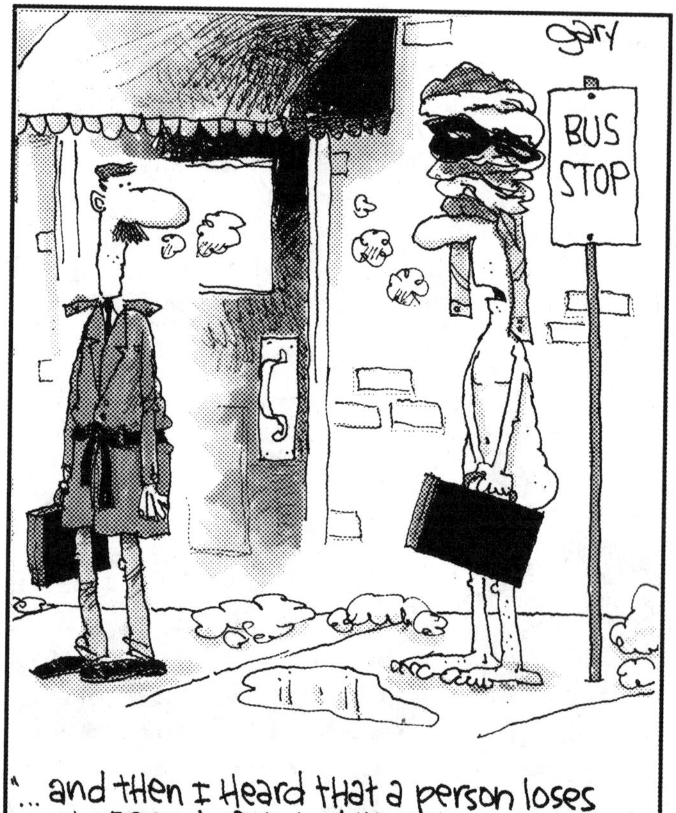
Gary
BUS STOP

"... and then I heard that a person loses ninety percent of his body heat through his head."

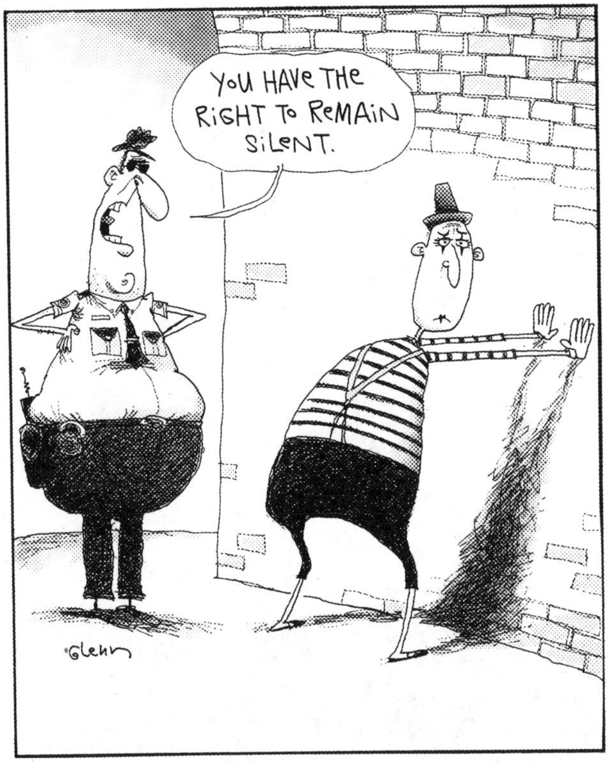
YOU HAVE THE RIGHT TO REMAIN SILENT.

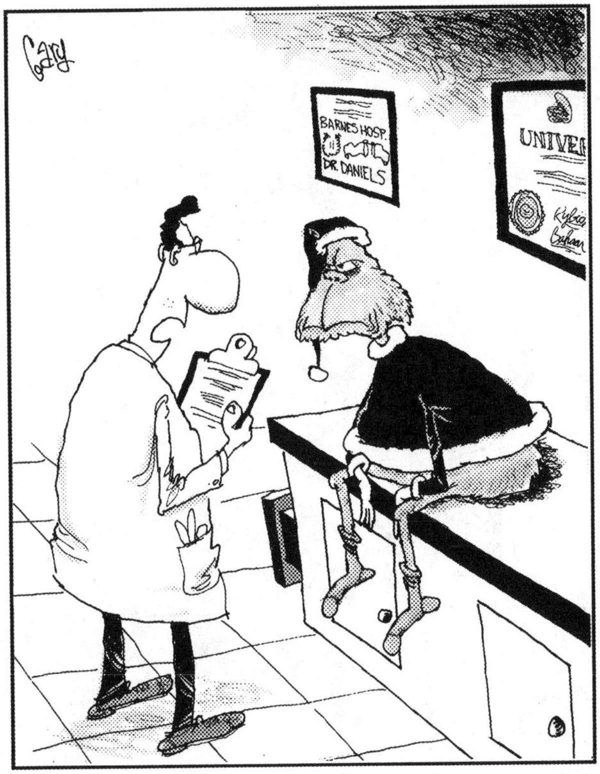
BARNES HOSP.
DR. DANIELS

"Mr. Grinch, the test shows the real reason your heart grew three sizes is due to the high fat content of Who roast beast."

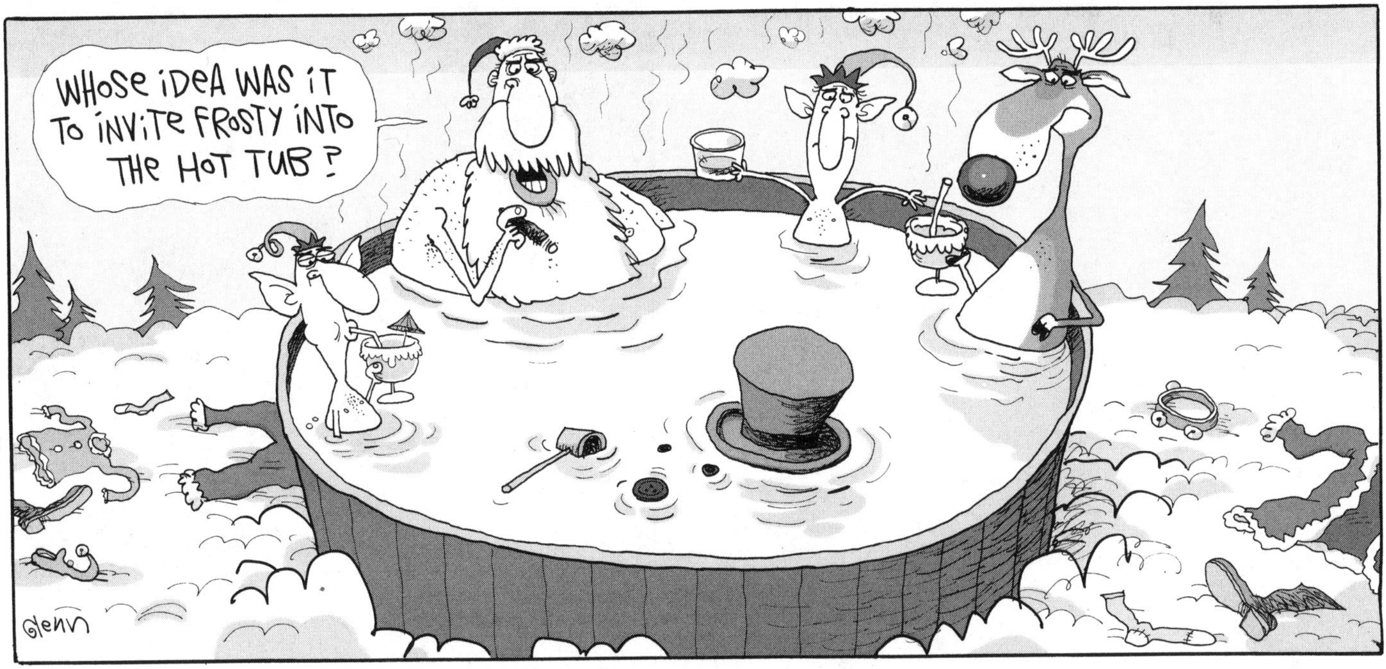
WHOSE IDEA WAS IT TO INVITE FROSTY INTO THE HOT TUB?

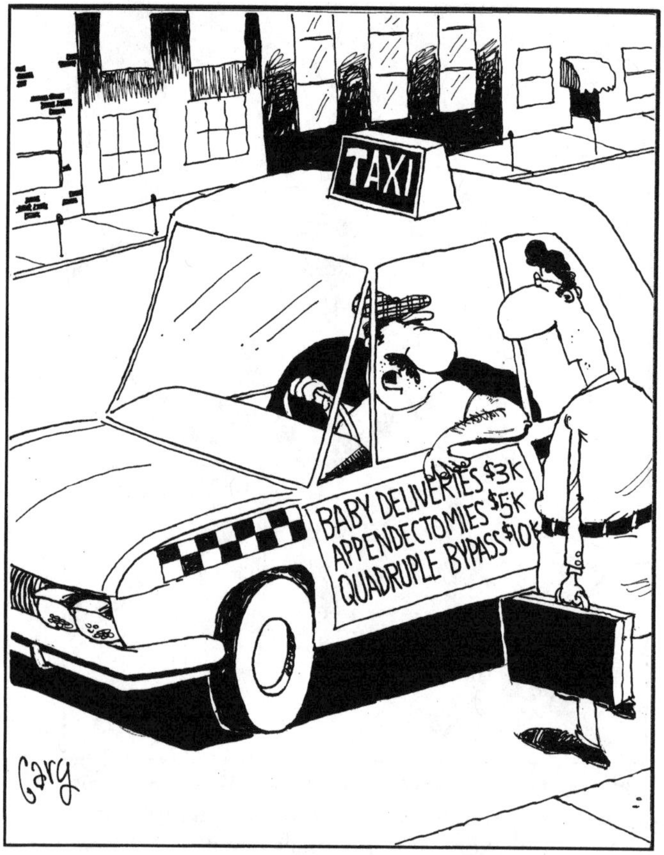
TAXI
BABY DELIVERIES $3K
APPENDECTOMIES $5K
QUADRUPLE BYPASS $10K
Gary

"I got the idea after delivering a baby last week in the backseat."

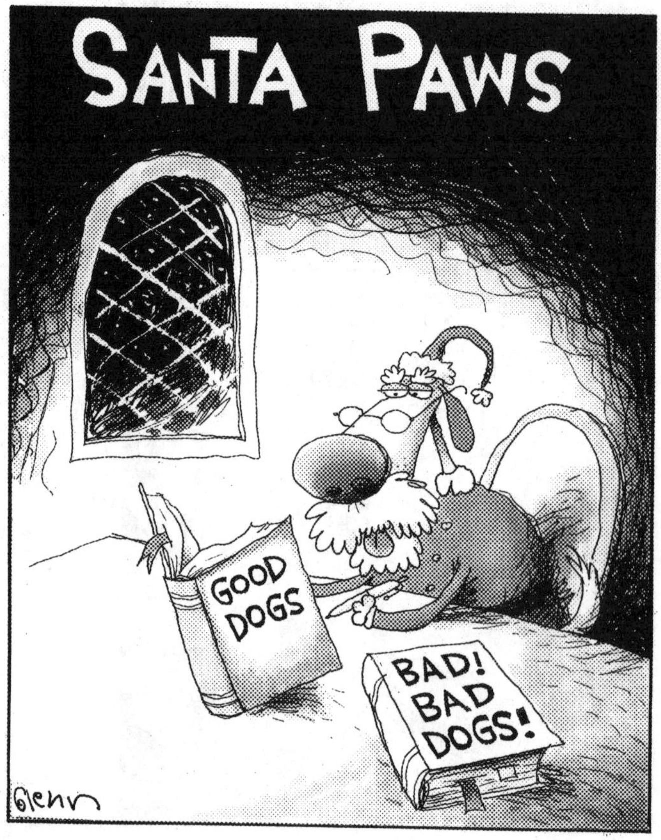
SANTA PAWS
GOOD DOGS
BAD! BAD DOGS!
Glenn

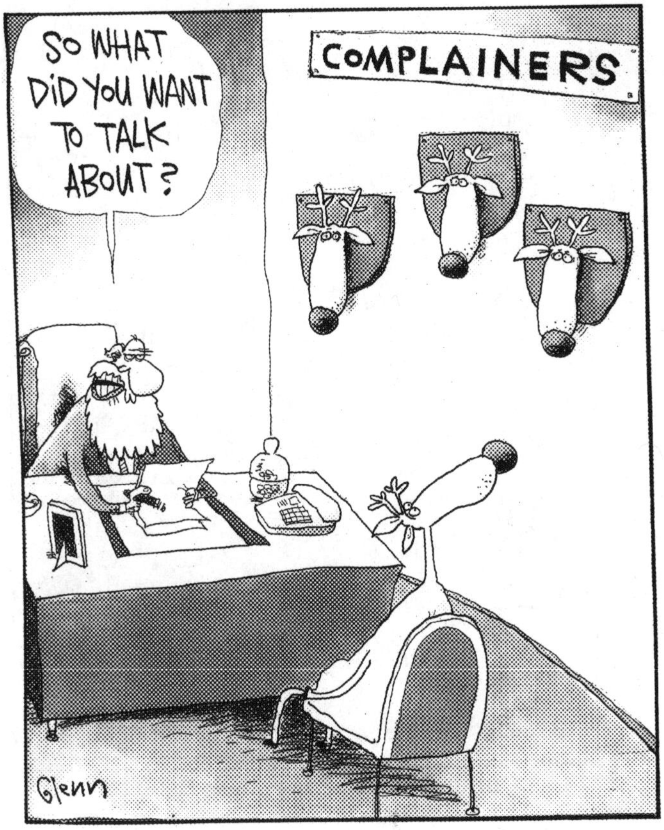
SO WHAT DID YOU WANT TO TALK ABOUT?
COMPLAINERS
Glenn

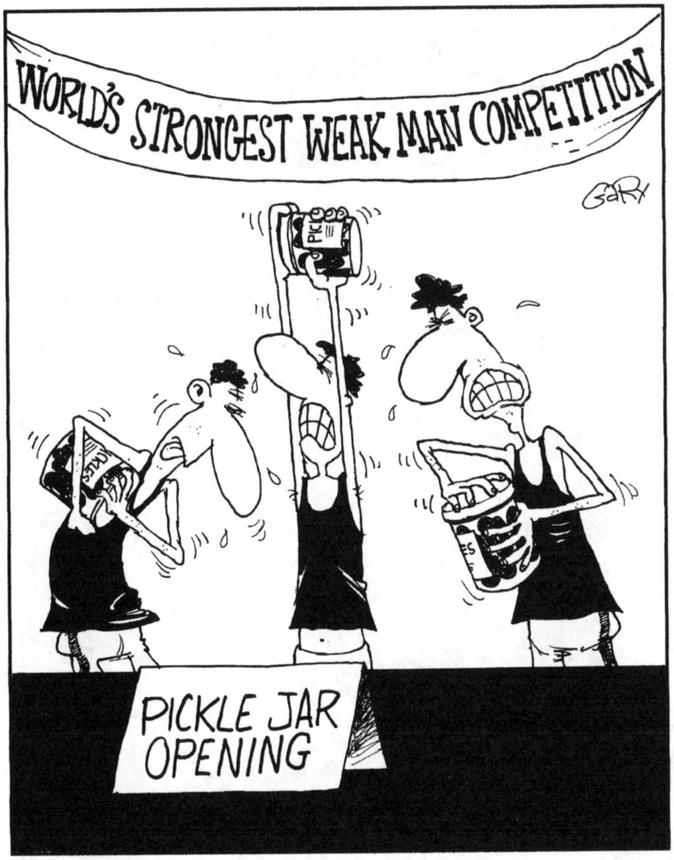
WORLD'S STRONGEST WEAK MAN COMPETITION
PICKLE JAR OPENING

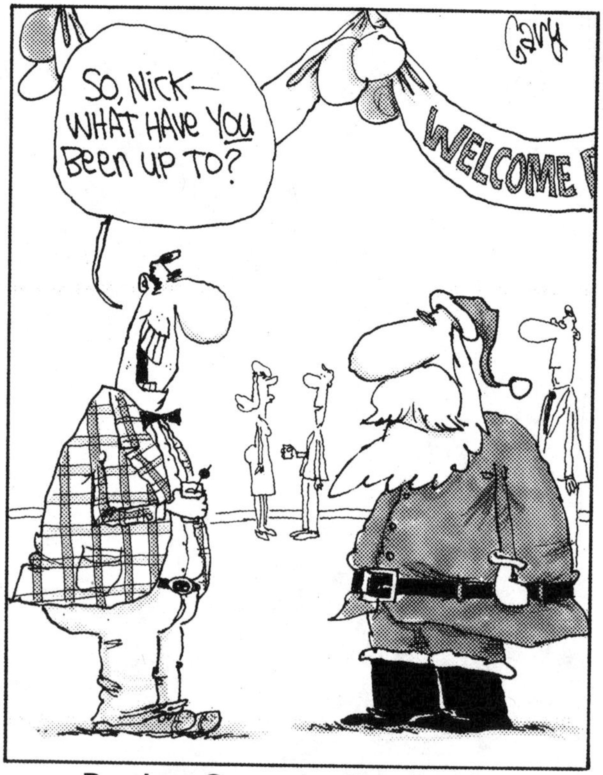
SO, NICK—
WHAT HAVE YOU
BEEN UP TO?
WELCOME
Gary

Dumbest Guy at the Class Reunion

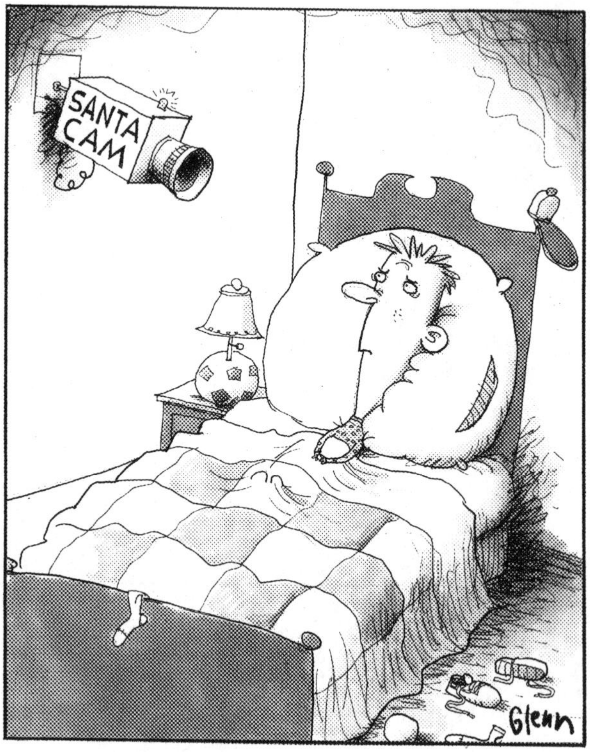
SANTA
CAM
Glenn

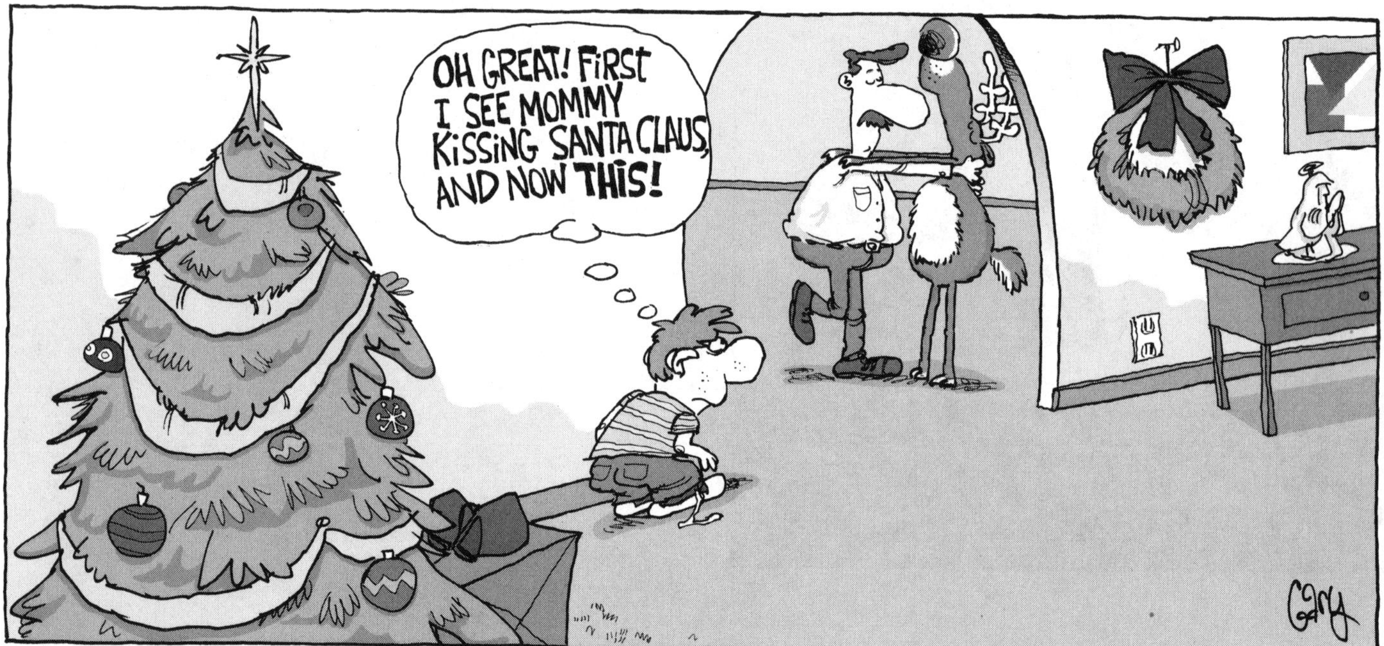
OH GREAT! FIRST
I SEE MOMMY
KISSING SANTA CLAUS,
AND NOW **THIS!**
Gary

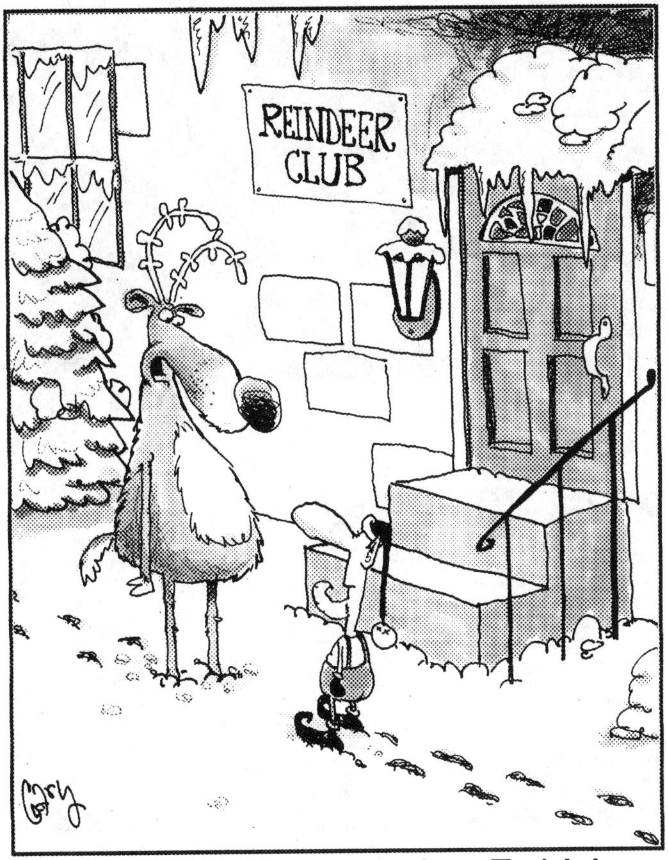
REINDEER CLUB
Gary

"Whoa, Barry, don't go in there. Tonight's featured reindeer game is elf-tossing."

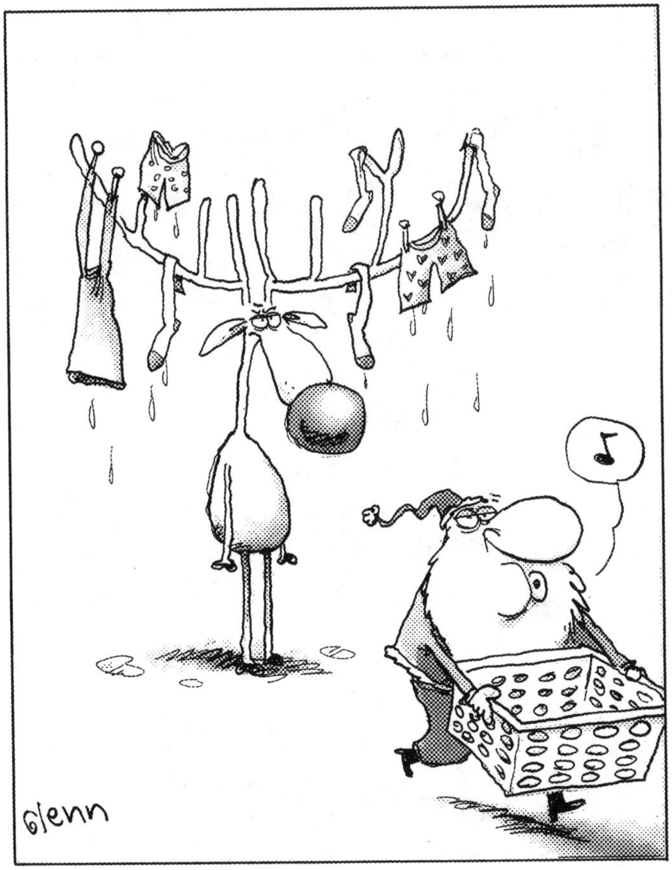
Glenn

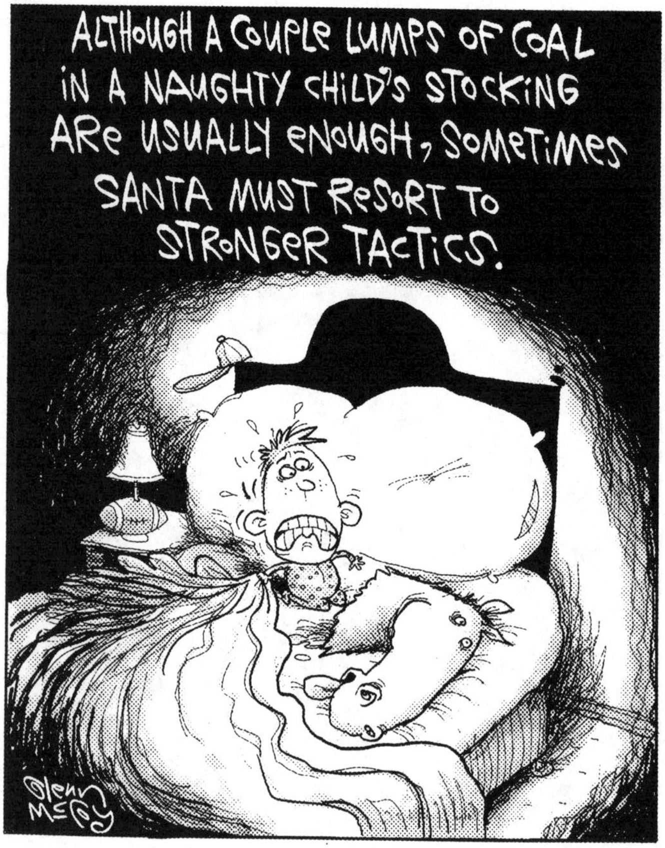
ALTHOUGH A COUPLE LUMPS OF COAL IN A NAUGHTY CHILD'S STOCKING ARE USUALLY ENOUGH, SOMETIMES SANTA MUST RESORT TO STRONGER TACTICS.
Glenn McCoy

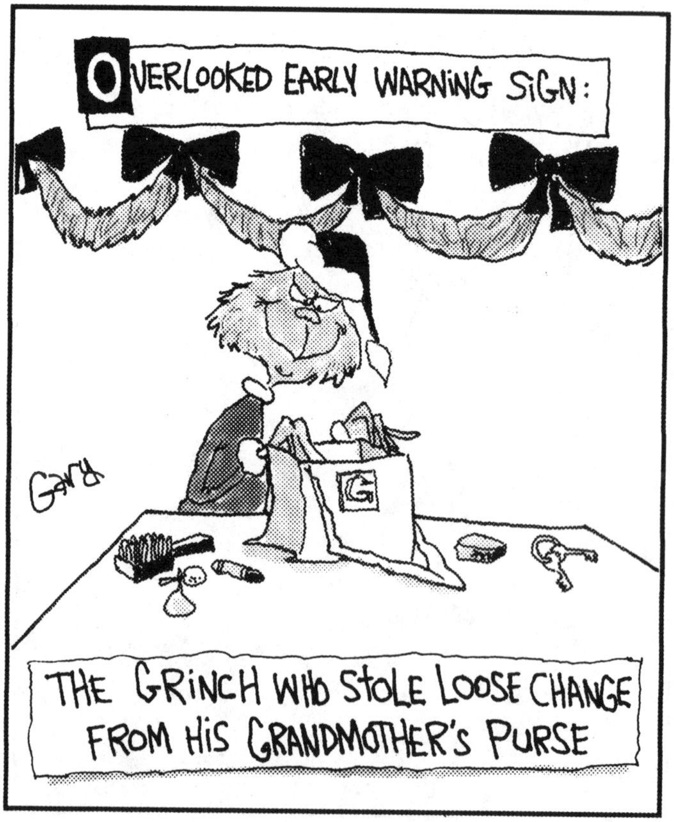
OVERLOOKED EARLY WARNING SIGN:
Gary
G
THE GRINCH WHO STOLE LOOSE CHANGE FROM HIS GRANDMOTHER'S PURSE

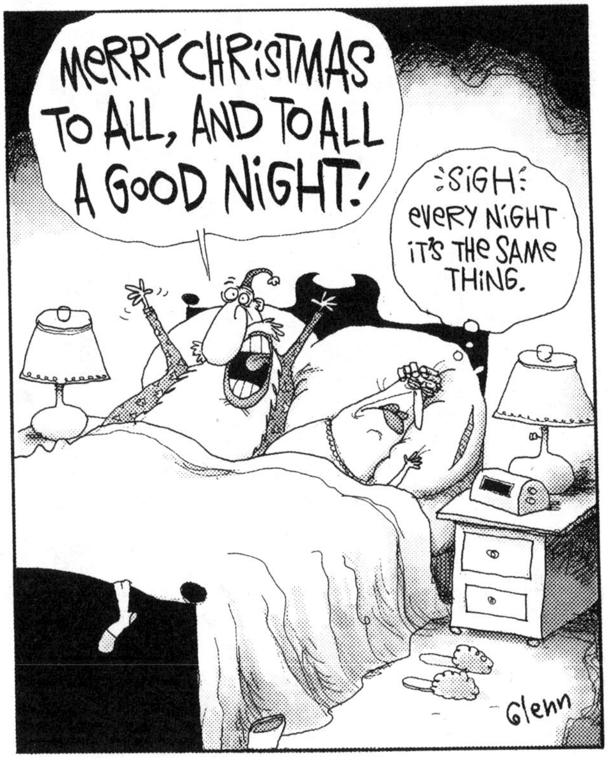
MERRY CHRISTMAS TO ALL, AND TO ALL A GOOD NIGHT!
SIGH EVERY NIGHT IT'S THE SAME THING.
Glenn

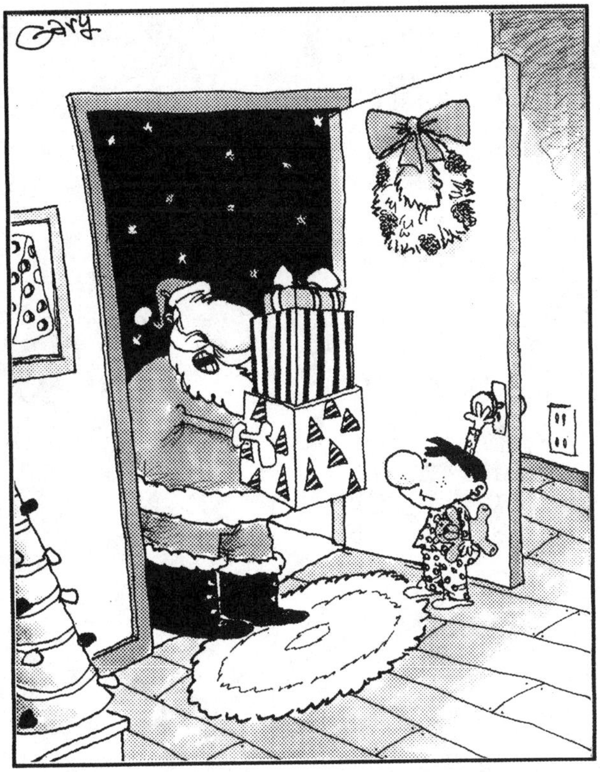
Gary

"I know, I know, but those chimneys just get my suit so filthy."

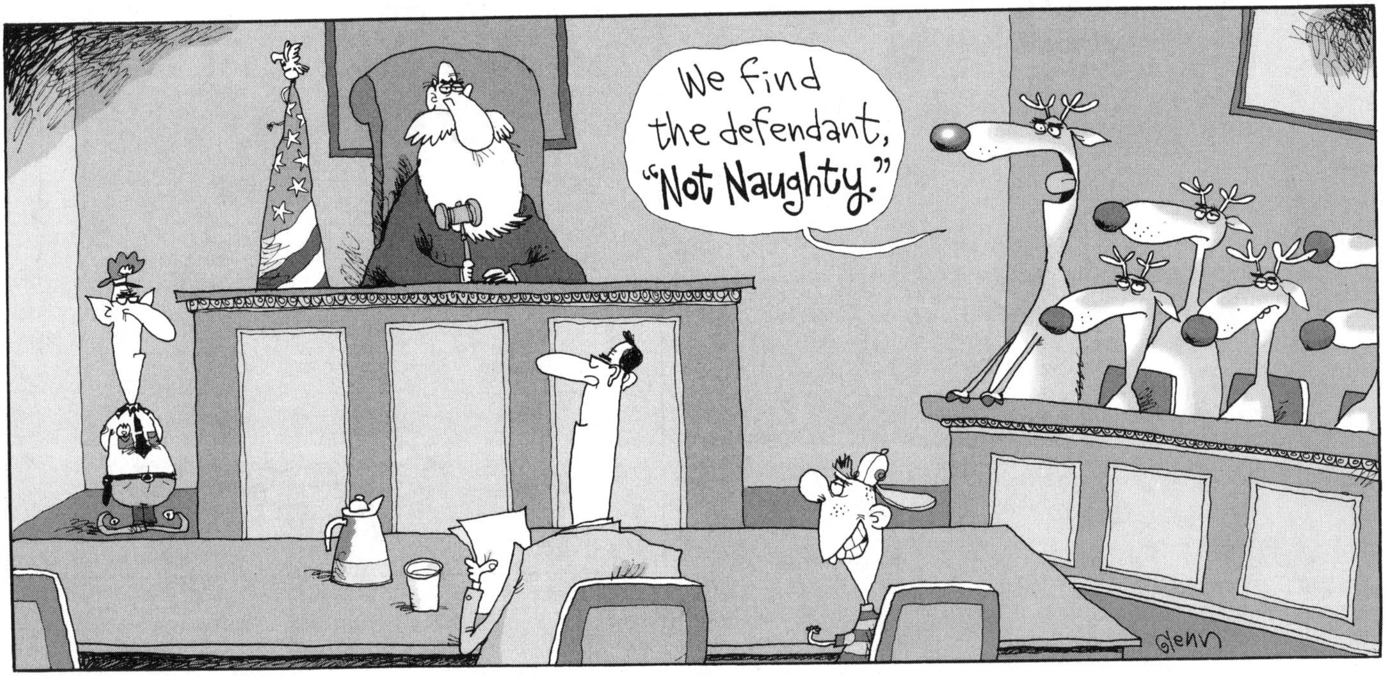
We find the defendant, "Not Naughty."
Glenn

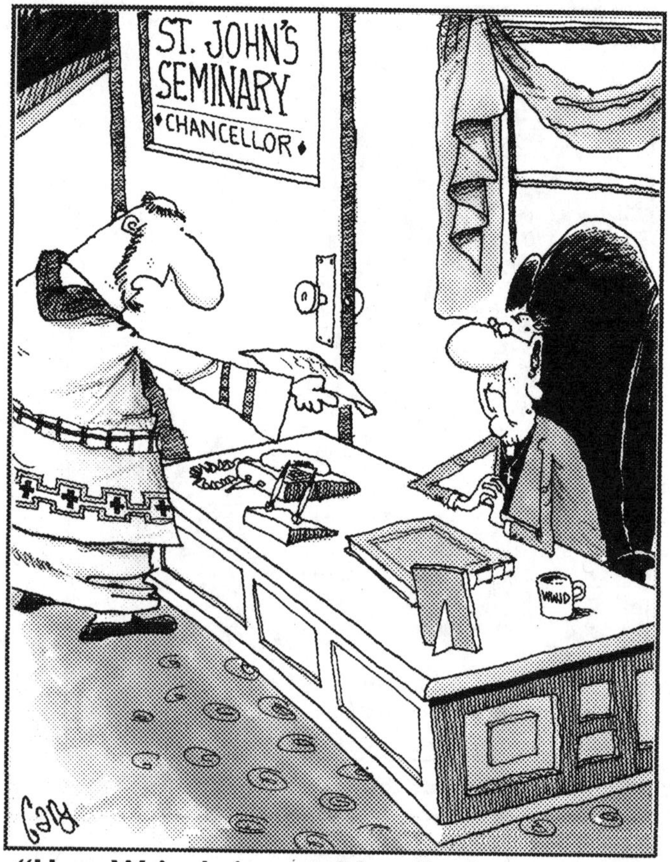
ST. JOHN'S
SEMINARY
CHANCELLOR

"Here. We're being sued for allowing prayer in school."

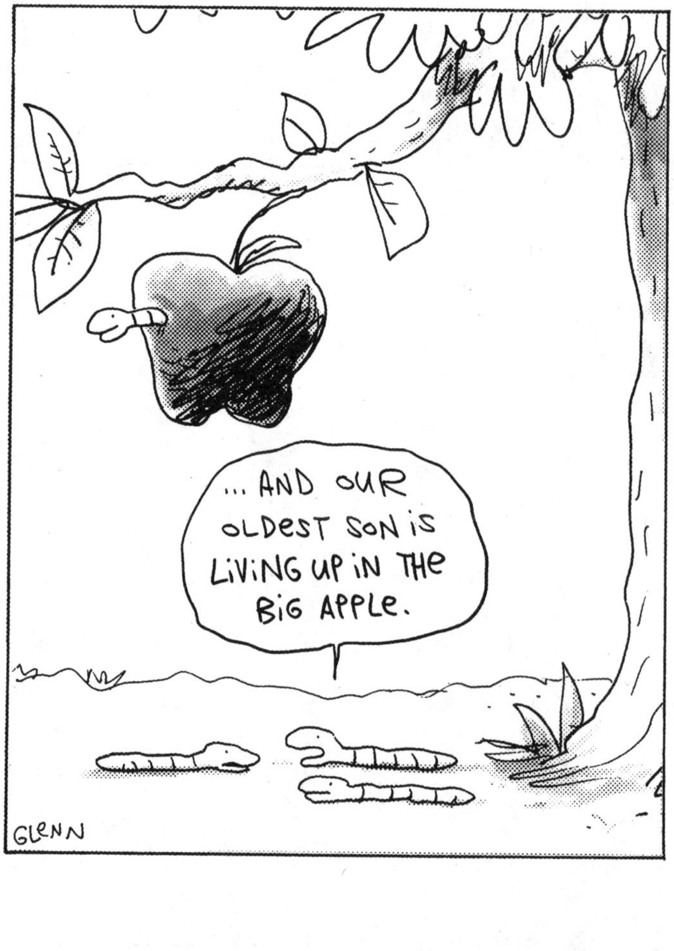
... AND OUR OLDEST SON IS LIVING UP IN THE BIG APPLE.

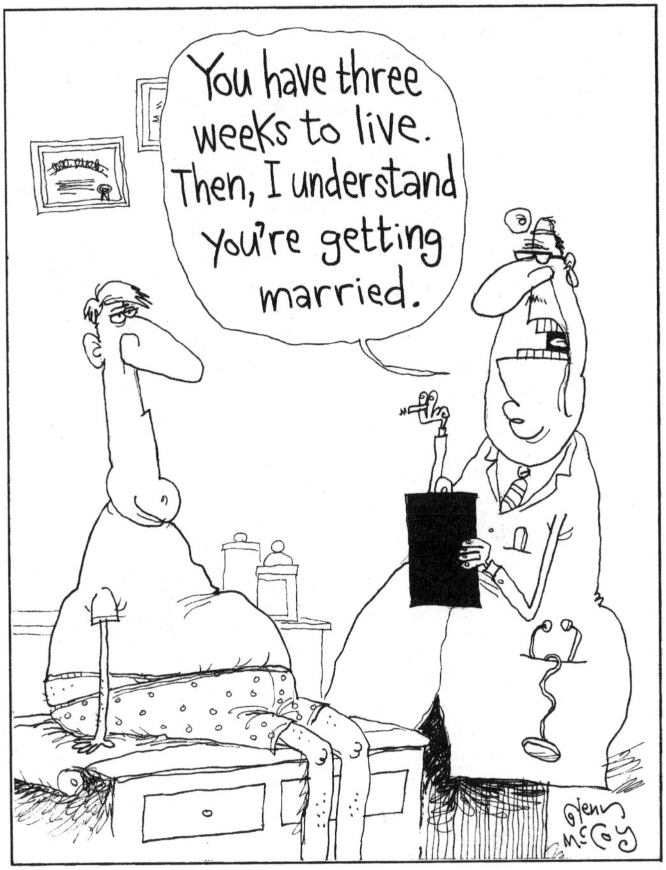
You have three weeks to live. Then, I understand you're getting married.

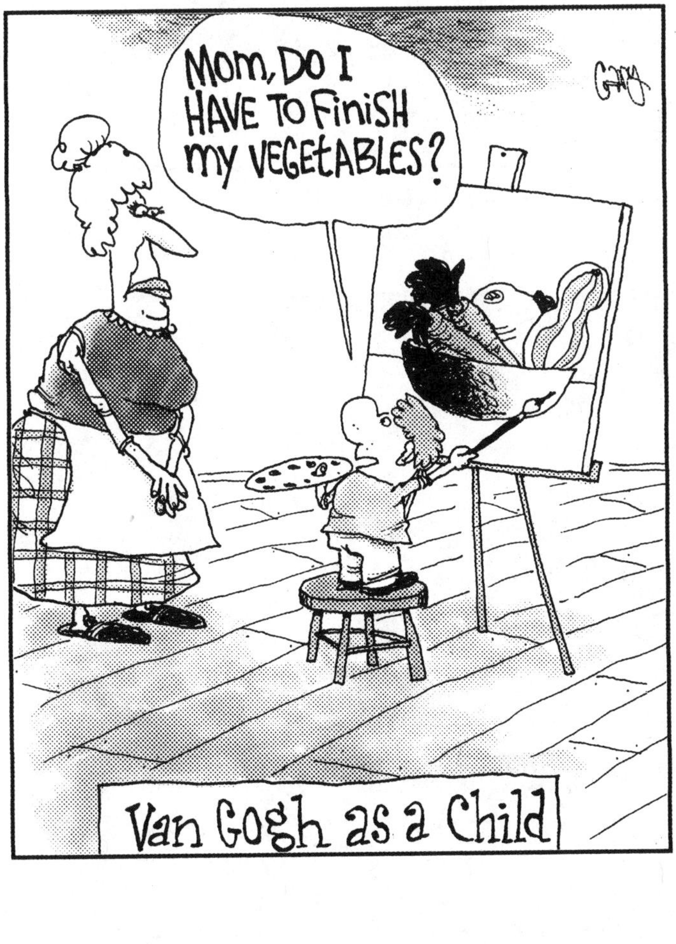
Mom, DO I HAVE TO FiNiSH my VEGEtABLES?
Van Gogh as a Child

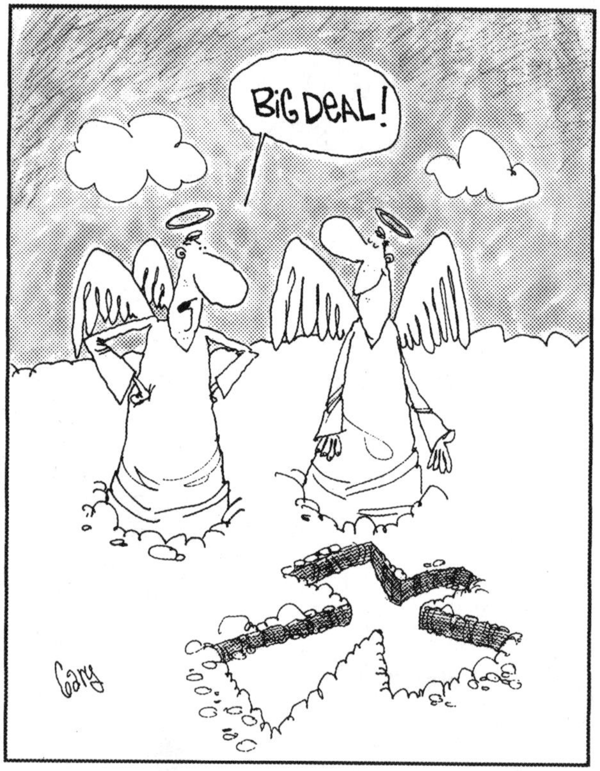
BIG DEAL!
Gary

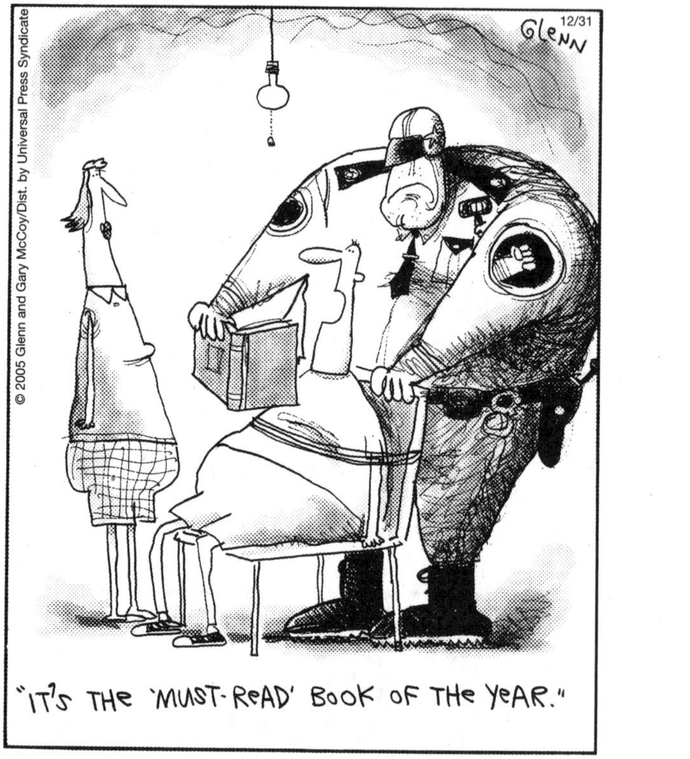
© 2005 Glenn and Gary McCoy/Dist. by Universal Press Syndicate
12/31
GLENN
"IT'S THE 'MUST-READ' BOOK OF THE YEAR."

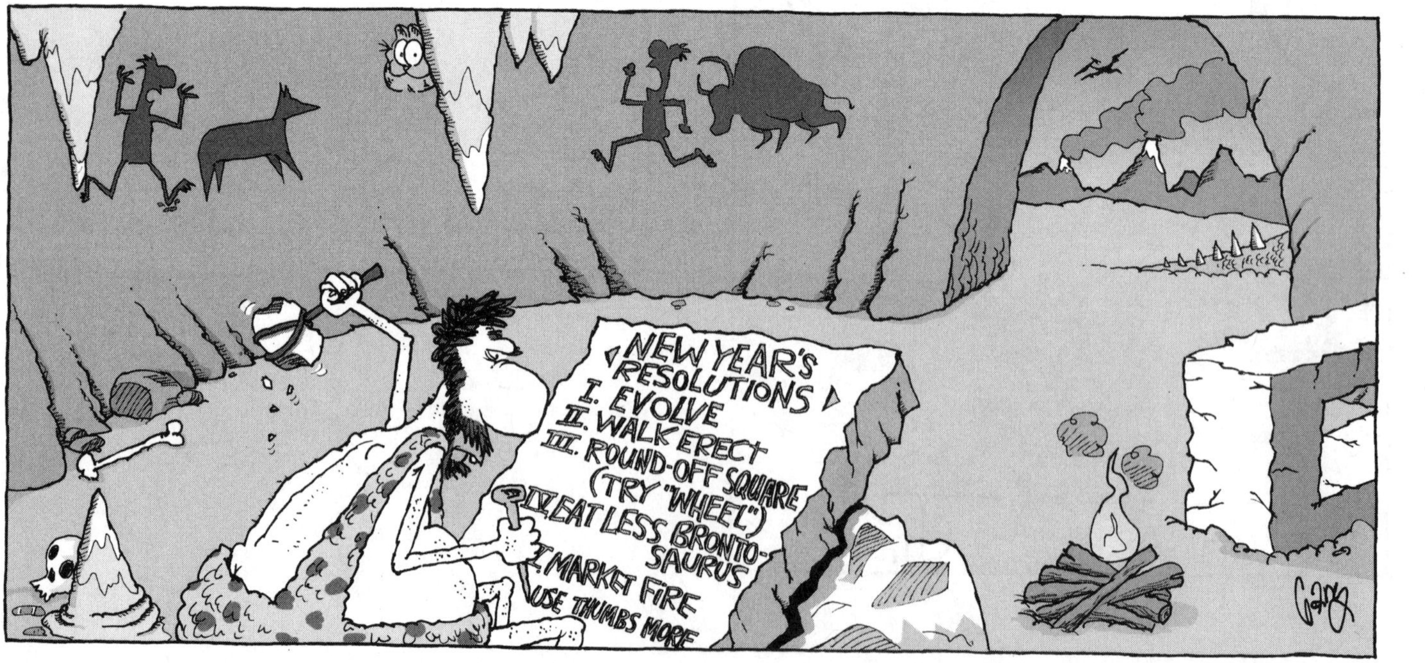
NEW YEAR'S RESOLUTIONS
I. EVOLVE
II. WALK ERECT
III. ROUND-OFF SQUARE (TRY "WHEEL")
IV. EAT LESS BRONTO-SAURUS
V. MARKET FIRE
USE THUMBS MORE
Gary

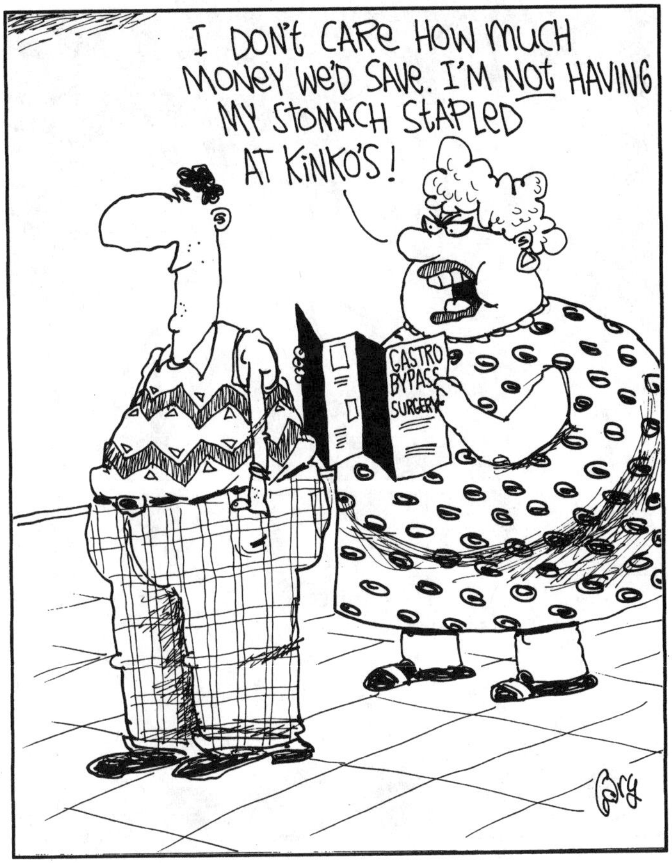
I DON'T CARE HOW MUCH MONEY WE'D SAVE. I'M NOT HAVING MY STOMACH STAPLED AT KINKO'S!
GASTRO BYPASS SURGERY

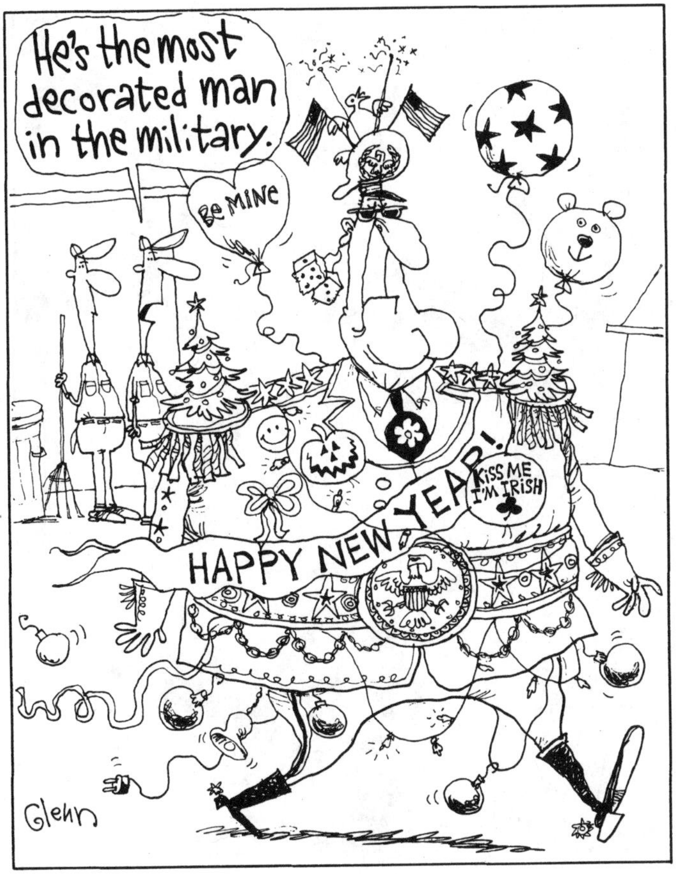
He's the most decorated man in the military.
BE MINE
KISS ME I'M IRISH
HAPPY NEW YEAR!
Glenn

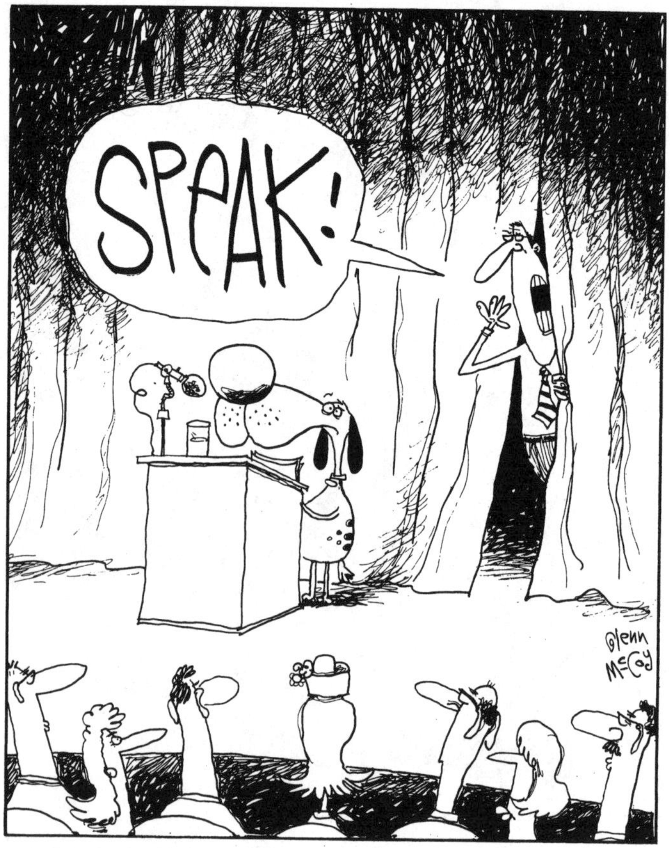
SPEAK!

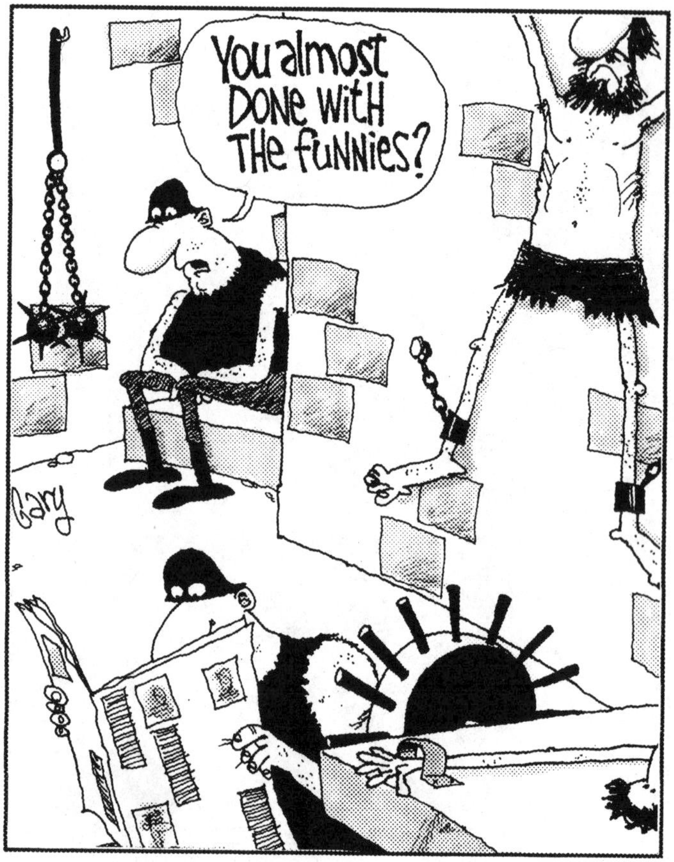
You almost DONE WITH THE funnies?

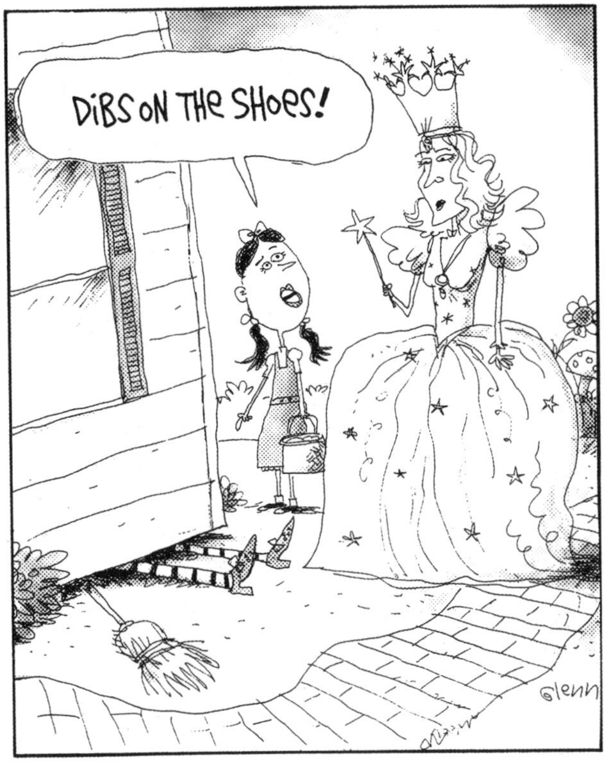
DIBS ON THE SHOES!

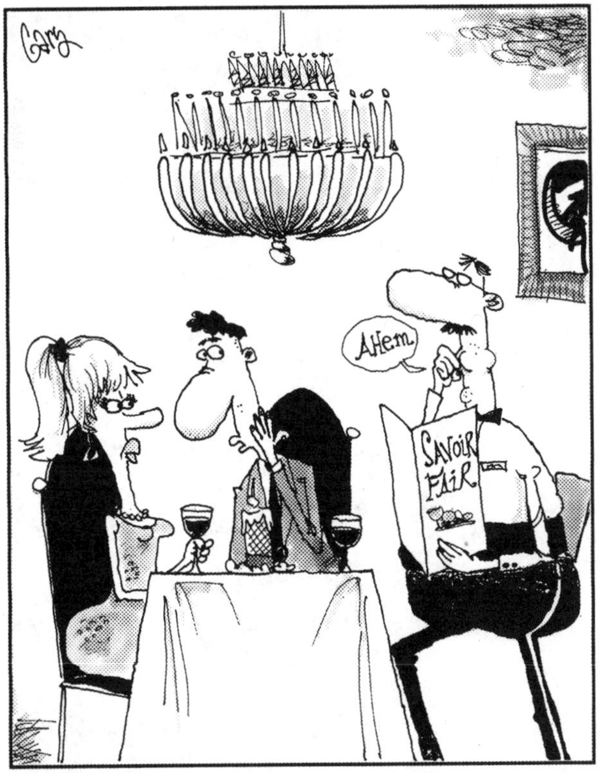
AHem.
SAVOIR FAIR

"The entire waitstaff of this restaurant is aspiring actors. Wait till you hear him read the au gratin potato special in Shakespearean fashion."

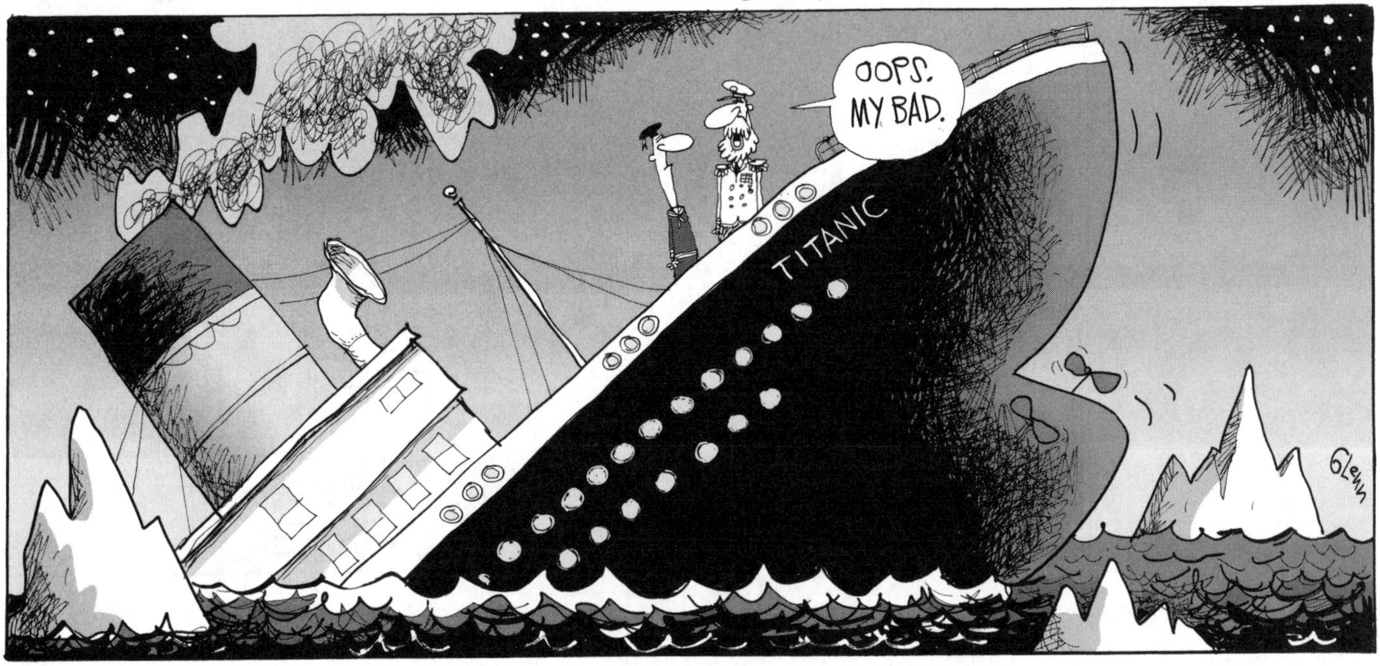
OOPS. MY BAD.
TITANIC

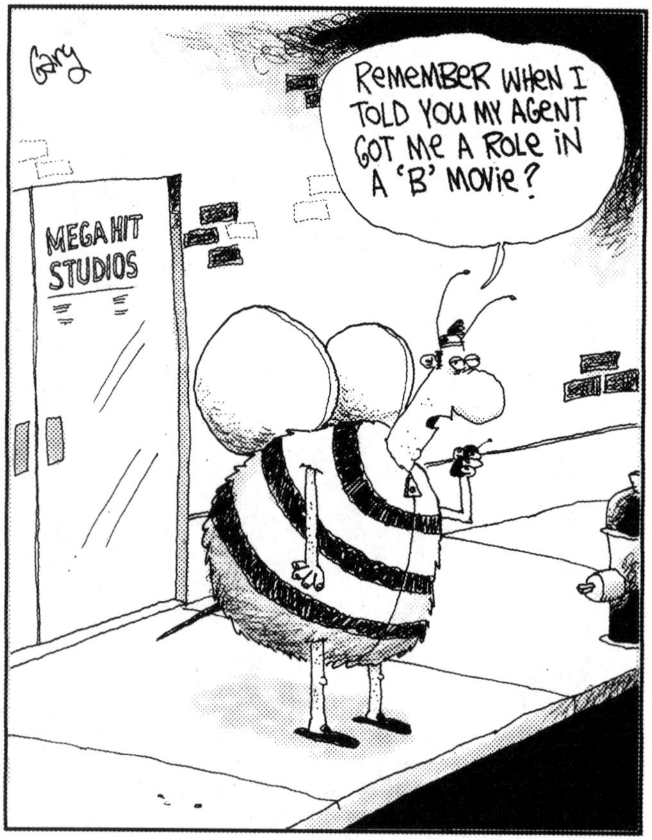
Gary
REMEMBER WHEN I TOLD YOU MY AGENT GOT ME A ROLE IN A 'B' MOVIE?
MEGA HIT STUDIOS

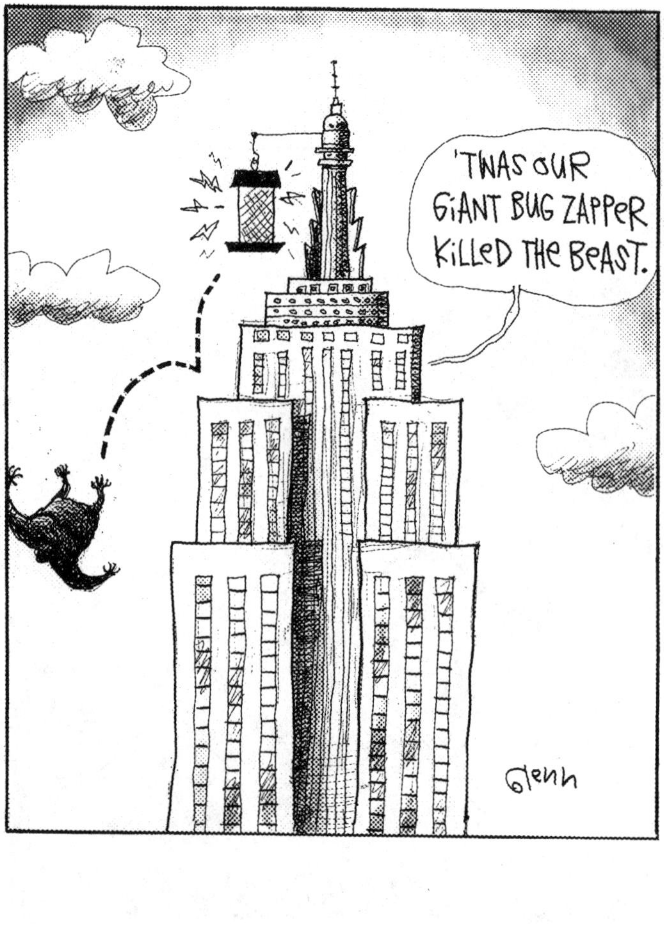
'TWAS OUR GIANT BUG ZAPPER KILLED THE BEAST.
Glenn

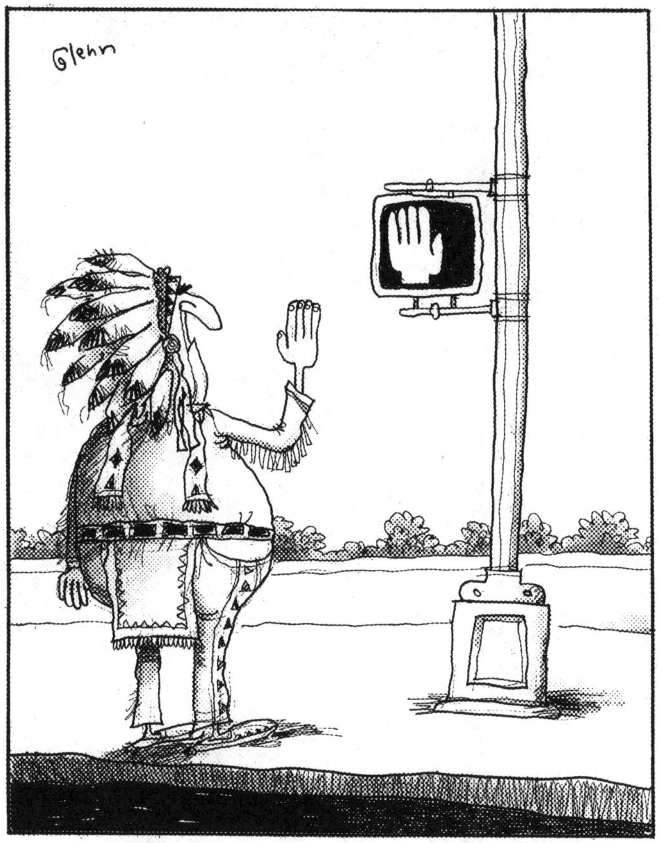
Glenn

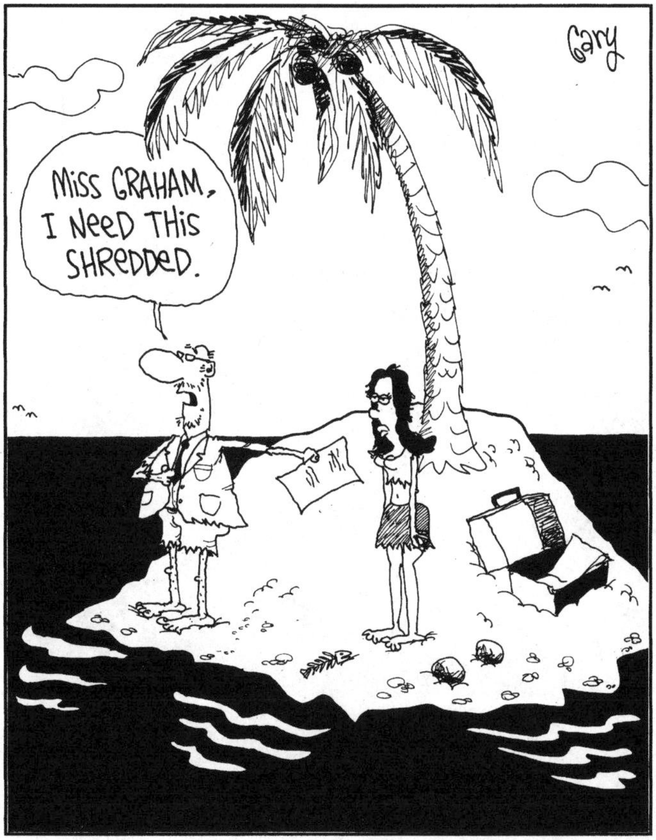
Gary
MISS GRAHAM, I NEED THIS SHREDDED.

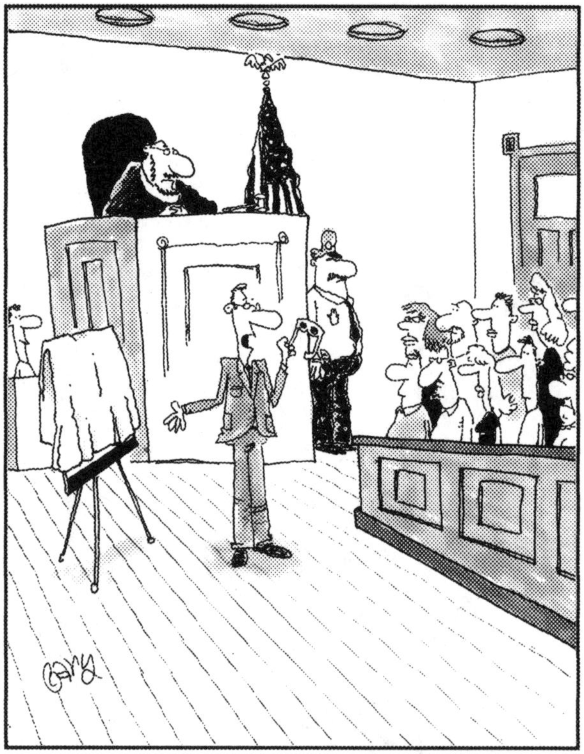
GARY

"I will now prove my client's innocence with the unveiling of Exhibit 'A.' But first I'd like to ask the jury to put on their 3-D glasses."

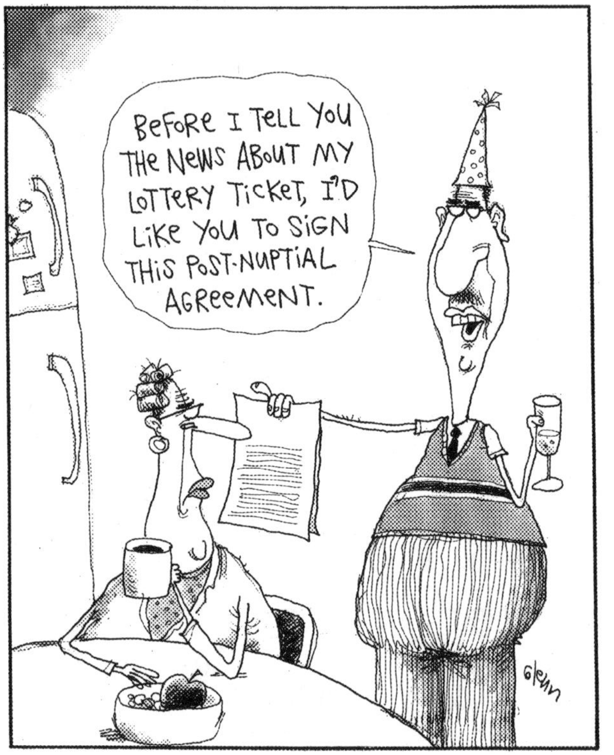
BEFORE I TELL YOU THE NEWS ABOUT MY LOTTERY TICKET, I'D LIKE YOU TO SIGN THIS POST-NUPTIAL AGREEMENT.
Glenn

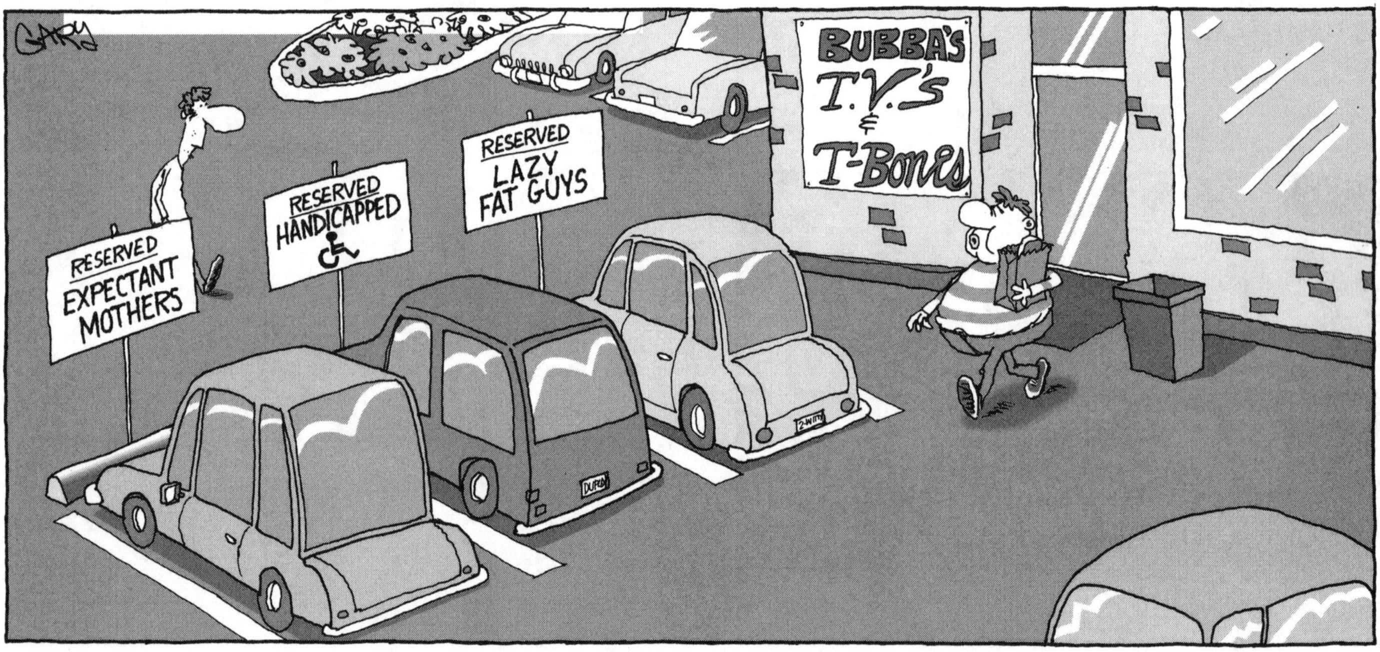
GARY
BUBBA'S T.V.'s & T-Bones
RESERVED LAZY FAT GUYS
RESERVED HANDICAPPED
RESERVED EXPECTANT MOTHERS

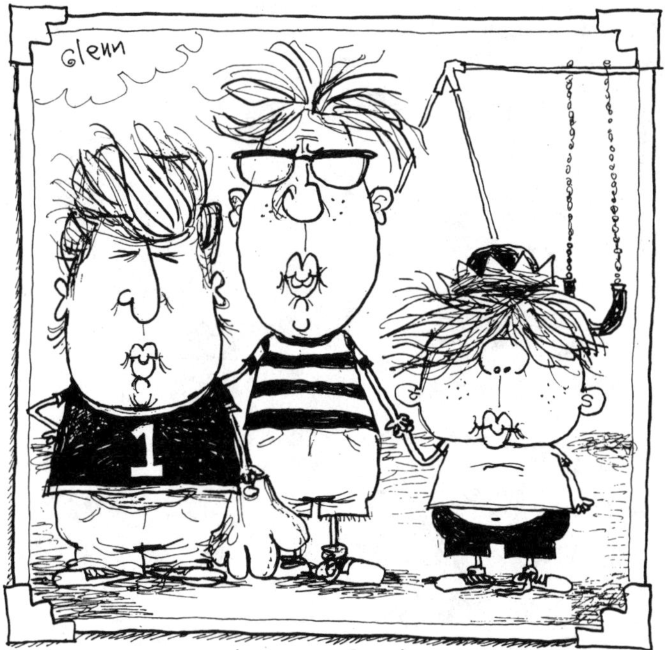
Glenn
1

An early photo of the Trump brothers from left to right: The Donald, The Jeff, and The Timmy.

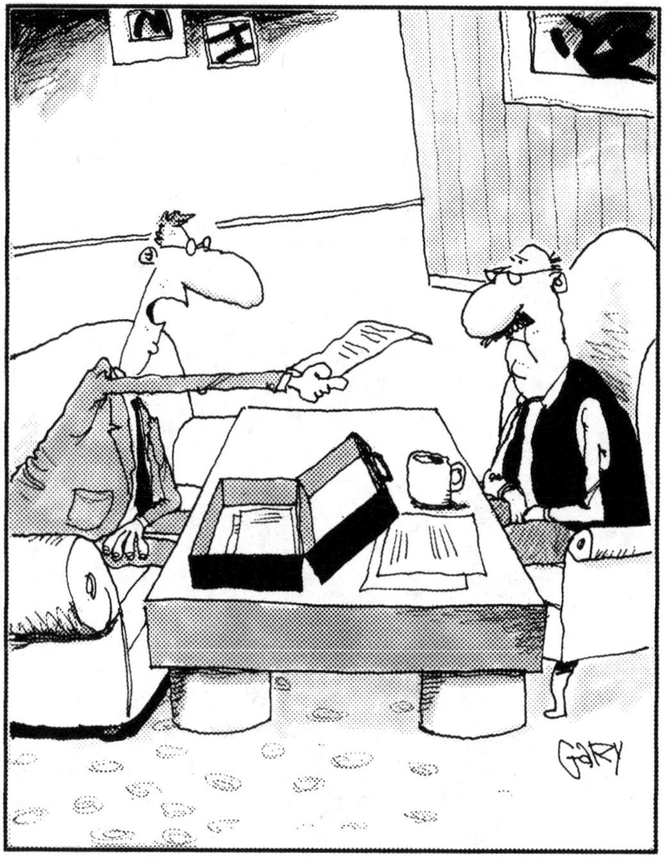
GARY

"... and I think this policy could come in handy. It protects against insurance salesmen who suddenly snap and begin beating you with their briefcase."

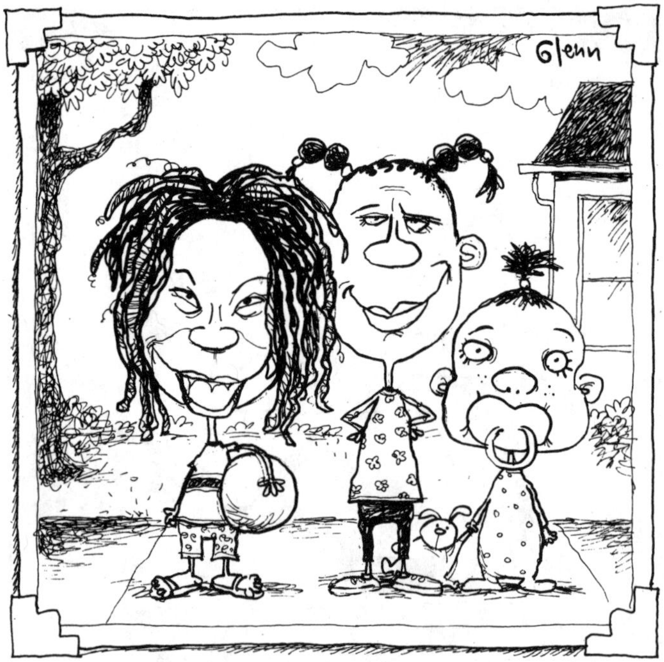
Glenn

An early photo of the Goldberg sisters from left to right: Whoopi, Yahoo, and Yee-Ha.

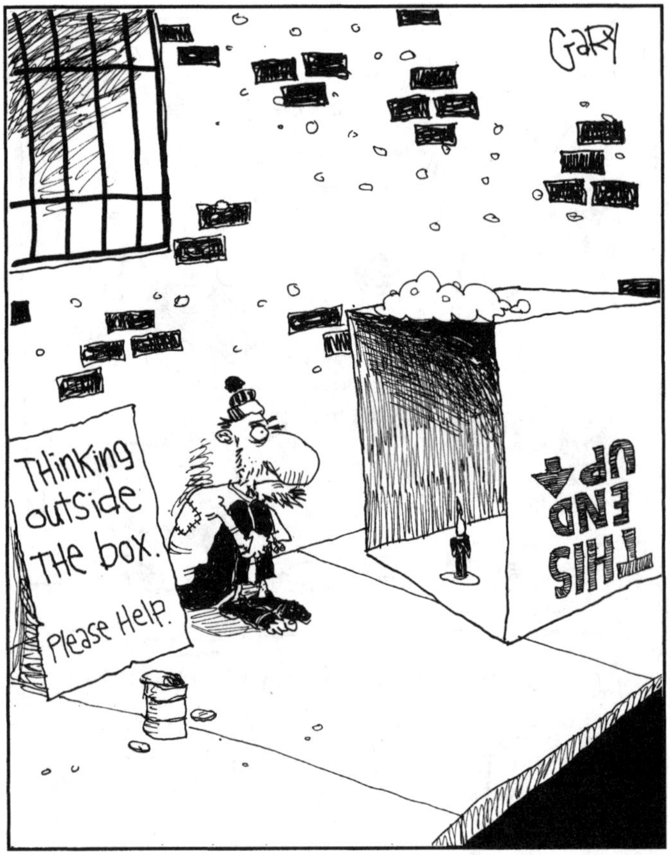
Gary
Thinking outside the box.
Please Help.
THIS END UP

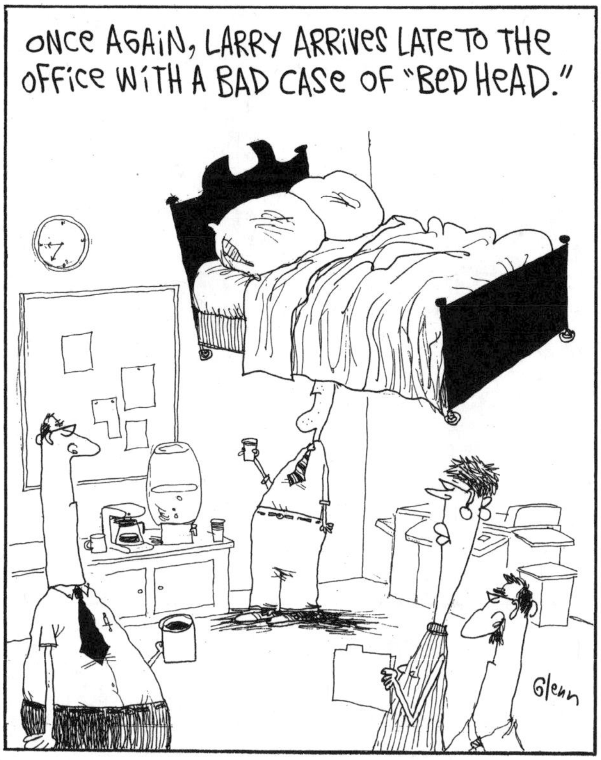
ONCE AGAIN, LARRY ARRIVES LATE TO THE OFFICE WITH A BAD CASE OF "BED HEAD."
Glenn

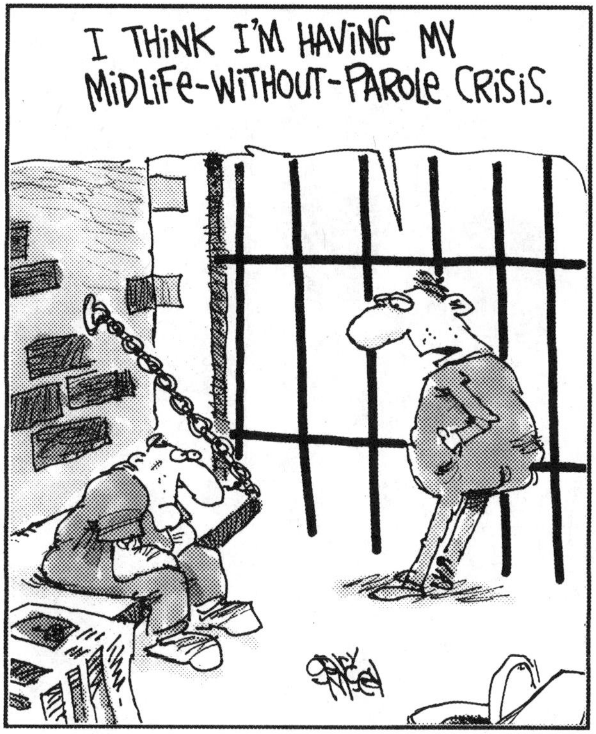
I THINK I'M HAVING MY MIDLIFE-WITHOUT-PAROLE CRISIS.

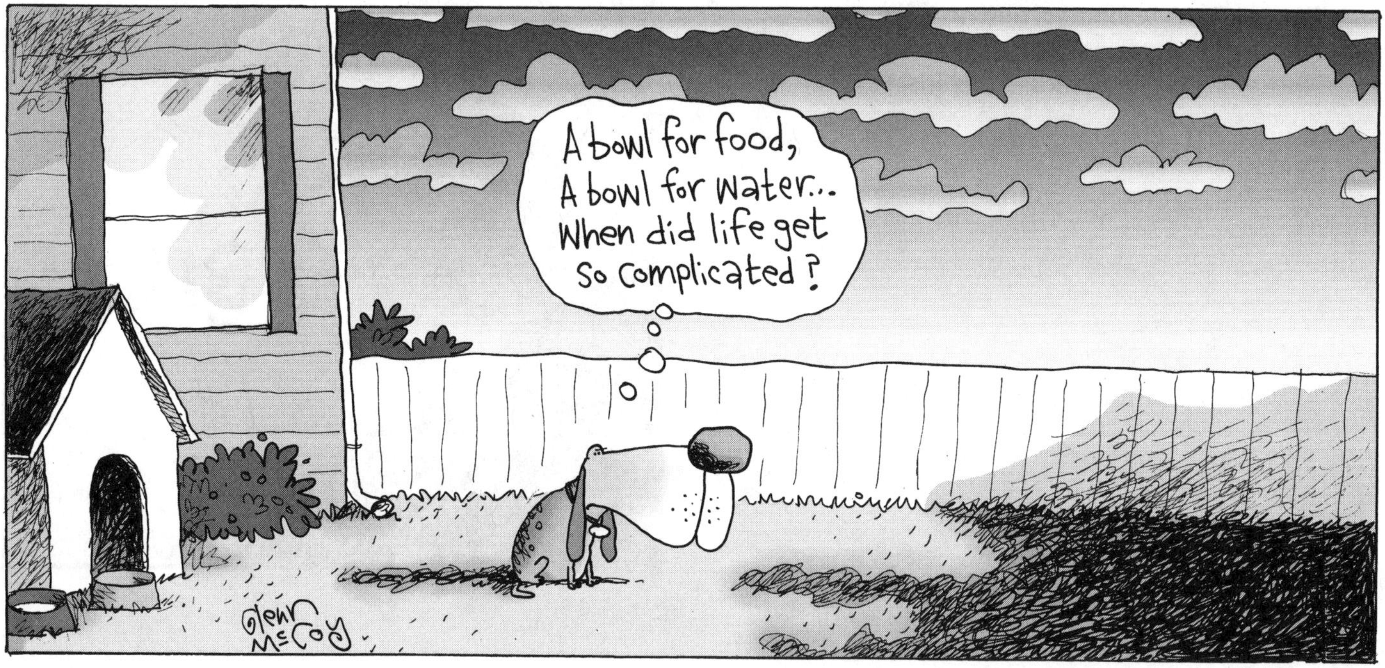
A bowl for food, A bowl for water... When did life get so complicated?
Glenn McCoy

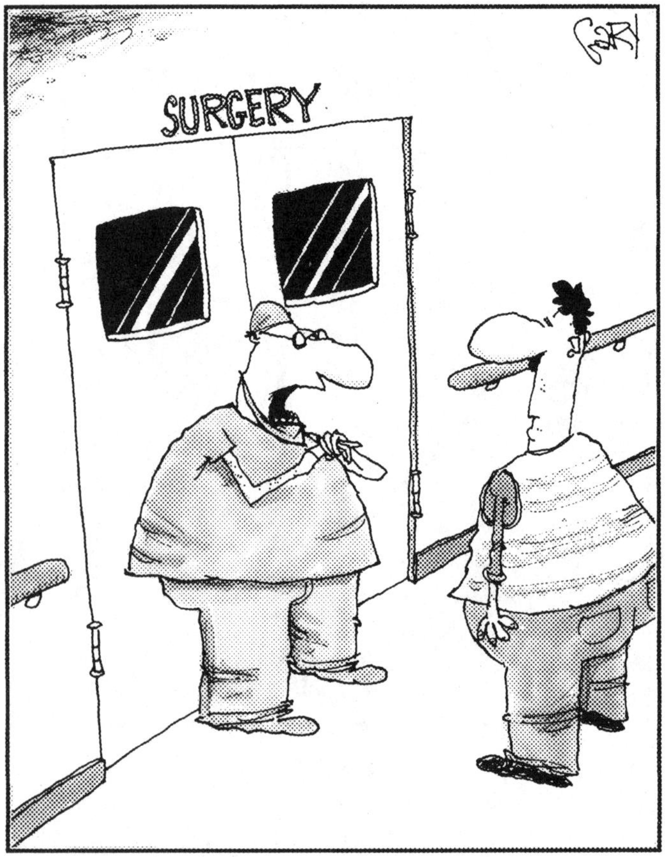
SURGERY

"I'm afraid we had some complications performing your wife's double bypass. So, we gave her a nose job instead."

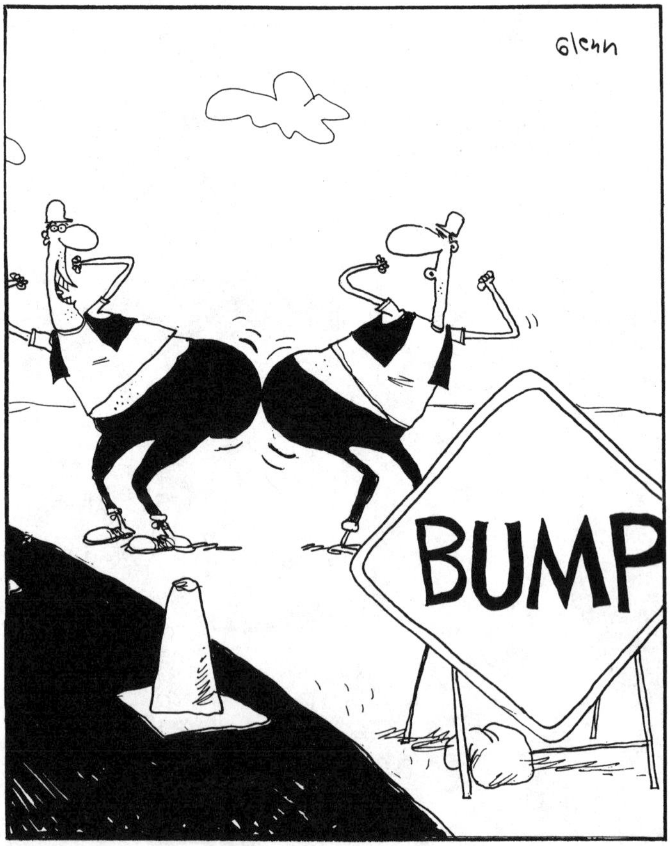
BUMP

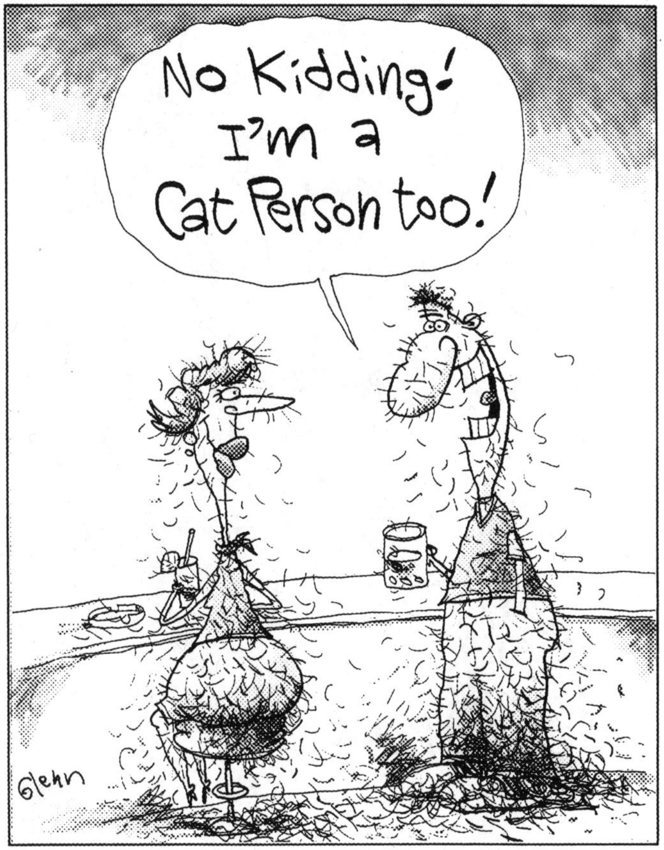
No Kidding! I'm a Cat Person too!
Glenn

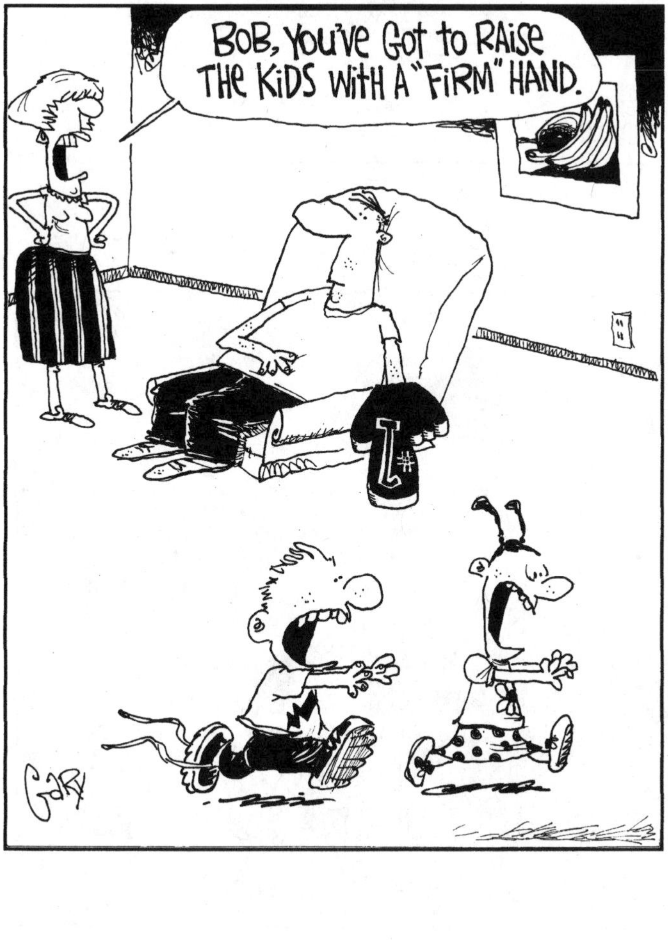
BOB, You've Got to RAISE THE KIDS WITH A "FIRM" HAND.
GARY

MEET The AUTHOR
THE 10 COMMANDMENTS
I. II. III. IV. V. VI. VII. VIII. IX. X.
Gary

YEP. THERE'S YOUR PROBLEM. YOU NEED A NEW BELT.
Glenn

CAN I BRING YOU A BOX FOR THE REST OF THAT?
Gary

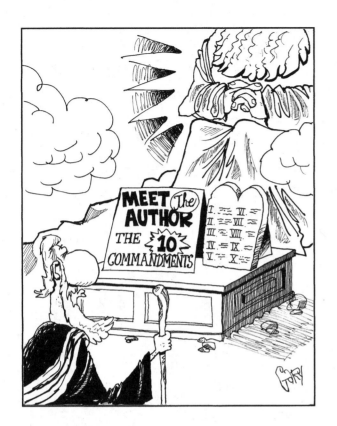

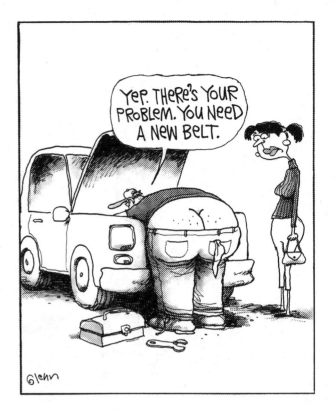

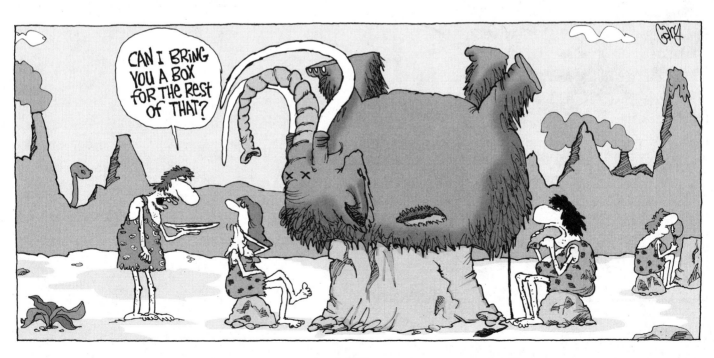

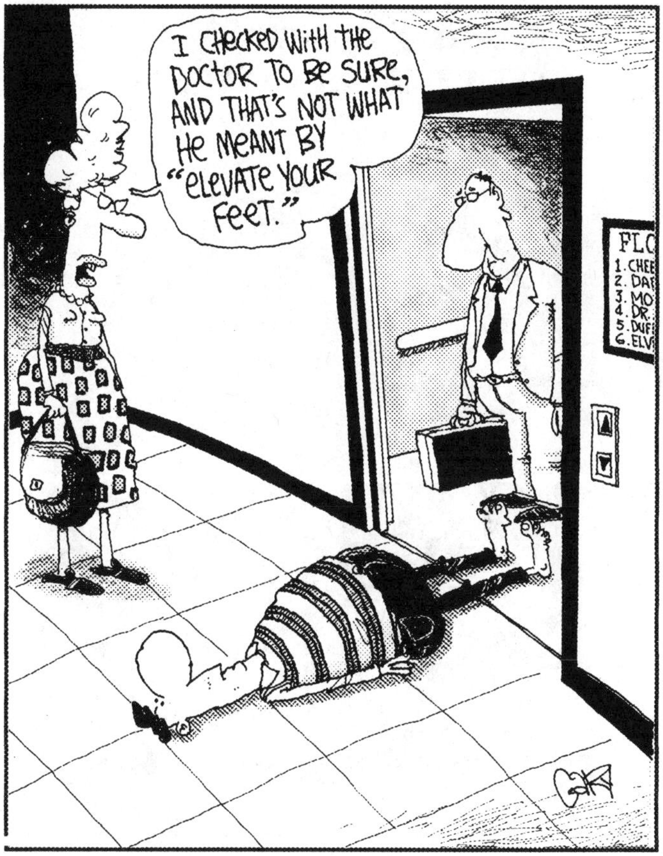
I CHECKED WITH THE DOCTOR TO BE SURE, AND THAT'S NOT WHAT HE MEANT BY "ELEVATE YOUR FEET."

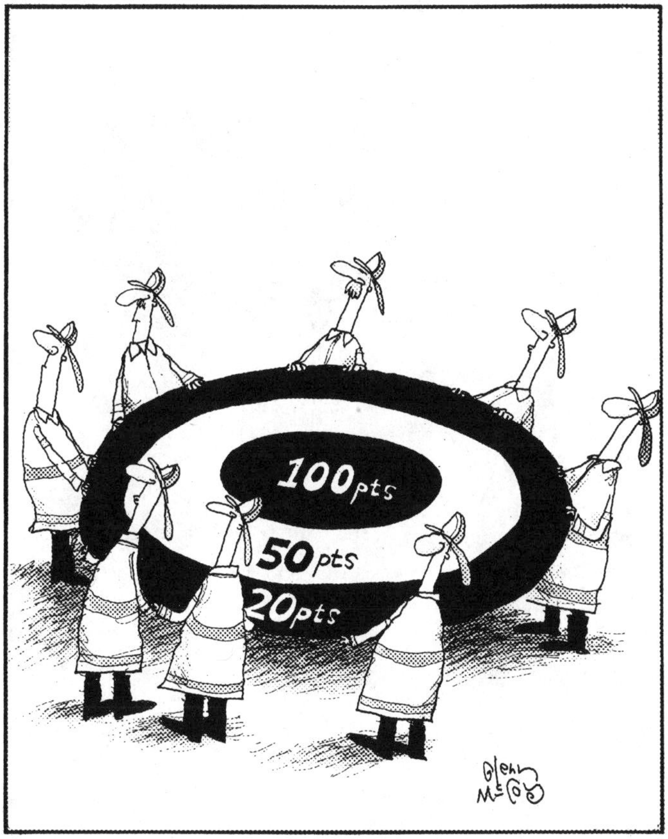
100pts
50pts
20pts

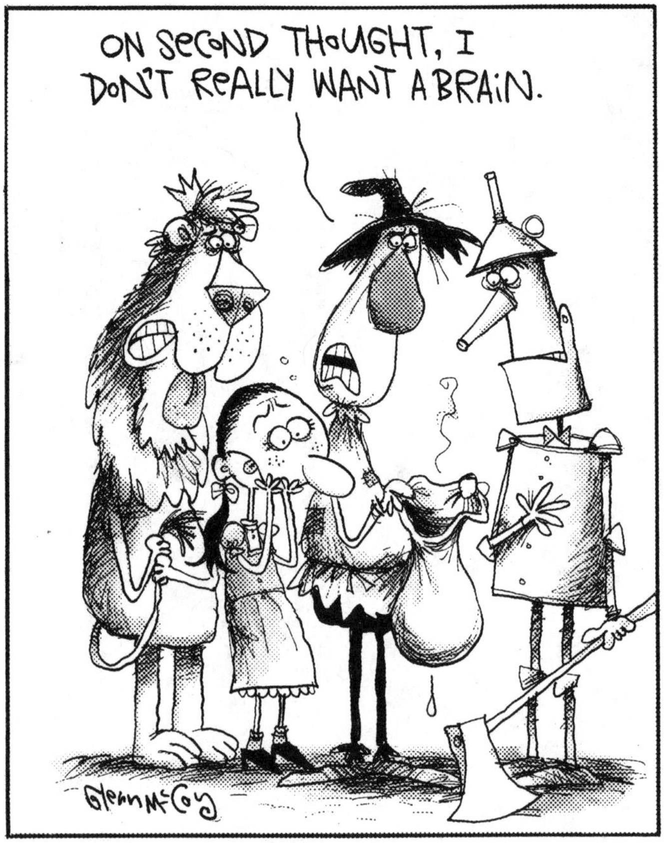
ON SECOND THOUGHT, I DON'T REALLY WANT A BRAIN.

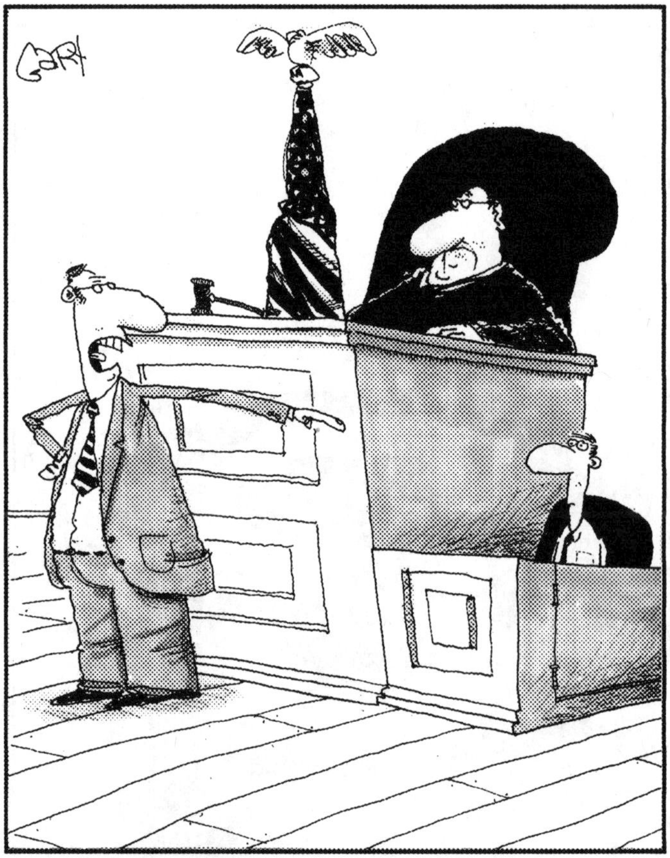

"Sir, let me remind you that you are under oath, AND you have a dentist appointment next Wednesday at nine."

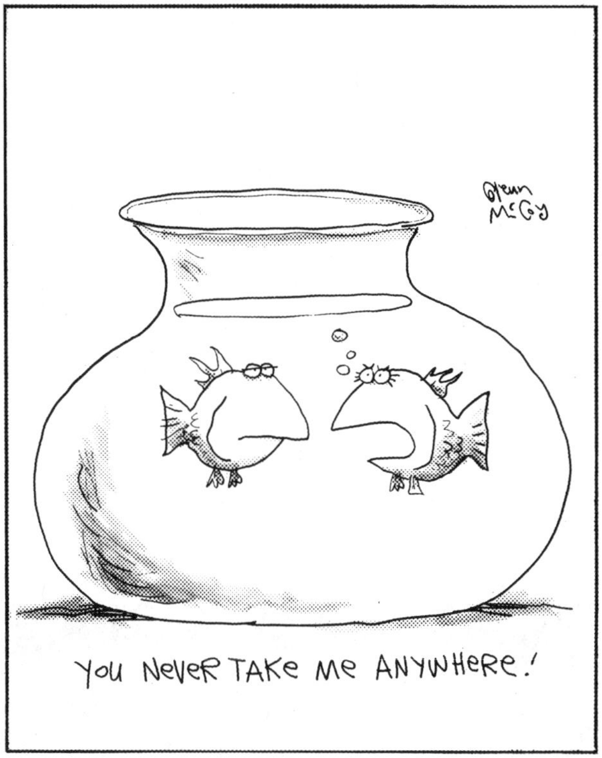
Glenn McCoy
YOU NEVER TAKE ME ANYWHERE!

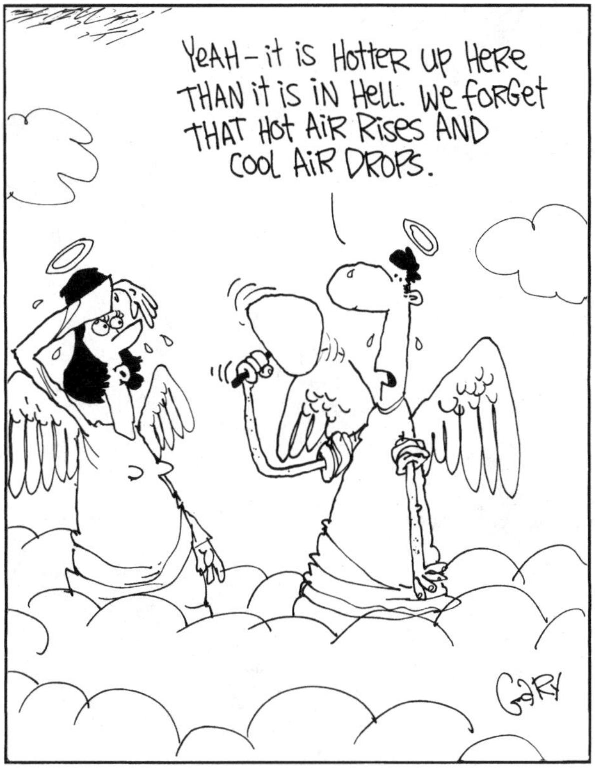
YEAH— it is Hotter up Here THAN it is in Hell. We forget THAT Hot Air Rises AND Cool Air Drops.
GARY

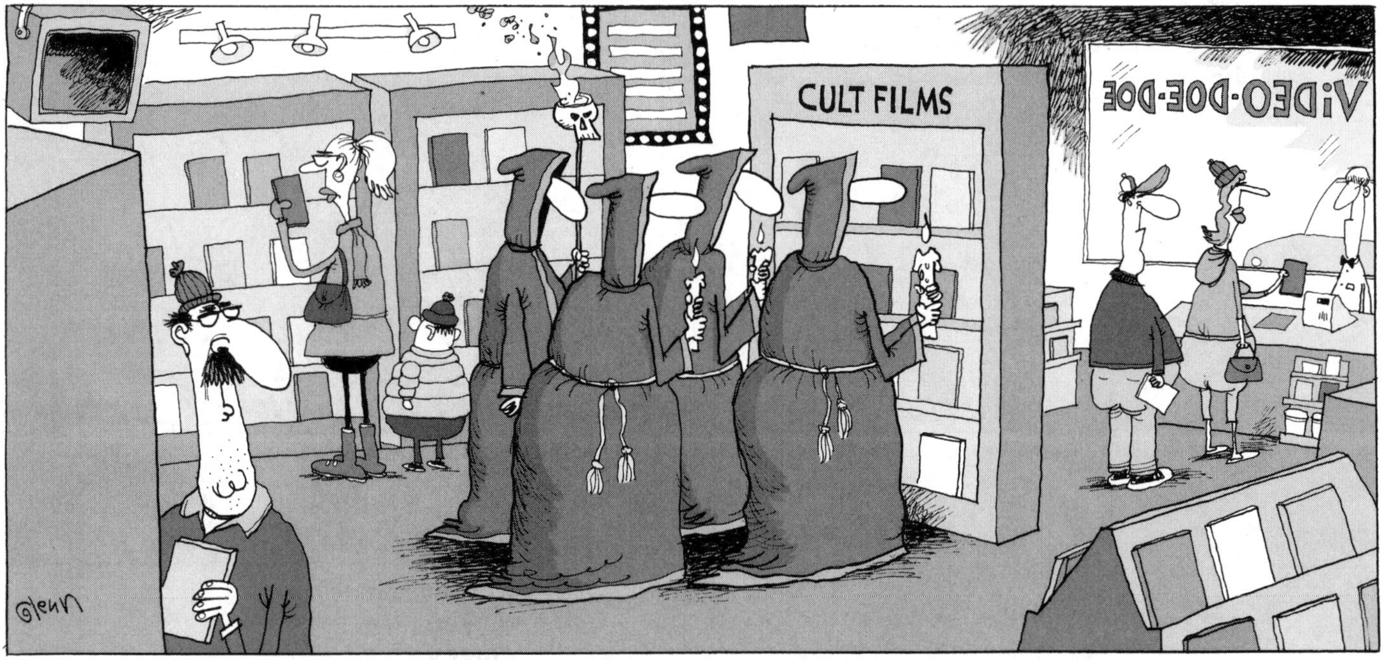
CULT FILMS
ViDEO-DOE-DOE
Glenn

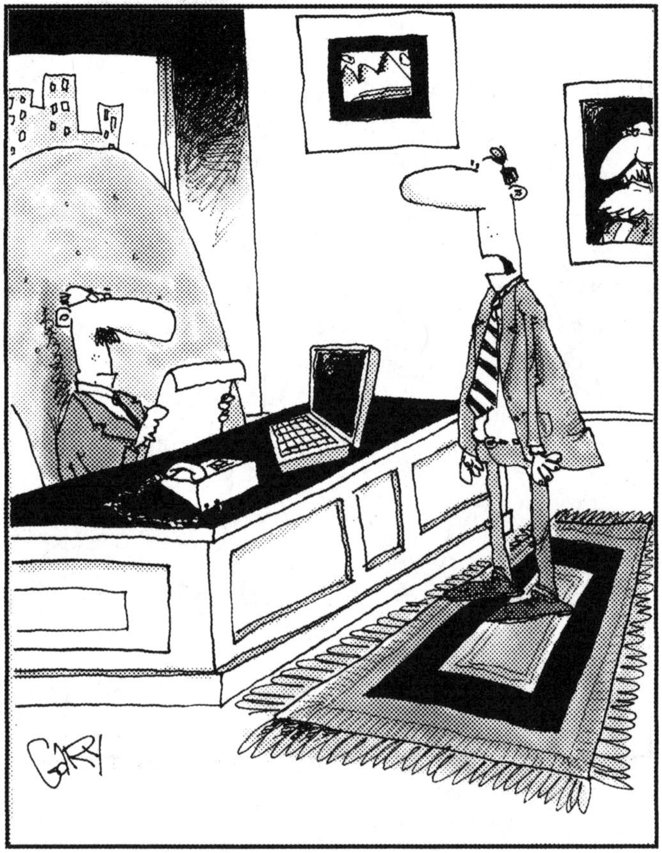
GARY

"No sir, that's not our mission statement. That's a statement that explains what the heck we're trying to say in our mission statement."

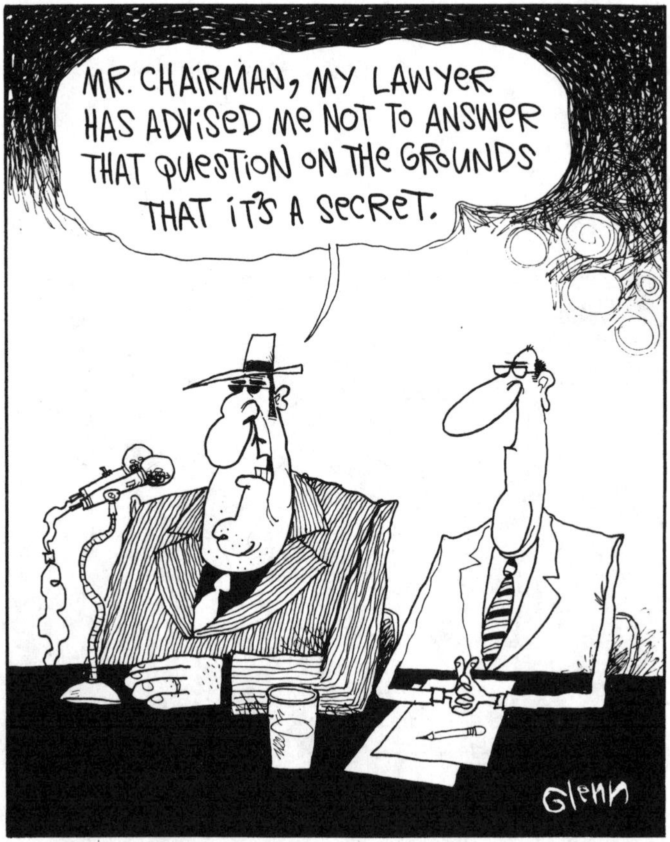
MR. CHAIRMAN, MY LAWYER HAS ADVISED ME NOT TO ANSWER THAT QUESTION ON THE GROUNDS THAT IT'S A SECRET.
GLENN

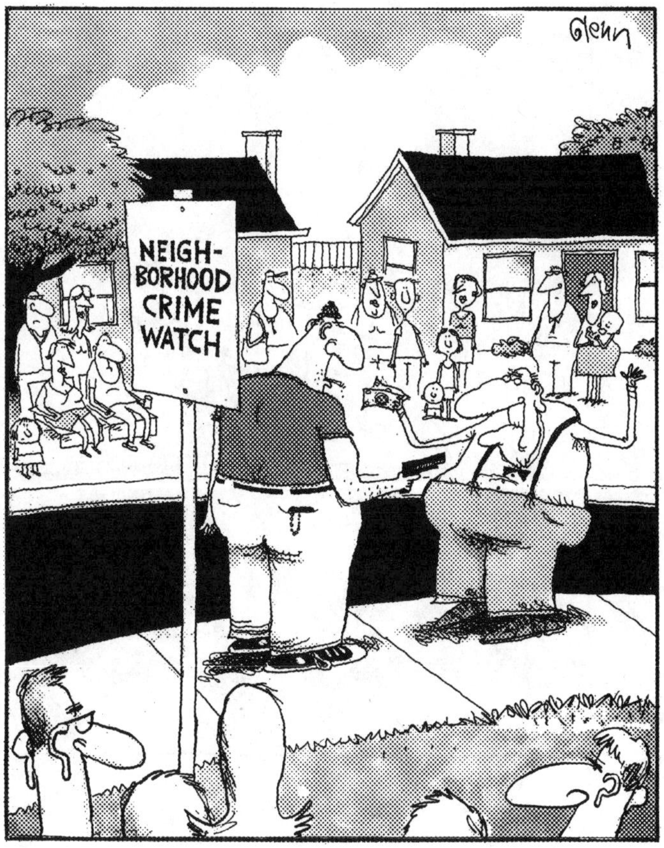
Glenn
NEIGH-
BORHOOD
CRIME
WATCH

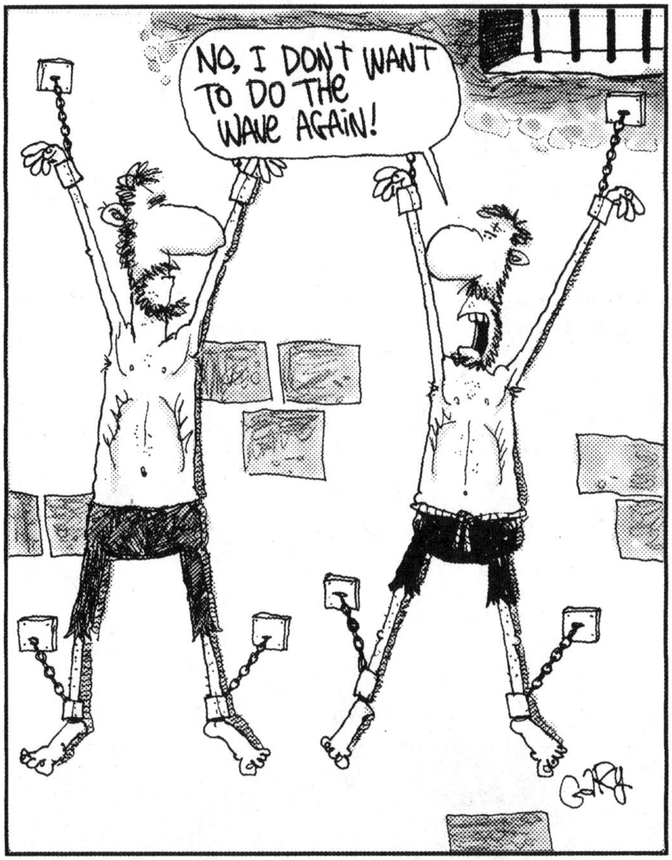
NO, I DON'T WANT TO DO THE WAVE AGAIN!
GARY

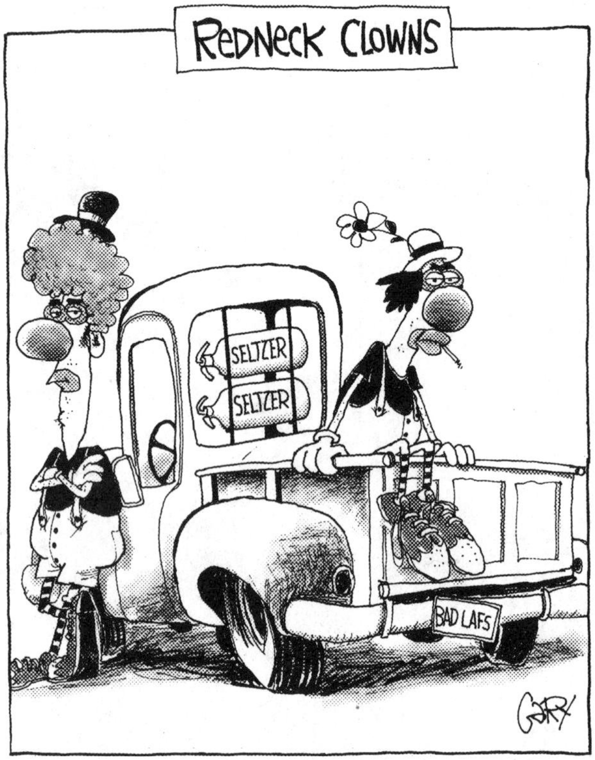
REDNECK CLOWNS
SELTZER
SELTZER
BAD LAFS
GARY

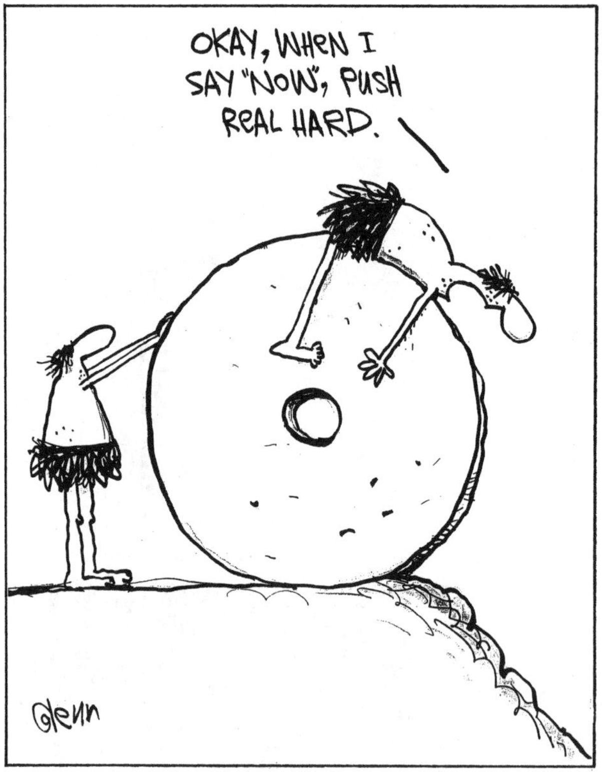
OKAY, WHEN I SAY "NOW", PUSH REAL HARD.
Glenn

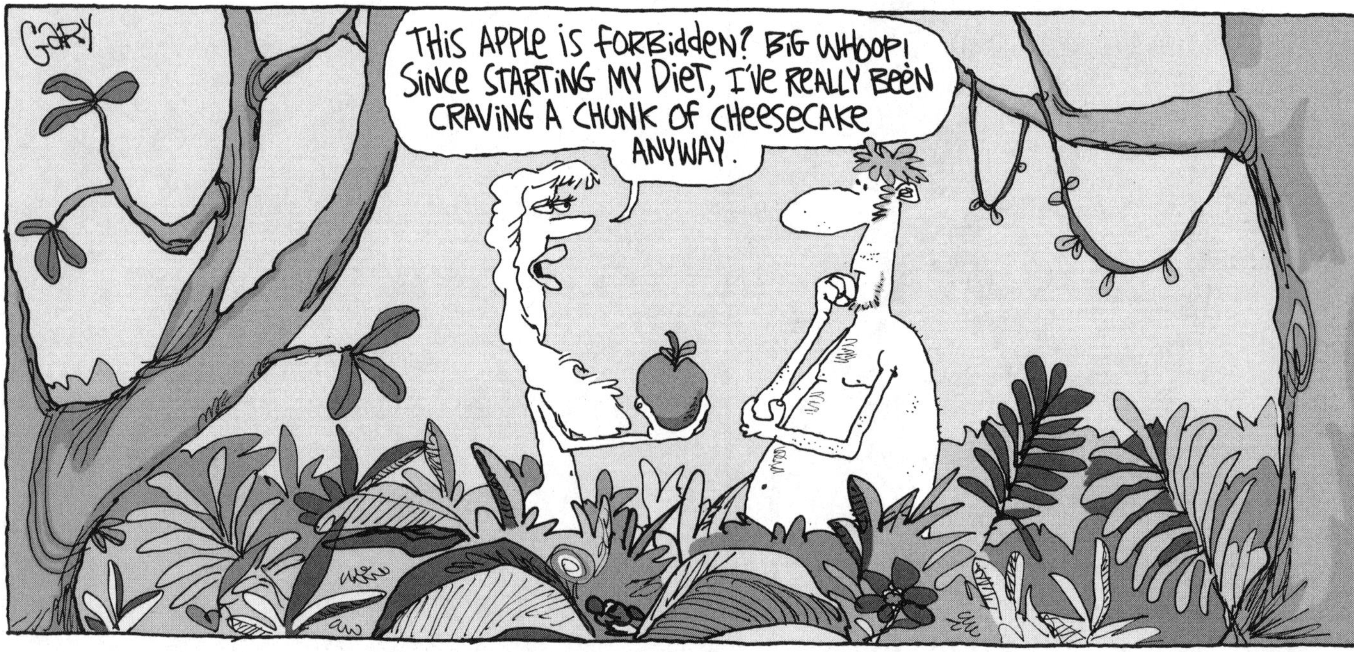
GARY
THIS APPLE IS FORBIDDEN? BIG WHOOP! SINCE STARTING MY DIET, I'VE REALLY BEEN CRAVING A CHUNK OF CHEESECAKE ANYWAY.

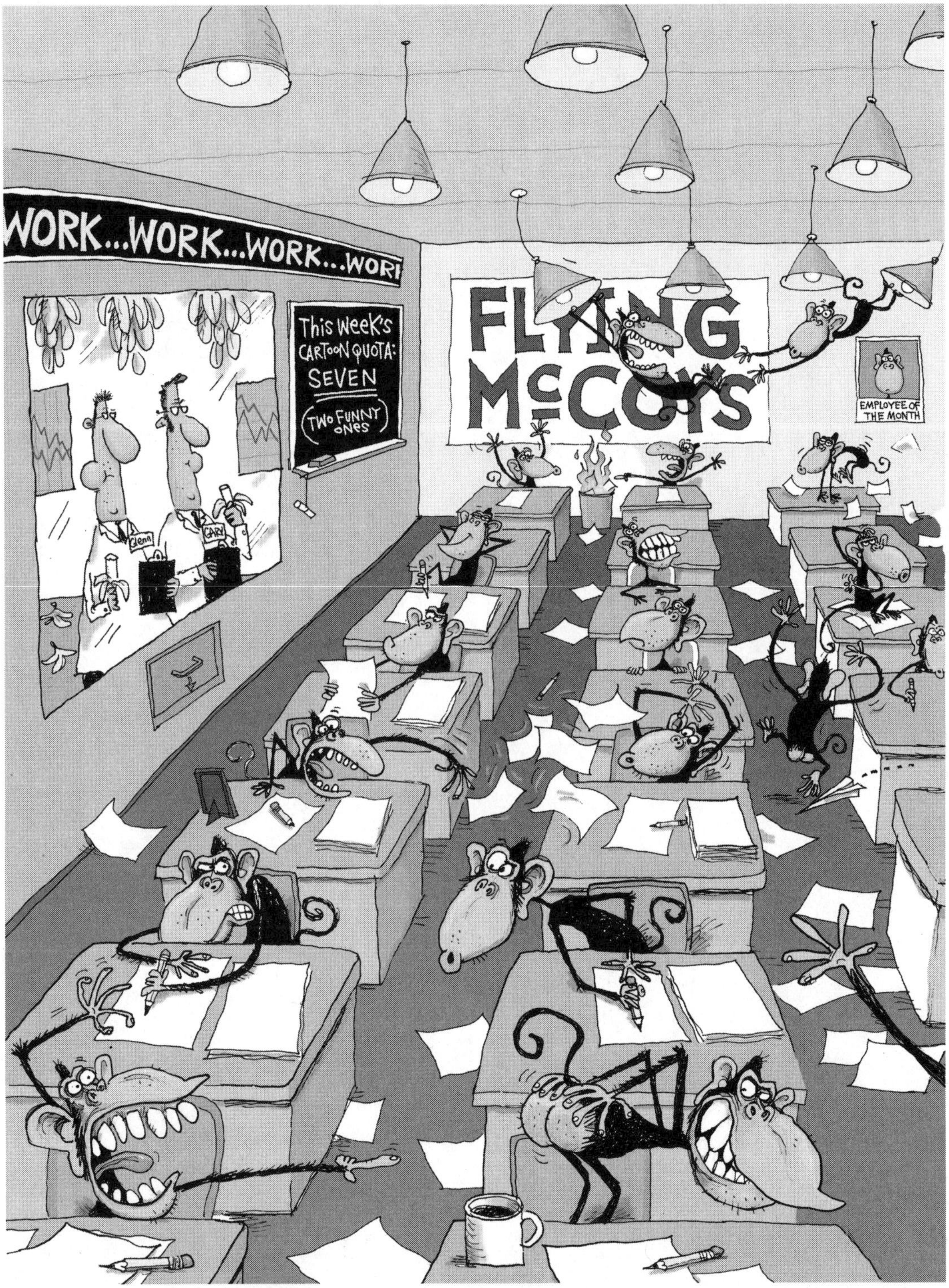
WORK...WORK...WORK...WOR
This Week's CARTOON QUOTA: SEVEN (TWO FUNNY ONES)
FLYING McCOYS
EMPLOYEE OF THE MONTH
Glenn
GARY

We're already hard at work on our next book!